Sick, and You Cared for Me
HOMILIES AND REFLECTIONS FOR CYCLE B

Published by Clear Faith Publishing LLC
22 Lafayette Road
Princeton, NJ 08540

ISBN 978-1-940414-00-3

First Printing November, 2014

Cover & Interior Design by Doug Cordes
Illustrations by Brother Mickey O'Neill McGrath

Sick, and You Cared for Me is printed on 60# Glatfelter Natural and the text is set in Fairfield and Scala Sans.

Printed in the United States of America

Sick, and You Cared for Me

HOMILIES AND REFLECTIONS FOR CYCLE B

EDITED BY DEACON JIM KNIPPER

Published by:
Clear Faith Publishing LLC
Princeton, New Jersey
2014

CONTRIBUTING AUTHORS

Fr. William J. Bausch

Rob Bell

Margaret Blackie, PhD

Rev. Joel Blunk

Fr. Greg Boyle, SJ

Fr. William J. Byron, SJ

Sr. Simone Campbell, SSS

Sr. Joan Chittister, OSB

Rev. Dr. David A. Davis

Deacon Bill Ditewig, PhD

Msgr. Michael Doyle

Michelle Francl-Donnay

Fr. James J. Greenfield, OSFS

Fr. Paul A. Holmes, STD

Fr. Daniel P. Horan, OFM

Deacon Greg Kandra

Deacon Jim Knipper

Michael Leach

Fr. Richard G. Malloy, SJ

Fr. James Martin, SJ

Rev Carol Howard Merritt

Rev. Penny A. Nash

Msgr. Walter E. Nolan

Christine Valters Paintner, PhD

Jan Richardson

Fr. Richard Rohr, OFM

Mary Elizabeth Sperry

Rev. Martha Sterne

Fran Rossi Szpylczyn

Patrick J. Wenrick

The opinions in each homily/reflection do not necessarily
represent the views of the other contributors.

DEDICATION

For my brother deacon,
Joseph J. Kupin (1951 – 2014)
Who had a passion for giving soulful homilies
and caring for all those he served.

"Christians have the duty to proclaim the Gospel without excluding anyone. Instead of seeming to impose new obligations, they should appear as people who wish to share their joy, who point to a horizon of beauty and who invite others to a delicious banquet."

Pope Francis

"Anyone who truly knows creatures may be excused from listening to sermons for every creature is full of God, and is a book."

Meister Eckhart

"No language about God will ever be fully adequate to the burning mystery which it signifies."

Elizabeth Johnston

"The test of a preacher is that his congregation goes away saying, not 'What a lovely sermon.' but, 'I will do something!'"

Francis de Sales

CONTENTS

FOREWORD   1
PREFACE   3

ADVENT SEASON

1ST SUNDAY OF ADVENT   7
DEACON GREG KANDRA

2ND SUNDAY OF ADVENT   11
REV. DAVID A. DAVIS

3RD SUNDAY OF ADVENT   17
FR. JAMES MARTIN, SJ

4TH SUNDAY OF ADVENT   23
FR. WILLIAM BAUSCH

CHRISTMAS SEASON

CHRISTMAS: MIDNIGHT   29
FR. RICHARD G. MALLOY, SJ

NATIVITY OF THE LORD: DAY   35
FR. DANIEL P. HORAN, OFM

HOLY FAMILY OF JESUS,
MARY AND JOSEPH   39
FR. JAMES J. GREENFIELD, OSFS

MARY MOTHER OF GOD   43
MARY ELIZABETH SPERRY

THE EPIPHANY OF THE LORD   47
FR. RICHARD G. MALLOY, SJ

BAPTISM OF THE LORD   53
DEACON GREG KANDRA

LENT

ASH WEDNESDAY   59
DEACON WILLIAM T. DITEWIG, PhD

1TH SUNDAY OF LENT   63
FR. WILLIAM BAUSCH

2ND SUNDAY OF LENT   69
ROB BELL

3RD SUNDAY OF LENT   75
REV. MARTHA STERNE

4TH SUNDAY IN LENT   81
FR. JAMES MARTIN, SJ

5TH SUNDAY OF LENT   85
REV. DAVID A. DAVIS

PALM SUNDAY   89
PATRICK J. WENRICK

HOLY THURSDAY   93
FR. GREG BOYLE, SJ

GOOD FRIDAY   97
DEACON GREG KANDRA

EASTER SEASON

EASTER VIGIL   103
MSGR. MICHAEL DOYLE

EASTER SUNDAY   107
FR. RICHARD ROHR, OFM

2ND SUNDAY OF EASTER   111
DEACON JIM KNIPPER

3RD SUNDAY OF EASTER 115
FR. PAUL A. HOLMES, STD

4TH SUNDAY OF EASTER 119
MARY ELIZABETH SPERRY

5TH SUNDAY OF EASTER 123
DEACON WILLIAM T. DITEWIG, PhD

6TH SUNDAY OF EASTER 127
FRAN ROSSI SZPYLCZYN

7TH SUNDAY OF EASTER 131
FR. DANIEL P. HORAN, OFM

ASCENSION OF THE LORD 135
MSGR. MICHAEL DOYLE

PENTECOST VIGIL 141
ROB BELL

ORDINARY TIME

2ND SUNDAY IN ORDINARY TIME 147
REV. DAVID A. DAVIS

3RD SUNDAY IN ORDINARY TIME 153
ROB BELL

4TH SUNDAY IN ORDINARY TIME 159
FR. DANIEL P. HORAN, OFM

5TH SUNDAY IN ORDINARY TIME 163
MSGR. WALTER NOLAN

6TH SUNDAY IN ORDINARY TIME 167
FR. WILLIAM J. BYRON, SJ

7TH SUNDAY IN ORDINARY TIME 171
FR. WILLIAM BAUSCH

8TH SUNDAY IN ORDINARY TIME 175
REV. CAROL HOWARD MERRITT

9TH SUNDAY IN ORDINARY TIME 179
MICHELLE FRANCL-DONNAY

10TH SUNDAY IN ORDINARY TIME 183
REV. PENNY A. NASH

11TH SUNDAY IN ORDINARY TIME 187
FR. RICHARD ROHR, OFM

12TH SUNDAY IN ORDINARY TIME 191
MARGARET BLACKIE, PhD

13TH SUNDAY IN ORDINARY TIME 195
REV. JOEL BLUNK

14TH SUNDAY IN ORDINARY TIME 201
FR. PAUL A. HOLMES, STD

15TH SUNDAY IN ORDINARY TIME 205
FR. JAMES J. GREENFIELD, OSFS

16TH SUNDAY IN ORDINARY TIME 209
FR. JAMES MARTIN, SJ

17TH SUNDAY IN ORDINARY TIME 211
JAN RICHARDSON

18TH SUNDAY IN ORDINARY TIME 215
REV. PENNY A. NASH

19TH SUNDAY IN ORDINARY TIME 219
PATRICK J. WENRICK

20TH SUNDAY IN ORDINARY TIME 223
FR. PAUL A. HOLMES, STD

21TH SUNDAY IN ORDINARY TIME 227
MICHELLE FRANCL-DONNAY

22ND SUNDAY IN ORDINARY TIME 231
REV. CAROL HOWARD MERRITT

23RD SUNDAY IN ORDINARY TIME 235
MICHAEL LEACH

24TH SUNDAY IN ORDINARY TIME 239
FR. JAMES MARTIN, SJ

25TH SUNDAY IN ORDINARY TIME 243
DEACON JIM KNIPPER

26TH SUNDAY IN ORDINARY TIME   249
FR. WILLIAM BAUSCH

27TH SUNDAY OF ORDINARY TIME   255
FR. PAUL A. HOLMES, STD

28TH SUNDAY IN ORDINARY TIME   259
DEACON GREG KANDRA

29TH SUNDAY IN ORDINARY TIME   263
FR. RICHARD ROHR, OFM

30TH SUNDAY IN ORDINARY   267
CHRISTINE VALTERS PAINTNER, PhD

31TH SUNDAY IN ORDINARY TIME   271
REV. DAVID A. DAVIS

32ND SUNDAY IN ORDINARY TIME   277
DEACON JIM KNIPPER

33RD SUNDAY IN ORDINARY TIME   281
REV. PENNY A. NASH

CHRIST THE KING   313
FR. RICHARD ROHR, OFM

THEMATIC CROSS REFERENCE   317
THE CONTRIBUTORS   319
THE CHARITIES   334
ACKNOWLEDGEMENTS   337

FEAST DAYS

MOST HOLY TRINITY   287
FR. RICHARD G. MALLOY, SJ

MOST HOLY BODY AND BLOOD
OF CHRIST   293
FR. WILLIAM BAUSCH

FEAST OF THE ASSUMPTION   297
FR. JAMES J. GREENFIELD, OSFS

SOLEMNITY OF ALL SAINTS   301
FRAN ROSSI SZPYLCZYN

FEAST OF ALL SOULS   305
JAN RICHARDSON

FEAST OF THE IMMACULATE
CONCEPTION   309
SISTER SIMONE CAMPBELL, SSS

FOREWORD

*T**he spiritual life is not* a template; it is a process meant to change our lives. There are stages in the spiritual life that move us from one level to another.

The first is compliance. The Ten Commandments dominate in this phase. Being spiritual in this phase depends on keeping a lists of do's and don'ts, on keeping the "rules"—whatever they are—on being perfect.

This kind of spiritual score keeping is a necessary but very immature stage. We concern ourselves with actions rather than attitudes. We worry about not insulting someone, perhaps, but not about wanting to insult them.

The point is that we don't make choices in this stage. Not real choices. We simply conform or rebel. We do what we're told and call ourselves holy for having done so. We do everything we're told but we never ask ourselves whether or not what we're doing has anything at all to do with the Beatitudes or not.

The second level of the spiritual life is awareness. It has more to do with becoming Christian than it does with going through the rituals of being Christian. This stage of spiritual development awakens in us the awareness that our role as Christian is to help make the world a just and peaceful place. We are not here simply to make ourselves paragons of organizational piety.

At the second level of the spiritual life, we come to realize that though God began the process of Creation it is our responsibility to complete it. Then we set out to become the kind of people we were put on Earth to be. We begin to go out of ourselves for the sake of the world rather than simply awarding ourselves gold stars for being regular observers of ancient rituals. "Do not wish to be called holy before you are holy," the Desert Monastics taught. It is holiness, not regularity, that we are now about in our spiritual life.

Finally, the third level of the spiritual life is transformation. It requires that we ourselves begin to "put on the mind of Christ." We ourselves begin to think like the Jesus of the Mount of Beatitudes who in the face of The Ten Commandments required love that was demanding, holier than laws could ever be. We face what it means to be just in an unjust world, meek in an arrogant one, humble in a domineering one, compassionate in a prejudiced one, full of grief for those who suffer from suffering not of their own doing, compassionate for those who are oppressed by the indifferent of this world.

Then the truly spiritual soul sees the world as God sees the world and sets out to make it right.

But that can happen only if we spend our lives immersed in the Scriptures, steeped in its passion for good, conscious of its struggles, in tune with the heart of God.

And how does that happen to us? Answer: It is the function of the Sunday homily to bring us face to face with the Jesus who walked from Galilee to Jerusalem raising women from the dead, curing the sick, contesting with the authorities in the of the poor. And to go and do the same.

And so, this book—a selection of homilies that break open the Christian tradition for our times and our lives. They goad us to compare our lives to the life of Jesus—and to grow into the best of ourselves.

Here begins the fullness of the spiritual life. Listen deeply and believe.

Sr. Joan Chittister, OSB
AUGUST 2014

PREFACE

In his homily for the 5th Sunday of Lent, my friend, Pastor Dave Davis, tells the story of a plaque that was located in the church where he first served so many years ago. It was affixed to the back of the pulpit where only the preacher could read the words and, thus, be reminded: "Sir, we wish to see Jesus." This is truly the message that comes forth from all congregations to their preacher, their pastor, their minister - that through effective and enriching preaching – they wish to see Jesus.

Church attendance continues to decline, and often the reason given is the congregation's lack of being spiritually nourished. Indeed, the people who come to church each week want to see Jesus! They want to walk away with a message that opens their lips, hearts and eyes in a Christo-centered fashion. And that is one of the answers I give when asked, "Why did you ever start this series of homiletic books?"

The other reason is to be able to raise money for charities that have been selected to benefit from each book. Through the gifts of each of the talented Contributors under the moniker of the *Homilists for the Homeless* we have been enabled to donate thousands of dollars in order to help feed the hungry, clothe the naked and visit the sick. Information on our Contributors, as well as the charities benefitting from this volume, can be found beginning on page 319.

After dedicating a full chapter in his exhortation, Evangelii Gaudium— The Joy of the Gospel— particular to preaching the Gospel, one cannot doubt the passion which Pope Francis has to effectively spreading the Good News. Long after the end of his papacy, Francis will be one who will be remembered for his love and compassion of those who live on the margins. While his own homilies are enriching, more importantly, his life has been shown to be one of including others and drawing them near. Recently, he said "It is not by proselytizing that the Church grows, but by attraction."

I hope that this book, along with our others, will 'attract' our readers to be more open to God's ever-presence in their lives so that we can fulfill our call to serve the hungry, the naked and the sick in our communities. For this call truly is the 'Good News' which Christ preached through his ministry.

May you and those you love be filled with the blessings that go with the gifted words within this volume.

Jim Knipper
08 SEPTEMBER 2014
NATIVITY OF THE BLESSED VIRGIN MARY

ADVENT SEASON

Isa. 63:16-17, 19; 64:2-7	*"Be watchful, be alert!"*
1 Cor. 1:3-9	
Mark 13:33-37	

Anyone looking for interesting holiday recipes may have stumbled upon a new word which has entered the American lexicon: "Cherpumple." It's a dessert, created by Los Angeles writer Charles Phoenix—a diet-destroying, gut-busting feat of cooking that seems guaranteed to induce sugar shock.

It's basically three different pies, stacked one on top of the other, and baked into one gargantuan "monster pie" with three layers—cherry, pumpkin, and apple, hence the name "cherpumple." The recipe has swept the internet and has become a sensation on YouTube.

I showed a picture of a "cherpumple" to my wife, and she agreed with me: it's absolutely disgusting.

Some things just aren't meant to be mashed together like that.

But I have to wonder if we haven't done something similar with Advent and Christmas. For all intents and purposes, we have managed to create one massive season—"Chradvent"—which conflates two distinct seasons into one. And it's beginning earlier and earlier each year.

In mid-November, I was amazed to walk by an apartment in my neighborhood in Queens and see the decked-out lobby, complete with a fully-lit

Christmas tree and wrapped gifts. The day after Thanksgiving, I noticed workers unloading Christmas trees to sell at a nearby flower shop. Even before Thanksgiving, it seems, we've started to celebrate "Chradvent."

Before everyone hops on that "Chradvent" bandwagon, I'd just like to take a moment to celebrate this season which so many have forgotten about—the season of Advent. We need to remember the reason for *this* season, and to hold on to Advent just a little while before surrendering to the craziness of "Chradvent."

The readings on this first Sunday of Advent alert us to something that is about to begin. A guest will arrive when we least expect him. The language is emphatic. "Be watchful, be alert!" Jesus tells his followers not to be caught off guard. His final word in this Gospel could not be more direct: "Watch!" Advent is that time of watching and waiting, of looking and seeking—hope-filled anticipation spread across four weeks.

We symbolize that, and ritualize it, with the Advent wreath. But we don't light all four candles at once. We go one at a time, so the light gathers and grows. If you have an Advent calendar, you don't fold open every window at once, but you go one small window at a time. Later in the season, we will sing the haunting refrain, "O come, O come, Emanuel, and ransom captive Israel…" We are captives awaiting freedom, prisoners held in dungeons of despair. But light is coming. Freedom is coming.

Jesus is coming.

But until he comes, we wait, and watch, and wonder, and pray.

We shouldn't rush it. This season is the time for taking stock, and making plans—a time of great expectations. Dorothy Day, in fact, compared it to a woman expecting a child. "She lives in such a garment of silence," Day wrote, "as though she were listening to hear the stir of life within her."

That brings me to a question all of us should ask during these coming weeks:

Are we listening?

Are we paying attention?

Are we looking to what will be—or are we already there?

If we jump right into the holiday season, we forget to wait, and watch, and wonder, and pray. We neglect the "joyful hope" that is so much a part of this beautiful season. When Christmas arrives, it will seem almost anti-climactic: one more day in a long litany of jingling bells and canned carols.

This year, resist the urge. Wait a while to get the tree or hang the wreath. Turn down the Christmas music. It's okay: it will be there in the middle of December, just as it was in the middle of November.

Instead, use these weeks to pull back, to retreat from the ho-ho-ho and fa-la-la-la-la. Find time to look within — to pray more deeply, and converse more intimately with the One who is coming. Ask Jesus: *How can I prepare for you? What can I do to welcome you into my life?*

If all of us do that, we may be surprised at the answers.

And we'll actually be able to hear the answer if we give ourselves over to the "garment of silence" which Dorothy Day wrote about.

"Cherpumple" is over the top, and unhealthy. And so, I think, is "Chradvent." So, do something sensible. Pull the two seasons apart, and live each of them as fully as possible.

Let's look forward to a merry Christmas.

But let's also use this opportunity, as well, to enjoy a blessed and holy Advent.

ISA. 40:1-5, 9-11

2 PETER 3:8-14

MARK 1:1-8

"Fear not to cry out: Here is your God!"

There is a tune in my ear that plays every time I read "Every valley shall be exalted." It is a tune that I learned in children's choir many, many years ago. A setting of Isaiah 40. It's not like I can remember the rehearsals, or what year it was, but I certainly remember the tune. It comes from somewhere deep within, and with a bit of clarity. "Every valley shall be exalted, every mountain made low, and all flesh shall see it together, for the mouth of the Lord has spoken it."

Like Advent itself, Isaiah 40 comes around every year, a call to worship here, an anthem there, a familiar solo…'Comfort ye!' But there's more to Isaiah 40, and more to the prophet's message, than a bit or a piece. It's more than a snippet. You and I don't get much chance to just sit with old Isaiah and take it all in, to hang there for a while, to listen, to look, or to let it well up within us from deep within.

While I was recently on sabbatical, I experienced some mountains. I climbed Twin Sisters in the Rocky Mountains by Estes Park, Colorado. I drove up Pike's Peak, and a few days later spent an afternoon on Kitchen Mesa above Ghost Ranch in New Mexico. I also took a cable car ride up Table Mountain in Cape Town, South Africa, and had a chance to hike up Stellenbosch Mountain. If I were to say that every view was different, that would be more than just stating the obvious. Upon reaching the top of Twin Sisters just after Labor Day, we sat in quite a snowstorm and could barely see each other. At the top of Pike's Peak, I learned the connection to the song "America the Beautiful" and watched as people seemed as drawn to the gift shop as they were to the view, especially the doughnuts touted as tasting better when made at that altitude. Clouds blew in so rapidly when we were on Table Mountain that we had to focus on the diverse vegetation and the beautiful wild flowers that were right at our feet. On Stellenbosch Mountain, I could see all the way to the Cape where the Atlantic and Indian Oceans meet. I sat there for a long time with my companions as they taught me more about the history of the South African nation. We sat and looked, and they pointed out the historic university town, the neighboring black township, the immigrant squatters' camp, the wine farms, and the millions of homes in the flats of Cape Town. A view from the mountaintop can be a whole lot more than you might expect.

Isaiah 40. It is an invitation to the prophet's mountain. Maybe not Sinai with Moses or Horeb and Carmel with Elijah, maybe not one of those famous biblical mountaintops, but the invitation from Isaiah is to come and to see and to hear. To come up and sit for a while and take in quite a view, not just a verse here or a quote there, but let the prophet point out some things. It's a whole lot more than you expect, sitting here and taking in Heaven and Earth and the promise of God. Isaiah 40. It's quite a view of creation.

The prophet is addressing the people of Israel at the time of captivity in Babylon. Their time of exile is coming to an end. The hope described is of a return to Jerusalem, as the time nears for restoration and rebuilding. God is faithful. God will feed, and gather, and carry the flock. God, the Holy One, the Creator of the ends of the Earth, has not grown weary. The nations of the world are nothing before the Lord, nor hardly a drop in the bucket. But you, O Jerusalem, herald of good tidings, do not fear, but lift your voice. The Word of the Lord stands forever. Here is your God!

In this wilderness, comfort, o comfort my people. In this wilderness, prepare the way of the Lord. In this wilderness comes a highway for our God, a highway of restoration and rebuilding and redemption. A highway destined for the Reign of God. Every valley shall be lifted up. Every mountain and hill be made low. The uneven ground shall be made level. The rough places will be made plain. All of it—valleys, hills, and rough places—will all be graded, shaped, and smoothed over so that it becomes this highway for our God. Creation itself is a pathway from the wilderness to the Reign of God.

You stand up here in Isaiah 40, stand with Isaiah and look out at the view, look out over creation, Look where the prophet points. Valleys, mountains, hills, rough places. It's beautiful alright, but the view is more than that. Can you see it? Can you hear it? Creation is singing, not simply a song in praise to the Maker of Heaven and Earth, but creation is singing and shouting and pointing and paving the way towards the direction of God's Glory, for the Glory of the Lord shall be revealed.

If you found yourself standing with Moses at Mount Sinai, I would think that the Glory of the Lord would be rather self-evident. It would be the awesome, earth-shaking, bush-burning yet not consumed, cloud-bearing, voice-speaking, law-giving, burning-the-face-of -Moses kind of glory. If you were hanging out with Elijah on the mountain, then any talk of God's Glory would come at Carmel after the fire of the Lord destroyed the burnt offering, the wood, the stones, and even licked up the water from the trench. But if you are with Elijah at Mt, Horeb, then God's Glory would come not in an earthquake, wind, or fire, but in a still small voice. I you're going to hang out with Isaiah up on his mountain and take in the view as he sees it, then it's going to be more than you might expect.

Valleys lifted up. Mountains made low. Power is given to the faint, and the powerless are strengthened. Then, Isaiah points to *a light to the nations. The eyes which were blind are now opened. I am the Lord, and that is my name. My Glory I give to no other.* Isaiah tells you to listen. *The sea roars and all that fills it. The desert and its towns lift up their voices. I will turn the darkness before them into light. When you pass through the waters, I will be with you. The flame shall not consume you. I will make a way in the wilderness, and rivers in the desert. Do not fear. Break forth into singing, O mountains. O forest and every tree in it. Good news to the oppressed: the brokenhearted will be bound up, liberty will be proclaimed to the captives, the prisoners will be released. The wolf and the lamb are now together. They shall not hurt, nor destroy on my holy mountain. For I am about to create a new Heaven and a new Earth.* When you find yourself on Isaiah's mountain, when you stop to take it all in, you will see that the Glory of the Lord is revealed in the peaceable Kingdom of God.

All of Creation is shaped into a pathway from the wilderness to the Reign of God. Creation is singing and shouting, pointing and paving the way in the direction of God's Glory where righteousness bursts forth in stunning colors, where justice rises on the horizon, and where peace covers the Earth like morning dew. When you sit with Isaiah, the prophet is pointing to the promise of God. It is the promise of restoration, rebuilding, and redemption. There will be a new Heaven and a new Earth. The view is so much more than you might expect!

Isaiah 40, like Advent, comes around every year. Maybe that's some part of the gift of God's graces. Images, words, and verses that are etched deep within, which come back with certain clarity, and for people of faith a certain mountaintop panorama comes into view, a certain song starts to play. You can't quite remember where you learned it, where you first saw it, but it is so familiar. Hopefully, you can't get it out of your head, or out of your heart. This is the promise of God. The glory of the Lord revealed as compassion, love, and mercy will break forth like the dawn in your life, as well as in mine. Christ Jesus himself will be made known afresh in the binding of the brokenhearted, as the hungry are fed and the naked are clothed, the sick and dying are cared for, the lost are embraced, sinners are forgiven, and finally, the first will be last and the last first. Isaiah 40, it comes around every year. Maybe that's some part of the Wisdom of God…God patiently waiting for us and for the world to change its tune, and to get a fresh perspective.

As you and I are sitting here with Isaiah, the old prophet, looking and listening, another Advent season is upon us. Not much seems to have changed. The songs and the jingles seem to still relay the message that life's purpose and meaning can be found right there in a purchase, among the stuff piled so high. The powers and principalities, the empires and the nations who opt for war and weapons and more troops press for more and more and more. The world's poor and suffering, the hungry far away, the hungry way close to home are still here. Creation is moaning, yearning for its own liberation while economics, politics, consumption, power, and might carry the day. The lost and the broken are all wandering far away from any sense of being a child of God, and are all longing for a love which can only come from God, there in the darkness as the Savior reaches and reaches and welcomes them home.

You and I are still sitting here with old Isaiah, looking and listening, and then Heaven and Earth start to sing. Heaven and Earth start to sing. *Fields, floods, rocks, hills, and plains. They repeat this sounding joy.* That tune, it comes from somewhere deep within. We've heard it before. The view from here is always more than you might expect.

3RD SUNDAY OF ADVENT

FR. JAMES MARTIN, SJ

Isa. 61:1-2, 10-11
1 Thess. 5:16-24
John 1:6-8, 19-28

"Rejoice always"

Here's a shocking thing that I learned during theology studies, specifically during our preaching class. "From time to time," said our professor, "it's okay *not* to focus on the Gospel when you're preaching on Sundays." What? Really? I thought you *had* to preach on the readings. "Well, yes," he said; "the church's documents on preaching recommend focusing on the *readings*—but that means not just the Gospel, but also the first and second readings; the psalms; or *even* the prayers of the Mass."

Today is a good time to exercise that freedom, because the second reading fits perfectly with Gaudete Sunday. The term, by the way, comes from the first words of the opening antiphon of the Mass, "Rejoice in the Lord always," which, oddly, we don't say. And the Latin for "rejoice" is *Gaudete*.

But that term may seem out of place if we look only at the Gospel, where John talks about the One who is to come: it sounds hopeful, but not really that *joyful*. John is approached by some priests and Levites who seem interested, curious, wondering, even hopeful about who he is. The Hebrew Scriptures had predicted the return of Elijah, so maybe this was him. But John makes clear he is only a voice in the wilderness, not fit even to do what a slave would do for the coming Messiah. So, as I said, hopeful, but not particularly joyful in tone.

It is today's second reading that fits the theme of joy much more closely. But it also may be somewhat baffling. Because at the beginning of the reading a strange little phrase upends the typical conception of St. Paul as a cranky, grumpy prude. Paul says, "Rejoice always." And, as we heard, he also says this in the opening antiphon from Philippians, "Rejoice in the Lord always!"

But how in God's name, literally, are we supposed to rejoice always? Does that mean that we're bad Christians if we're not always happy? Well, let's look at that passage a little more carefully.

By common consent, First Thessalonians is the earliest of Paul's letters and, therefore, the earliest writing in the entire New Testament. It was most likely written in Athens or Corinth around A.D. 50. As such, it *predates* the four Gospels and the Acts of the Apostles. Here, Paul is writing to the Christian community that he had founded in Thessalonica, located in the Roman province of Macedonia, on the northern shore of the Aegean Sea. In his brief letter, he encourages his fellow believers to have confidence in the second coming of Jesus, which they thought would happen within their lifetime.

Unlike some of Paul's other letters, he's not responding to any heated theological debate raging within the Christian community in the region. Nor is he scolding his fellow Christians for some litany of horrible sins. Instead, he is mainly encouraging them to lead holy lives. The beginning of the letter, in fact, contains generous praise of the conduct of the Christians in Thessalonica, whom he says are an example to other churches in the region. So it's a very gentle letter.

Now back to that remarkable phrase, which is part of a triad of Christian practices: "Rejoice always, pray without ceasing, give thanks in all circumstances; for this is the will of God in Christ Jesus for you."

You could spend a lifetime meditating on that one sentence. You could spend a lifetime meditating on just the words "rejoice always." But is it possible?

Realistically, what does it mean to "rejoice always"? Well, first of all, it doesn't mean that you cannot be sad about suffering or that you have to ignore the tragedies in the world around you. But at first blush, Paul's words certainly seem to imply this to be the case. I mean, we encounter sadness in our lives and we see sadness in other lives, as well as great injustice. Think of all the sick people we know, or the great economic disparities in the world. How can we be "rejoicing"?

Well, Thessalonica in the time of St. Paul was hardly a paradise. Under the heel of Imperial Rome, many in the town were living as slaves. Those who were free may have been poor, illiterate and unable to obtain what we would consider even basic medical care. The Thessalonians would have fully understood the meaning of suffering. And the Christians among them would have known persecution, something that Paul alludes to in the first few lines of his letter. Paul knew about suffering, too. So how could Paul ask them to turn a blind eye to the realities of life?

He wasn't. St. Paul was pointing to something *deeper*. It is easy to be joyful when you are happy. Or to be joyful during those fleeting moments when the world seems like a fair and just place for everyone. But how can you be joyful in sad times, and in the face of injustice? You can be joyful because joy is deeper than happiness and is not about a thing or an object, but about something else: God. Joy is happiness in God.

One of the most vivid memories I have as a Jesuit novice was being invited to a predominantly African American church in Boston. Before this, I had never been in such a church. Yet, from the moment the choir began singing the entrance hymn, an African-American spiritual, I felt swept away into a chorus of joy. Years later, during my time working in

Eastern Africa, I would experience that same ebullience in the songs of the churches in the Nairobi slums, where Kenyans would be packed shoulder to shoulder as they shouted out the words of Swahili hymns.

What these two groups had in common was not simply the color of their skin, but their abiding confidence in God.

Joy, deeper than happiness, is a virtue that finds its foundation in the knowledge that we are loved by God. For Christians, the knowledge that Jesus has been raised from the dead is a constant cause for joy, even in tough times. This does not mean that suffering does not bring sadness. Of course it does. But suffering is not the last word—in Jesus's life, or in ours. And that knowledge can lead us to a deeper joy. Even in the midst of difficulties.

Sadness is an appropriate and natural response to suffering. And God desires that we be honest about our sadness, and share it in prayer with God. The knowledge that God is with us, however, and that God accompanies us, can lead us to a confident joy that can carry us through difficult, and sometimes unbearable, times.

Likewise, the passage "rejoice always" does not mean that we should simply "look on the bright side" in the face of injustice. The anger that rises within you over an unjust situation is a sign that God is moving you to address that injustice. God speaks to you through your anger at what you see, through your disgust over what you have read, or your shock over what someone has told you. How else would God move you to action? This is particularly the case when it is an injustice visited upon another person, since anger over an injustice to yourself (rightful though the anger may be) may be tinged with selfishness and a sense of wounded pride.

"Let's say you passed a homeless person sitting beside a fancy restaurant; diners come out, after having spent hundreds of dollars on their meal, but fail to give the person even a glance, let alone a few dollars or a kind word." You might be angry or sad. You would probably be moved to give the that person some of your own money, and maybe even spend some time with him. But you certainly wouldn't say to yourself, much less to him, "Be happy!" Witnessing the injustice, you would try, as far as you could, to lessen it. Out of such strong emotions and holy anger are born great works of charity.

Where is the joy, then? It comes from a loving trust in God, in the awareness that God is working through the compassion you feel, in the knowledge that God desires a just world where the poor are treated fairly, and in the trust that God will help those who heed His voice to help bring about justice. So, there is joy.

Of course, this is what John the Baptist is talking about in the Gospel today. "Make straight the way of the Lord" means not physically leveling a path that Jesus can walk on; but bringing justice into the world, making things "right" with God; preparing a just world, and repenting of greed. So his message is not just a hopeful one, but a joyful one, as well.

But, let's go back to St. Paul. One important key to his suggestion is that all three parts of his triad of Christian practices are bound together. Rejoice always. Pray without ceasing. In all circumstances, give thanks. So: joy, prayer and gratitude—they're all connected.

Joy, for example, springs from gratitude. When we recall things, events or people for which and for whom we are grateful, our joy increases. Prayer also supports the other two virtues. A contemplative awareness of the world, and an attitude of prayerful attentiveness, make it easier to see life's blessings. Finally, joy moves us to gratitude.

Likewise, our gratitude over good news can lead to joy. Joy can also move us to prayer. In our joy we want to be with God, to share our joyful life, gratefully, in prayer—just as we would share joy with a friend. Thus, each virtue supports the others in a complex spiritual interplay. Prayer awakens gratitude. Gratitude leads to joy. And joy moves us to prayer. In this way, we are able to follow Paul's gentle advice to the Thessalonians from almost 2,000 years ago.

Many modern believers think of St. Paul not as the Apostle of Joy, but as the Apostle of Gloom. He is usually characterized solely as a stern moralizer, intent on frustrating authentic human emotions, obsessed with tamping down human sexuality. Yet, here in his earliest letter, Paul is recommending something positive.

There were other Christian communities that needed to hear sterner words. But to the Christians of Thessalonica and to Christians today, the Apostle Paul advises three things. The first of these is joy.

So on this Gaudete Sunday, I say to you, St. Paul says to you, the church says to you, and Jesus Christ says to you: "Rejoice always!"

4TH SUNDAY OF ADVENT

FR. WILLIAM BAUSCH

2 SAM. 7:1-5, 8-12, 14-16
ROM. 16:25-27
LUKE 1:26-38

"Be it done unto me according to your word."

In the *Philadelphia Museum of* Art there is a painting of the Annunciation by an artist named Henry Ossawa Tanner. It shows Mary as a young girl sitting on her disheveled bed, and there is this light in front of her. It must be right after the angel has spoken to her. And Mary is just sitting there, looking at the light with her mouth open, dumbfounded. She has this look on her face that says, "What, are you kidding? How can this be?" She is stunned, confused, scared to the point that the angel is compelled to say, "Do not be afraid."

There is a similar fresco at St. Michael's Chapel at Rutgers University. It depicts the topsy-turvy aspect of the event, as the angel appears to Mary upside down, uttering the word "blessed" backwards, indicating that Mary's life would be thoroughly upended.

And it would be. What God is asking is incomprehensible. In addition, in her tiny village, where everyone knows everyone else, and many people are related to one another, everyone knows that she and the man who is already her legal husband have not yet begun to live together. And all of them can count to nine. What will they say about her? What kind of nasty looks will they cast her way when her precious child is born too soon?

It is all too much: too much at stake, too much to ask. Yes, like so many others before her, Mary has just experienced the truth: that it's a fearful and messy thing to be encountered by God, to discover a mission, a conscience, to stand at the crossroads. As a Jew, Mary knew well enough the ancient stories. She thinks of Moses, who tried to duck his call by saying he was no natural leader like his brother Aaron. Pick him. Or Isaiah, who protested his call to be a prophet by saying he'd make a lousy one. Or Jonah, who ran the other way when told to go to Nineveh. They wanted to be close to God, but not that close. Mary, too, knew that to flirt with God had its unspeakable joys but also its cost.

What I'm trying to do with these insights is to wean you away from those gorgeous Annunciation paintings of a serene Mary, robed in Renaissance attire, glowing with a halo and accompanied by cherubs in a resplendent room whose windows show a Tuscan landscape. The reality is quite the opposite.

Mary's sitting on a disheveled bed with hair undone trying to recover from what was like a slap in the face, realizing fully what it meant to say yes to God and fearful of the consequences. She knew what it wound up costing Moses and Isaiah and Jonah—that is closer to the truth, and, therefore, it made her yes, when she got around to it, all the more open and generous and heroic.

What I'm trying to do is to present to you this gospel as a "Mary Moment" to contemplate. The Mary Moment is one we all know: that sudden stop-in-your-tracks episode. Perhaps it's the loss of a family member or friend, a flash of self-disgust while watching online porn or engaged in loveless sex or binging. Maybe it's a movie or book or tender insight that made us pause, an incident that slowed us down, made us realize for a fleeting moment that a certain shallowness has entered our lives, that life is really about more than celebrity dances and Facebook and divorces and fashion, and *Hot in Cleveland* and endless stimulation—that we have other choices we should make.

A man relates a simple story. "One spring afternoon," he says, "my five-year-old son, David, and I were planting raspberry bushes along the side of the garage. A neighbor joined us for a few moments. Just then David pointed to the ground. 'Look, Daddy! What's that?' he asked.

"I stopped talking with my neighbor and looked down. 'A beetle,' I said. David was impressed and pleased with the discovery of this fancy, color-ful creature. Then my neighbor lifted his foot and stepped on the insect giving his shoe an extra twist in the dirt. 'That ought to do it,' he laughed. David looked up at me, waiting for an explanation, a reason. That night, just before I turned off the light in his bedroom. David whispered, 'I liked that beetle, Daddy.' 'I did too,' I whispered back." The man concluded his story by saying. "We have the power to choose."

We have the power to choose how we will respond to every living thing that crosses our path. We have the power to love one another or not.

There are these Mary Moments when we are confronted with such an opportunity to choose, to realize that we can be better persons. We don't always have to use people. There are people who live on the edge, are poor or suffering, who need our concern and ministrations. There's a bad habit we need to deal with, an indifference we need fired up, an addiction that calls for attention, a relationship that needs healing, a priority that needs to be put in place. We need to embrace the holiness we secretly desire, no matter how much others make fun of us. The "Me" life, the shallow life, the surface life, is killing our souls, and yet, all the while, in the background, we vaguely sense that an angel is confronting us. These are Mary Moments.

Can we say yes? It's not easy. There will be a cost—Mary knew that, hence her fear—and there will be indescribable peace and joy. Mary also knew that when later she sang to cousin Elizabeth, "My spirit rejoices in God my Savior, for he has looked with favor on the lowliness of his servant...for the Mighty One has done great things for me and holy is his name."

But perhaps today, in the light of this familiar gospel now seen with fresh eyes, we can reconsider, perhaps even ask Mary to intercede for us—that, perplexed and fearful as we sit on the edge of our beds, we too may find courage to say "yes," to surrender to:

> *live simply,*
> *give generously,*
> *care deeply,*
> *speak kindly,*
> *to walk by faith and not by sight,*
> *to utter fearfully but firmly, "Be it done unto me according to your word."*

CHRISTMAS SEASON

CHRISTMAS: MIDNIGHT

FR. RICHARD G. MALLOY, SJ

ISA. 9:1-6
TITUS 2:11-14
LUKE 2:1-14

| *"For a child is born to us."*

A Red Sox fan walks into a New York bar where the Boston fans meet to watch the Red Sox games. On this particular day, the Red Sox were playing the Yankees. When a Red Sox batter hit a home run, the Red Sox fan would yell, "Bartender, give everyone in the house a drink on me—except for that guy over there in the Yankees hat." The guy in the Yankees hat says to the Red Sox Fan, "Thank You." Later on, the Red Sox turn a crucial double play and, the Red Sox fan yells, "Bartender, give everyone in the house a drink on me—except for that guy over there in the Yankees hat." The guy in the Yankees hat says to the Red Sox fan, "Thank You." In the ninth inning, the Red Sox catch up and then go ahead of the Yankees by three runs to win the game. The Red Sox fan yells, "Bartender, give everyone in the house a drink on me—except for that guy over there in the Yankees hat." The guy in the Yankees hat says to the Red Sox fan, "Thank You." Then the Red Sox fan says to the bartender, "What's the matter with that guy? I insult him and all he does is thank me. Is he nuts, or what?" The bartender replies, "No. He's not nuts. He's the owner!"

The "owner" of the world has come, and, although he is more likely a Cubs or Phillies fan than a Yankees rooter, Jesus has come to bring us joy and peace. St. Paul tells us: "The grace of God has appeared, saving all."

We are saved from despair, discouragement and depression, saved from all that threatens us with destruction and death, and saved from horror, hate and hell. He comes to heal us, and make us whole. He comes to reestablish the people of Israel, and inaugurate the Reign of God. He comes to free us from all ill, and to set us free to live and to love. This is our God. This is Jesus, the one whose name means "God Saves!"

The prophet proclaims, "The people who walked in darkness have seen a great light; upon those who dwelt in the land of gloom, a light has shone. You have brought them abundant joy and great rejoicing." The Lord of all is born for us this night, born in our hearts, born in our lives, born in our social systems and cultures. Born to save and transform all. Isaiah sings, "For a child is born to us, a son is given us; upon his shoulder dominion rests. They name him Wonder-Counselor, God-Hero, Father-Forever, Prince of Peace."

Many of us of a certain age remember the stunning proclamation bursting forth in the original *A Charlie Brown Christmas* (1965). Little Linus recites from the King James Version of Luke's Gospel: "And, lo, the angel of the Lord came upon them, and the glory of the Lord shone round about them: and they were sore afraid. And the angel said unto them, 'Fear not: for, behold, I bring you good tidings of great joy, which shall be to all people. For unto you is born this day in the city of David a Savior, which is Christ the Lord. And this shall be a sign unto you; Ye shall find the babe wrapped in swaddling clothes, lying in a manger.'"

DePaul University New Testament scholar, John Dominic Crossan, notes that Luke's Gospel is really quite radical. The angel speaks to those on the margins of society, the shepherds and the 'pagan magicians,' i.e. magi. The shepherds were rough guys who knew how to protect the sheep from wolves and rustlers. Shepherds carried weapons and were seen as 'dangerous outsiders.' The angel announces the arrival of the Messiah, the King long awaited by the people of Israel. The titles of this King are a striking insult to the reigning powers. Lord, Savior, Prince of Peace. Caesar Augustus held these titles. Anyone claiming them was in for trouble. It's like saying, "The Commander in Chief, POTUS, The most powerful man on Earth," is born for you this day." According to Crossan, Jesus comes to bring "peace through justice" as opposed to the Roman "peace through victory" (http://bustedhalo.com/features/busted-john-dominic-crossan).

There was a time when Christmas stopped war. It happened December 24, 1914. Curiously, this fact wasn't highlighted in my high school history books in the 1970's. Winter 1914 was cold, wet and miserable in the trenches. The Germans began lighting up their Christmas trees. They sang Christmas songs, and the English troops began singing back. John McCuthceon's haunting ballad captures the miracle of this moment when Christmas songs stopped the slaughter. Peace permeated the land as "in two tongues one song filled up that sky."

> *My name is Francis Tolliver, I come from Liverpool.*
> *Two years ago the war was waiting for me after school.*
> *To Belgium and to Flanders, to Germany to here*
> *I fought for King and country I love dear.*
>
> *'Twas Christmas in the trenches, where the frost so bitter hung,*
> *The frozen fields of France were still, no Christmas song was sung*
> *Our families back in England were toasting us that day*
> *Their brave and glorious lads so far away.*
>
> *I was lying with my messmate on the cold and rocky ground*
> *When across the lines of battle came a most peculiar sound*
> *Says I, "Now listen up, me boys!" each soldier strained to hear*
> *As one young German voice sang out so clear.*

"He's singing bloody well, you know!" my partner says to me
Soon, one by one, each German voice joined in harmony
The cannons rested silent, the gas clouds rolled no more
As Christmas brought us respite from the war

As soon as they were finished and a reverent pause was spent
"God Rest Ye Merry, Gentlemen" struck up some lads from Kent
The next they sang was "Stille Nacht." "Tis 'Silent Night'," says I
And in two tongues one song filled up that sky

"There's someone coming toward us!" the front line sentry cried
All sights were fixed on one lone figure trudging from their side
His truce flag, like a Christmas star, shown on that plain so bright
As he, bravely, strode unarmed into the night

Soon one by one on either side walked into No Man's Land
With neither gun nor bayonet we met there hand to hand
We shared some secret brandy and we wished each other well
And in a flare-lit soccer game we gave'em hell

We traded chocolates, cigarettes, and photographs from home
These sons and fathers far away from families of their own
Young Sanders played his squeezebox and they had a violin
This curious and unlikely band of men

Soon daylight stole upon us and France was France once more
With sad farewells we each prepared to settle back to war
But the question haunted every heart that lived that wonderous night
"Whose family have I fixed within my sights?"

'Twas Christmas in the trenches where the frost, so bitter hung
The frozen fields of France were warmed as songs of peace were sung
For the walls they'd kept between us to exact the work of war
Had been crumbled and were gone forevermore

My name is Francis Tolliver, in Liverpool I dwell
Each Christmas comes since World War I, I've learned its lessons well
That the ones who call the shots won't be among the dead and lame
And on each end of the rifle we're the same.

Do yourself a favor and google the version of the song on Youtube. (http://www.youtube.com/watch?v=QTXhZ4uR6rs). It is the most moving Christmas song I have ever heard. The miracle is that the truce went on for days. They couldn't get the soldiers to go back to killing. They eventually had to replace the troops to get the war going again. Joseph Persico, in his book on World War I, reports that there was one German soldier who would not participate in the truce. His name: Adolph Hitler.

Christ is born again this Christmas. He is the one who made our world, and he asks us to treat his world with respect and one another with care. He calls us all to live in love, to practice peace, to join in justice, and to let God reign in our war weary world. Let us be peacemakers and heralds of joy as we stroll unarmed into this Silent Night. Let us pray.

NATIVITY OF THE LORD: DAY

FR. DANIEL P. HORAN, OFM

IsA. 52:7-10
HEB. 1:1-6
JOHN 1:1-18

"...and the Word was God."

In a sense, it is true to say that, 'Jesus is the reason for the season.' But it may not be true in the way that we are typically accustomed to thinking.

Most people who express such reminders, either literally or on bumper stickers, tend to reinforce an error that stands at the other end of the continuum from the over-commercialized, idol-of-shopping holiday that Christmas has become. Such 'Jesus is the reason for the season' people tend to focus on the birth of a little boy, the celebration of a particular person, the coming of *Emmanuel*, which, of course, is a good thing. But the message usually stops there.

The birth of Jesus may be the occasion for our celebration, but the love of God is really the fullest 'reason for the season.'

What we celebrate today is not just a birthday, nor some other kind of 'special day' for Jesus, but the nearly inexplicable and almost incomprehensible love of God. What we celebrate today, what remains the truest reason for the season, is that God so desires to be in relationship with us that God planned, from all eternity, to forego Divinity to become one of us as one among us.

In order to understand what this means in a practical sense, I invite you to imagine sitting in front of a computer (for most of us, this won't take much effort). You're logged into your email account, Facebook page, E-Harmony profile, or Twitter feed. Through one, or maybe all of these media sites, you are receiving messages, communications, missives of some sort from a loved one, or at least one you want to love. You get to know a lot about this person: their likes and dislikes, priorities, goals, vision for the future, what this person may think of you, and so on. But you don't get it all. There is still something missing.

Perhaps you and this person both recognize that something still feels off and, because you want the other to reveal him or herself to you and vice versa, you talk on the phone or through video chat. Your picture of the beloved becomes clearer, an image, their face, something more personal begins to be seen. But it's still not enough.

Eventually the other person says, "I really want to meet you in person, I'll come to you, and then we can go get some coffee." And for the first time, what had once been a true yet partial encounter experience now becomes an 'in the flesh' meeting. So many things that couldn't be communicated in earlier ways can now be disclosed and received in overt and implicit ways. Now you really can start to know the other and allow, if you're willing, the other to know you. In the end, this shift in the relationship illustrates the difference between "knowing *about*" someone and truly "*knowing*" someone. *This* difference, *this* shift in the relationship, is exactly what Christmas is all about.

The authors of the Letter to the Hebrews and the prologue to John's Gospel both make this point in today's readings. "Long ago, God spoke to our ancestors in varied and partial ways," the Letter to the Hebrews begins. It's not that other people haven't known God over the centuries, it's just that they knew God incompletely, just as one might only know about someone from social media, email, and phone calls today. "No one has ever seen God," John's Gospel proclaims, but now God has come to meet us directly in this person Jesus of Nazareth. God has decided to take the 'relationship to the next level,' and has drawn near to us.

Far too often, we who are so familiar with the Bible can zone out or presume that we already know the meaning of certain passages; therefore, we miss some important details which are present in the text. Such is the case, I believe, with John's prologue. Yeah, we get the Word and John the Baptist and the darkness, and we identify what seems like the climactic point in John 1:14: "And the Word became flesh and dwelt among us." But the prologue still continues and goes on for four more verses. I think that the real pinnacle of the prologue comes at the actual ending of the passage in John 1:18 when we are told who exactly this Word really is. The Word-made-flesh, this Jesus Christ, is *truly God*, the image of the invisible God, the expression, or "pressing-outward" (as in the Greek *exegesis*) of the Father, whom nobody had previously seen.

The joy of this season, as well as its 'reason,' is found in the recognition that God so loved creation that God became part of that very same world. Communicating through angels, in Scripture, through burning bushes and prophets no longer sufficed. In order to be fully in relationship with us, God had to become one of us. The first reading from Isaiah calls all people to sing for joy and celebrate God's action and, indeed, we have cause for rejoicing. What was unclear has been made visible, and the mystery of what God is like, how God loves, what is important to God is revealed in the life, actions, and sayings of Jesus.

But that's not all. We believe that Jesus Christ is both fully-God *and* fully-human. So if Jesus reveals to us who God is, he has also revealed to us who we are, or rather who we should be. Yet, do we celebrate *that* today? This is in part why I am so hesitant to talk simply about 'Jesus is the reason for the season.' There is a way in which such a phrase can allow us to wiggle out of our responsibility to take seriously the meaning of God becoming incarnate. We might, with or without realization, prefer to imagine Christmas as a little boy's birthday party, more than humanity's meeting up with God for the first time in person. This meeting up with God should challenge us to consider the ways in which we are, or are not, being fully human just as much as we get to see who God is in God's fullness. Perhaps the greatest gift we can give on Christmas is to try to be more fully human by following more closely in the footprints of Jesus Christ.

HOLY FAMILY OF JESUS, MARY AND JOSEPH

FR. JAMES J. GREENFIELD, OSFS

GEN. 15:1-6; 21:1-3
HEB. 11:8,11-12,17-19
LUKE 2:22-40

"And the child grew... and the grace of God was on him."

One of my homiletics professors, Fr. Bob Waznak, SS, suggested that if we take the Feast of the Holy Family in a sentimental way then we would conjure up an artificial family. You know, the photos we see of smiling, cheerful families. The result could be the "first family of Nazareth"—Joseph holding a lily in one hand and a carpenter's tool in the other, Mary looking perfectly accessorized, and Jesus gazing lovingly at his holy parents, eagerly awaiting their next command. Waznak concludes that we would get "the Waltons of Nazareth."

But we all know that this feast is not for perfect families at all. I was once at a convention when the speaker asked if there were anyone in the meeting room who had *not* come from a dysfunctional family. No one raised a hand. My point here is that this feast is for those of us who know that we are not perfect and did not come from a perfect family or upbringing.

I was at a parish in Camden, NJ, for the Fourth Sunday of Advent, and school children were dressed as angels as they brought forth the Christmas crèche figures—all of them but Jesus, who would obviously arrive in a few days. What struck me so profoundly was the figure of Mary, whose outstretched arms were waiting to hold the little figurine of Jesus. I thought to myself how many other mothers have those same outstretched arms waiting for their babies or children—to come home from the hospital, to come home from war, to deal with an addiction. There are also women desirous of becoming mothers, as they struggle with infertility.

Fast forward to the scene in Luke's Gospel for today, and we also see two wisdom figures, almost like Temple lights—Simeon and Anna—burning brightly with outstretched arms. Simeon had waited a long time to receive Jesus, to hold him. He sings his song of gratitude once he meets this baby whom he believes will change the world. Anna, the only woman in the Gospel who is called a prophetess and who had fasted in the Temple night and day during her long widowhood, spoke of Jesus as one who would redeem Israel. These two elders, whose lives are spent in waiting and wondering, remind us that life does not always unfold in the way we may want. But, enter Jesus into the mix, and we experience a new way to 'grow up,' develop, and age, making peace with ourselves, our families, and our world.

Here is where Luke masterfully sets the theme of his Gospel: this little baby will grow to adulthood and have special concern for the poor and forgotten. Pope Francis, in *The Joy of the Gospel*, says this:

> *Salvation came to us from the "yes" uttered by a lowly maiden from a small town on the fringes of a great empire. The Savior was born in a manger, in the midst of animals, like children of poor families; he was presented at the Temple along with two turtledoves, the offering made by those who could not afford a lamb; he was raised in a home of ordinary workers and worked with his own hands to earn his bread ... [His preaching] was "The Spirit of the Lord God is upon me, because he has anointed me to preach good news to the poor."*

And so, these two grandparent figures, seemingly out of place and forgotten in the midst of the Temple, remind us that ours is a God of surprises, that grace abounds on the margins as much as in the mainstream, and how God's choice to be born poor calls us to choose friendship with the poor at every turn. Furthermore, it is Anna and Simeon who tell us to look beyond great empires and find God among the lowliest and downtrodden. How similar is the clarion message of Pope Francis who challenges powerful nations, including our own, and wants our great Church to be poor for the poor! Giant empires, no; gentle hearts, yes!

Simeon's song that Jesus is a "light to reveal God to the nations" reminds us that the revelation of God in Jesus is the source of true light for our world. This kind of light is totally and completely a gift from God. In this Christmas Octave, we recognize that we cannot simply manufacture this sort of revelation, which drives back the darkness of the world and makes it a better place, without the light of Christ. It reminds me of the Persian proverb: "The candle says to the darkness, I beg to differ."

Simeon also says to Mary "this child is destined for the fall and rise of many in Israel, and to be a sign that will be contradicted (and you yourself a sword will pierce) so that the thoughts of many hearts may be revealed." At the end of the chapter we learn that Mary ponders all of this in her heart. How many other mothers, just like Mary, need to balance pains, tensions, and contradictions within their hearts? As disciples, we are brought into this similar dynamic as we seek to wrestle with the issues of our own day in like fashion.

A New York Times editorial titled "Why, God?" and published on Christmas Day featured Kevin O'Neil, a Redemptorist priest, who wrote about celebrating Christmas amid so many harsh realities in our world. He quoted a contemporary theologian who described mercy as entering into the chaos of another. He went on to say that "Christmas is really a celebration of the mercy of God who entered the chaos of our world in the person of Jesus, mercy incarnate. I have never found it easy to be with people who suffer, to enter into the chaos of others. Yet, every time I have done so, it has been a gift to me, better than the wrapped and ribboned packages. I am pulled out of myself to be love's presence to someone else, even as they are love's presence to me."

As we celebrate the Feast of the Holy Family, we are invited to be the face of mercy, to be outstretched arms for others—not in any idealized, 'Walton family' kind of way. As St. Paul writes about putting on Christ, he leads us to find our merciful self by way of a metaphor: clothing ourselves with compassion, kindness, humility, meekness, and patience. With these attributes, the Word of God can dwell in our lives, our families, and our world.

Merry Christmas!

MARY MOTHER OF GOD

MARY ELIZABETH SPERRY

Num. 6:22-27
Gal. 4:4-7
Luke 2:16-21

"Mary kept all these things, reflecting on them in her heart."

People call this time of year a season of wonder. We decorate our homes and public spaces with gleaming lights, bright colors, and shining ornaments which captivate our senses and fuel our imaginations. Even the oldest among us begins to view the world through the eyes of a child.

Just one week ago, on Christmas, we celebrated the birth of our Lord Jesus Christ. But now it seems as though most of the world has moved on from that celebration. Though some people began preparations in mid-autumn and celebration in the first days of December, their Christmas spirit expired at midnight on December 25th. Instead, they have turned their attention to after-Christmas sales, New Year's resolutions, and even Valentine's Day (if store displays are to be believed). But in the Church, we continue to celebrate Christmas through the Baptism of the Lord.

Today's Gospel, a Gospel of the Christmas season, presents two very different models from what the world gives. The models in the Gospel have not rushed past the meaning of the Christmas celebration, eager to get on with what is next. First, the Gospels present the shepherds. After hearing the angel's proclamation of God's faithfulness in sending the promised Messiah, they do not dawdle in preparation. They leave their flocks immediately, and hasten to Bethlehem to see the baby who will save the world. Once they encounter Jesus, they return home praising God, and giving witness to God's fidelity. Having seen God's goodness in their own lives, they reach out to share this Good News with everyone they meet.

The second model is Mary, whom we honor today as the Mother of God. Luke tells us that, in the depths of her heart, Mary reflected on all that had happened to her—the announcement that she would bear the Son of God, her visit to her kinswoman Elizabeth, the journey to Bethlehem to register in the census, Jesus's birth, and the shepherds' visit. Unlike all too many people today, Mary did not move on to the next event or distraction as quickly as possible. Instead, she took time to embrace the wonder of what God had done for and through her. She allowed her heart, her being, her life, to be filled with the wonder of the presence of God. This reflection helped to allow the meaning of what had happened to become part of her life.

Together, Mary and the shepherds shared the gift of wonder. Though their lives were simple, they saw the presence of God in the world around them. They opened their ears to hear the voice of the angel. They did not let their fear keep them from following God's path. Too often, our eyes and ears and hearts are clouded, unable to experience the wonder of God's creation and of the myriad of gifts that God gives us each day.

But in this holy season, with our attention captured by the sights, sounds, and scents of the season, we take the time to reflect once again on the wonder of the incarnation. We are created in God's own image and likeness. Though our sinfulness separated us from His love, God loved us so much that He sent His own Son to be one of us, to live among us, to die as one of us, so that we might live forever with Him. This is the mystery that we celebrate in this holy season, the mystery that gives meaning to our lives.

Following the example of Mary and the shepherds, we are called to reflect on all the good things that God has done in our lives, and to give witness to His faithfulness. But before we can reflect on the good things that God has done, we have to notice them—a task that may be more difficult than we realize. So many things distract us, and keep us from paying attention to what God is doing in our lives: from the electronic gadgets that have become necessities, to the noise and pace of our everyday lives. We live in a culture that glorifies busy-ness, assuming that the busier you are, the more important you must be.

Trying to accomplish too much within a limited amount of time keeps us from noticing the wonders that God gives us. That is why the Church takes weeks to celebrate Christmas, and why it gives us Mary and the shepherds as models in this season. The example of the shepherds reminds us of the need to make our search for God a priority over our worldly cares. Following the example of Mary by taking time to reflect, allows us to move past the hectic pace of of the holiday season to focus on the meaning of what we celebrate.

But we cannot allow our reflection to be entirely self-focused. Reflecting on the good things which God has done in our lives should spur us to action on behalf of others. We must take notice of our brothers and sisters, also made in the image and likeness of God. The generosity and kindness that mark the Christmas season cannot be limited to our circle of acquaintances, nor should be packed away with the lights and tinsel. Instead, they must become part of our daily lives as we seek ways to serve others, to care for their needs, and to help create a kinder and more just world.

As we begin this new year, let our resolution be this: to live with eyes and hearts open to all that God has done, and is doing in our lives. For at least a few minutes each day, let us stop to look at the world's beauty and wonder, to reflect on God's presence in our lives, and to seek ways to witness God's faithfulness through our words and actions. For this year, may we resolve to follow the example of the shepherds, and of Mary—rejoicing in the wonder and giving witness to God's love.

THE EPIPHANY OF THE LORD
FR. RICHARD G. MALLOY, SJ

<table>
<tr><td>Isa. 60:1-6
Eph. 3:2-3, 5-6
Matt. 2:1-12</td><td>*"Magi from the East arrived in Jerusalem"*</td></tr>
</table>

A guy bought his wife a beautiful diamond ring for Christmas. After hearing about this extravagant gift, a friend of his said, "I thought she wanted a new car." "She did," he replied. "But where was I going to find a fake Ford?"

The Three Kings brought gifts to Jesus. A few days ago, many of us experienced the joy of receiving a gift that we don't need, nor will we remember that gift at this time next year. But the best gift is to give to those in need. More importantly, our faith calls us to structure our society in ways that reduce the need for charity. God wants us to go beyond charity, and give one another the gift of justice.

Many years ago, I lived and worked in a parish in North Camden, NJ. It was Christmas Eve, 4:00 PM, and about 16 degrees outside. He appeared at the Rectory door with worn shoes, no shoelaces, nor any socks. His coat was wide open. He had no hat, no gloves, no scarf. He told me he lived with an infant and a three-year-old in rundown housing on Elm Street, a block over from the Church. It was near the end of the month. Food was scarce, but that wasn't the main problem. No toys. "Christmas," he said, as his eyes met mine with a look that mixed a mild fear of rejection with avid anticipation. I smiled, asked him to wait, and headed down to rummage through the new to "brand new used" toys in Holy Name Rectory's basement.

I was filled with gratitude to all who gave as I looked at an almost empty basement that was bulging two weeks before with brightly wrapped gifts. Many people began appearing after Thanksgiving with dolls and trucks, mittens and hats, "for the children." Their cars had braved the territories they had heard were so dangerous, the streets of North Camden. Sr. Linda spent the last days of Advent going from home to home, distributing everything from Teddy bears to Barbie dolls, but there were a few things left. I carried an armful, including a battered yet serviceable Big Wheel, up the rickety steps.

His eyes opened wide as I handed him the haul. "What's your name?" "Jesús," he replied. "Can I give you a hand carrying this stuff home?" I asked. "No. No. *Está Bien*," he said, as he scooped up all his short arms could hold. "I can handle it." As he neared the bottom step, a Fischer-Price something or other fell out of his arm, as he tried to guide the Big Wheel with his free hand. I again offered to accompany him. This time he agreed to let me bear some of the burden, even though there was really not that much to carry. After all, he was only 39 inches tall, a little 7 year old man of the house, out gathering Christmas gifts for his Hispanic family.

Jesús and I entered the tiny, one-room apartment where his family lived. His little brother let out a whoop, jumped on the Big Wheel, put it in forward, raced across the floor and promptly slammed into the wall, narrowly avoiding the small, sparsely decorated Christmas tree and waking his baby sister. Picking up the infant, Jesús's mother thanked me. I told her to thank those who had given so generously and enabled us to distribute what few toys we had. She made me coffee, *Café Bustelo*, hot and sweet. We chatted. They were new to the neighborhood. She said she'd bring her husband to Mass to meet me. He was at work that Christmas Eve, washing dishes in a ritzy restaurant in Philadelphia.

As I left, she said she would pray for me. God knows I could use the prayers. As I walked home, I wondered who would pray for her. Who would make those Christmas prayers for peace and justice effective in her life, and the lives of her husband and children? I wondered who would give not only toys at Christmas, but also justice in January and July. As I walked in the bitter, dark December 24th cold, I wondered who would save Jesús and his mother, Maria, in North Camden, NJ?

Then and now, there were and are too few toys in the lives of kids like Jesús. No nights at the movies, no trips to the Jersey shore, and he probably never saw the inside of the Camden Aquarium, unless his mother hit the Lottery.

In 2013, one out of four children in the USA under the age of six lives in poverty. Overall, 22% of children in our country are poor. In 2013, the poverty line for a family of four was $23,492. In the developed world, only Mexico (26%), Chile (24%) and Turkey (23%), have higher child poverty rates than our United States. After the debacles at the close of the Bush II presidency, the government blew $750 billion to bail out Wall Street. In March 2009, the Dow Jones Average went down to 6,626. By 2014, the Dow was back up, by over 16,000. But no conservative commentator calls the $750 billion "welfare." In the Spring of 2014, while Wall Street rode high, Main Street had yet to fully recover. Middle class wages have stagnated since 1973, and in 2014 politicians voted down what would have been an increase in the minimum wage from $7.25 to $10.10.

Corporate welfare costs this country. The NFL is a non-profit corporation. Government subsidies to corporations total some $80 billion. Over 48 companies received more than $100 million. GM took $1.7 billion, while Shell, Ford and Chrysler all walked away with $1.0 billion. Prudential, Boeing, Microsoft, Amazon, and Casinos in Colorado and NJ milked the taxpayers for more than $200 million each. *Forbes*, no lefty journal, asks, "Where is the outrage over Corporate Welfare?" Since 1976, the *Fortune 500* took 16,000 subsidy awards, mostly tax breaks, totaling some $63 billion. That's billion with a capital "B."

Jesús's family in Camden, NJ, saw very little of this government generosity for the rich. The future of the church in our country depends, to a large degree, on how we do justice for Latinos and everyone else in the USA. 50% of Catholics in the USA, under the age of 25, are Latinos. The Three Kings, Caspar, Balthazaar and Melchior remind us we need to do justice for all peoples. Epiphany celebrates that Christ came for all peoples.

Years ago, Dr. Howard Thurman, theologian, civil rights activist and Dean of the chapels of Howard and Boston Universities, penned these beautiful lines:

> *When the song of the angels is stilled,*
> *When the star in the sky is gone,*
> *When the kings and princes are home,*
> *When the shepherds are back with their flock,*
> *The work of Christmas begins:*
>
> *To find the lost,*
> *To heal the broken,*
> *To feed the hungry,*
> *To release the prisoner,*
> *To rebuild the nations,*
> *To bring peace among brothers,*
> *To make music in the heart.*

In many Latino countries, such as Puerto Rico, the kids get their gifts on the Feast of the *Los Tres Reyes* (The Three Kings). Jesus came to bring love, peace and justice to all the world. Let us begin the work of Christmas. Let us give one another the gifts of justice and peace. Let us pray.

ISA. 55:1-11
1 JOHN 5:1-9
MARK 1:7-11

"I will baptize you with water, but he will baptize you with the Holy Spirit."

At home, I have a little green book that someone gave me as an ordination gift: it's the *Rite of Baptism for Children*, with all the prayers and readings for the sacrament. In the back, there's a notation I scribbled on the inside cover: "Margaret Flanagan. July 1, 2007. First baby baptized." I wrote that down in the book so I'd never forget. It was a big day for Margaret—and for me.

Of course, the biggest day for baptism is the one we've just heard in the Gospel: the baptism of Jesus. I don't know that John the Baptist wrote it down in the back of any book. But we do have this account in the Gospels, and we hear it once again and are reminded: this is where it all began.

Baptism was the beginning of Christ's public ministry—and for the rest of us, our own baptism marks the beginning of our own lives as Catholic Christians. Most of us were baptized when we were infants, so we don't remember it. And the chances are, if you have been a part of a baptism—as a parent or a godparent, or just as a relative looking on—there's a lot going on that you may not have noticed.

This Sunday, the Feast of the Baptism of the Lord, is a good opportunity for us to notice what we may have been missing—to look beyond the water, the oil, the prayers, the crying babies, and the christening gown that was worn by your great grandmother's second cousin. This Feast is a chance to reflect on what this sacrament means —and, in particular, how it is celebrated.

It comes down to the "Three C's of Baptism": Creation, Commitment, and Community.

The first 'C' is Creation. One of the things you notice about the Baptism ritual is that, unlike most of our liturgies, it doesn't begin with a hymn, a song, or a prayer. It begins, instead, with a question:

   "What name do you give your child?"

It sounds obvious. But those seven words are deceptively simple. Everything that follows flows from them. Baptism, the first sacrament of initiation, is fundamentally about who we are—and who we will be. To be baptized is to be defined in a new way: as a Catholic Christian. We are transformed. As the rite states, we become a new creation. Having a name, an identity, is critical to that. In Genesis, you'll recall, one of the first things Adam did was name everything around him. In naming their child, parents continue what began in Genesis—and, in effect, declare that they are continuing God's creative work in the world.

So yes: baptism is about creation—in all its beauty, joy, and wonder.

The second 'C' is Commitment. It is the commitment of parents—and, significantly, godparents. Being a godparent entails *commitment*: a commitment to the Catholic faith, and to living that faith with fidelity, enthusiasm and joy. That means living it in such a way that their godchildren will see what they do, how they pray, what they value, how they love and they will say: "I want to be like that."

Finally, there is the third 'C,' Community. Early on within the rite, the priest or deacon says, "My children, the Christian community welcomes you with great joy." The Church celebrates this sacrament as a *community*—because as a community, we pray together, rejoice together, grieve together, and we grow together. The Christian life isn't lived in isolation. And we don't celebrate our sacraments that way, either. The guidelines for baptism make this clear: "All recently born babies should be baptized at a common celebration on the same day." This is why we baptize several children together on the first Sunday of every month. It is an experience to be shared.

The Scriptures acknowledge as much. In today's Gospel, St. Luke mentions other people who were there and baptized along with Jesus. It wasn't something he did alone. He had his community around him.

And so do each of us. And that community is wider and greater and more wondrous than we realize. Because of baptism, I'm connected to you, and you're connected to me. And we're all connected to a billion other believers—even to little Margaret Flanagan, the girl in the back of my baptism book.

That connects us, as well, to the man baptized in the Jordan two thousand years ago. Near the end of the Baptism Rite, there's a prayer reminding us that because of baptism, we call God our Father. Because of it, too, we call Jesus our brother—the one who showed us by his example how to begin the great mission of the Gospel, through water and the Spirit. Today *his* mission is *our* mission. The same Spirit which accompanied him also accompanies us as we strive to live the Gospel, to love beyond all measure, and to make the world new. Baptism gives us the grace that we need in order to do that. It has made each of us a new creation.

As we recall the baptism of Christ, and its significance for our own baptisms, let us strive every day to be that "new creation;" to embrace our commitment to our baptism and all that it entails; and to support and welcome those in our community whom are celebrating this sacrament.

Creation. Commitment. Community. I might also add a fourth "C," one which underlies all the others: Charity—the great bond of love that uplifts us, inspires us, and inflames our hearts.

These are the raw ingredients of what it means to be a Christian.

Or, as the Baptism Rite puts it so plainly, but so beautifully:

> *"This is our faith. This is the faith of the Church. We are proud to profess it, in Christ Jesus, our Lord."*

LENT

ASH WEDNESDAY

DEACON WILLIAM T. DITEWIG, PhD

JOEL 2:12-18
2 COR. 5:20-6:2
MATT. 6:1-6, 16-18

"Rend your hearts."

In the verses leading up to today's first reading, the prophet Joel paints a picture of complete devastation. Beginning with recounting a plague of locusts which has blighted the landscape, destroyed fields and crops, caused fires and destruction, he describes a world in which "joy has withered away from among all people." Stop and consider the impact of this tragedy for a moment.

Some years ago my family and I were living on the island of Guam in the Western Pacific Ocean where I was stationed while in the Navy. In that part of the world typhoons were an annual commonplace occurrence. Sometimes these massive storms would be close enough to cause some wind and rain damage, but rarely did they hit our small island directly. That all changed with the coming of a Super-typhoon named 'Pamela.'

In those days, a storm was classified a typhoon when its winds exceeded 75 miles per hour. If those winds doubled, the storm was reclassified as a super-typhoon. With winds over 225 miles per hour, Super-typhoon 'Pamela' hit the tiny island of Guam directly for nearly three days.

The damage to the island was devastating. I have been told that it took more than twelve years for birds to return to the island. The storm had picked up walls of sand from the ocean and the beaches, and scoured the landscape of vegetation. Seventy-five percent of the structures on the island had their roofs torn off, and most windows were blown out. The human toll was blessedly small: one man suffered a fatal heart attack during the storm.

The aftermath was perhaps even worse than the storm itself. Most areas of the island were without power for weeks; supplies to make repairs had to be flown in from thousands of miles away. The daytime temperatures were in the nineties, and the humidity was over ninety percent as well. Life was generally miserable.

I mentioned that the windows had been blown out. Most nights, families would gather by candlelight, trying to keep children occupied and restore a sense that things would be OK. Sitting around the candle, with plywood or plastic sheeting covering the holes that had once been windows, we would hear a noise approaching. At first we thought it was some kind of vehicle, making a noise not unlike a street sweeper. But then, as the noise grew, we realized that it was something else entirely. They were swarms of insects, our own plague of locusts. Since our window barricades were not airtight, the house would soon have dozens of these creatures "passing through" as their swarm searched for food. Sometimes we would have several of such swarms each night, and this lasted for weeks. The birds were gone, but the insects were not.

I thought about all of this while pondering our reading from Joel today. His description of the devastation around him is powerful and poignant. In the midst of such devastation, whether it is caused by natural disasters or by human invasion, cruelty, and violence, we turn inward because all that is outside of us is destroyed. Listen again to the voice of the Lord: "Yet even now, says the Lord, return to me with your whole heart, with fasting, and weeping, and mourning. Rend your hearts, not your garments, and return to the Lord, your God."

A people with nothing soon realize that what matters most lies within, what our Jewish ancestors constantly referred to as "the heart." In Jewish writing, "the heart" includes what we would call our conscience, our innermost being, where we "are alone with God." What God is constantly reminding us is that he wants a real and true relationship with us. God's focus is not simply on the external aspects of religious practice, but on the interior life. External religious practice, without an interior conversion of heart to God, is a lie. After a plague of locusts, violence, devastation, and with the loss of everything we think we know and have, when we have truly "hit bottom" in our lives, we turn to that which matters the most: our innermost heart and our relationship with God.

We hear the same message from Christ in today's Gospel. Christ reminds us strongly that it is our inner conversion of heart which God seeks. I have always loved the passage that says we are to wash our faces, and to take every effort to not show to others that we are fasting—all on a day when we get ashes smeared on our foreheads! It has become popular to observe this practice by many groups of Christians, and not just we Catholics anymore. It's not simply all the people who will go to work or school today with ashes proudly displayed. You see the ashen Cross displayed on Facebook pages, on internet sites, blogs and on Twitter. It has become a public badge of religiosity. In other words, exactly what Jesus tells us NOT to do!

So, what does this all mean to us today?

First, with this celebration, we begin the sacred season of Lent. Our songs and prayers will remind us often about the significance of these "forty days." It can be funny sometimes to listen to people trying to calculate those forty days! "Do we count the Sundays?" "Do we count the days between Ash Wednesday and the First Sunday of Lent"? On and on, we in the West tend to think so literally about things that we miss the real point. Think of all the times in the Old Testament and the New Testament where we read about the number forty.

In Hebrew numbers, every number has a symbolic meaning, and "forty" is the number of human testing and preparation for a future mission taken on for God. So, for example, the rains came down for forty days and nights during the Great Flood; what happens afterward? God forms a new Covenant with Noah. We see the people wandering in the desert for forty years before they enter the Promised Land to begin their new life of freedom. In the New Testament, Jesus—following his Baptism—goes into the desert for forty days to be tempted by the Devil before returning and beginning his new public life and ministry. That's what Lent is for us: a time of preparation and testing leading to our renewed Covenant, our new mission in the Risen Christ at Easter. Today is the first step on that journey.

As we prepare to receive the ashes today, may we keep in mind their true significance. Remember that in every life we experience times of our own devastating "plague of locusts," which can turn us away from God and to the brink of despair itself. We can believe that there is nothing left, that all is ashes and ruin. That is our starting point, and it turns our hearts to God.

After receiving the ashes, and after you have returned your whole heart over to God, follow Christ's command and "wash your face" and "do not look gloomy like the hypocrites." It's not the ashes that will save us, but hearts given over to God.

1ˢᵗ SUNDAY OF LENT

FR. WILLIAM BAUSCH

GEN. 9:8-15

1 PETER 3:18-22

MARK 1:12-15

"The kingdom of God is at hand."

*W*e priests, like many others, pass around in-house jokes and bloopers. In my early days it was said of one pastor that he was inaccessible on weekdays and incomprehensible on Sundays.

Or there's that snide thing they say about us preachers: "A preacher is someone who talks in other people's sleep."

And we all remembered the earnest priest who concluded a wedding ceremony with, "Go, the Mass and the marriage are ended."

Our all-time favorite is the one where, at a funeral homily, this priest, gesturing toward the casket, intoned solemnly, "What we see before us is the mere shell. The nut is gone."

Despite that delightful nonsense, I want to turn serious on this first Sunday of Lent and share some evocative themes. To keep you awake, I am going to do this is by telling you some stories, three of them to be exact, two that are about us and one that is about Jesus. I ask you to listen, not with TV ears and hearts, but with faith ears and hearts. These stories are not to entertain. They are stories that offer images to put us in the mood for Lent.

My first story concerns a Dr. Scott Peck, who was, way back, a celebrated, best-selling author and psychiatrist—some older folk here may remember his name. He once told a story about counseling a man who was a career sergeant in the army stationed in Okinawa in the 1940s and 50s. This sergeant was in serious trouble because of his excessive drinking and was being counseled by Dr. Peck. In their sessions the sergeant denied that he was an alcoholic, or even that his use of alcohol was a problem. "There's nothing else to do in the evenings in Okinawa," he said in justifying his behavior, "except drink."

Peck then asked him if he liked reading, and the sergeant said he loved to read. So the doctor asked him if he couldn't read a book instead of going out drinking.

"Nah," said the sergeant, "the barrack's too chaotic with all the guys."

"You could go to the library," Peck suggested.

"No, the library's too far away," was the response. Confronted with the fact that the library was no farther away than the bar, the sergeant claimed he wasn't really that much of a reader after all. The doctor suggested fishing, which the sergeant liked, but he said he wasn't available in the day and Okinawa didn't have night fishing. Peck came back with an offer to put the sergeant in touch with a number of people who were enthusiastic night fishers, and suddenly the sergeant said that, well, he wasn't much of a fisherman either.

"So," Dr. Peck said, summing things up, "There are things you could do here besides drink, but given the choice, you're going to choose drinking over any of them."

"Guess that's right," said the sergeant.

"But since it's getting you in all kinds of trouble, seems like you've got a pretty severe dilemma on your hands."

With anger the sergeant answered, "This island would drive anyone to drink!"

It's a story, but we surely get the point and recognize that the sergeant is us, routinely rationalizing our less-than-Christlike behaviors. It's a story, a parable, made for Lent; for Lent, like Dr. Peck, is here to tell us to stop kidding ourselves, to confess our sins, not our excuses. It's time to strike our breasts and call it like it is, crying out, "O God, be merciful to me, a sinner!"

My second image-story is a familiar one to all of us these days. It's about a mother named Sue who was standing at the kitchen sink, working diligently on dinner preparations, her mind totally committed to the task at hand, peeling potatoes. Her middle son, three-year-old Steven, was playing nearby. Within a few moments she felt a tug on her skirt proceeded by the words, "Mommy…" She nodded something like "un-huh" or "yes?" and went on peeling the potatoes. There were more tugs on her skirt and more little sounds: "Mommy…" Again, she gave a brief verbal comment and yet stayed right at her task.

Five minutes passed. Steven continued to chatter and then she felt those tugs on her skirt again. This time the tugs seemed harder and more persistent. She finally put her potatoes down in the sink and bent down to her son. Steven took her face in his two little chubby hands, turning her directly to his line of vision and said, "Mommy, will you listen to me with your eyes?"

That rings a bell, for there we are: multitasking, treating the people who have needs, the people we love, like they're a distraction from "what really matters." You know: cell phone to the ear, attention to the computer screen, fingers to the text board, head turned toward the TV. And all the while, all that our loved ones want is that we listen with our eyes so that they know they are important to us; and the poor, the sick, and the needy want to hold our faces to their line of vision so that, like Mother Teresa, we see them and respond to them.

So never mind the grand schemes of "doing something for Lent." There's these telling little spiritual challenges right in front of us, laden with the invitations to a deeper spirituality.

Now, for the Jesus story.

Father Bob Roberts received a call from a hospital. The operator informed him that Mary, a member of the church, wanted to see him because her child had just died.

Fr. Roberts sped off in his car to a hospital several miles away. He had a vague idea who Mary was. She had been involved in the young adult group, so he knew her enough to say "hello." Yet he couldn't ever remember seeing her with a child, so he was shocked to hear that her child had died.

When he got to the hospital, he was directed to a dark, quiet corridor where he found Mary, just outside of her son's room. "Thank you so much for coming," she said. As he and Mary paused in the hall, she told him the heartbreaking story of her son, Jimmy. Jimmy had been born with multiple physical and mental handicaps. As they spoke they went into the room where Jimmy's body lay. All the tubes and wires were still connected to him. Fr. Roberts was totally shocked by what he saw. Jimmy was tiny, much smaller than a normal seven-year-old boy. His little body was badly twisted and deformed. The priest found it difficult even to look at him without wincing.

But not Mary. She looked upon her son with eyes of uncompromised love. She touched his face and spoke quietly to him, even though he couldn't hear anymore. She tenderly kissed his cheek many times. Mary told Roberts how much Jimmy had meant to her, and how much she would miss him. Then the priest had a kind of epiphany. He realized that where he saw Jimmy as someone marred in his appearance, almost beyond human resemblance, Mary saw him as a beautiful, lovely human being, and she lavished undeserved, unabashed, unquenchable love on her child.

We get the picture, don't we? Jesus sees us the same way. However we are, however others see us—unlovely, broken, sinful—Jesus loves with a redeeming, unquenchable love. And while for Lent we confess our sins and do our penances as we should, we must remember that Jesus' compassion, forgiveness, and love are also a part of the Lenten equation.

End of stories and end of homily, but I have a parting suggestion. If you want to carry around a kind of spiritual mantra or image for Lent, how about picturing Jesus as little Steven and hear him saying to you what Steven said to his mother: "Listen to me. Listen to me with your eyes!" That is, "Put aside the distractions and give me your full attention these 40 days of Lent. Yes, listen to me with your eyes—and with your heart."

2ND SUNDAY OF LENT

ROB BELL

GEN. 22:1-2, 9-13,
15-18

ROM. 8:31-34

MARK 9:2-10

"Take your only son, whom you love, and sacrifice him there..."

*T*his passage is a classic example of the kind of story that you find in the Bible which causes many people to ask, *"What does a story like this, about a man named Abraham and his son, possibly have to teach us?"* And to be more specific, *"What kind of God would ask a man to sacrifice his son?"*

That's the question, isn't it? The answer is found by looking into a brief history of religion, and bringing to light some details of the story.

Early humans came to the realization that their survival as a species was dependent upon things like food and water. In order for food to grow, it needs sunlight and water in proper proportions. Too much water and things wash away, but not enough and plants die. Too much sunlight and plants wilt, yet not enough and they die. These basic observations brought people to the conclusion that they were dependent upon *unseen forces for their survival, and for which they had no control.* This was actually a monumental leap for that time!

The belief (I use that word intentionally) arose that these *forces* are either on your side, or not. But how do you keep these forces on your side? The next time you have a harvest, you take a portion of that harvest and you offer it on an altar as a sign of your gratitude. Because you need the forces (gods and goddesses) on your side. Now imagine what happened when people would offer a sacrifice, but then it didn't rain, or the sun didn't shine, or their animals still got diseases, or they were unable to have children. Obviously, they concluded that they hadn't offered enough! And so they offered more and more and more. *Anxiety* was built into this form of religion from the beginning. One never knew where you stood with the gods. The thought became that the gods are angry, demanding, and if you don't please them they will punish you by bringing calamity.

But what if things went well? What if it rained just the right amount and the sun shined just the right amount—what if it appeared that the gods were pleased with you? Well then, you'd need to offer them thanks. But how would you ever know if you'd properly showed them how grateful you were? How would you know you'd offered enough? If things went well, you never knew if you'd been grateful enough or offered enough. But if things didn't go well, then clearly you hadn't done…enough. Either way, there was *Anxiety*.

Now, stay with me here, because this is where things get dodgy: Whether things went well or not, the answer was always *sacrifice more. Give more. Offer more.* This was because you never knew where you stood with the gods. And so you'd offer part of your crop. Then you'd offer a goat and maybe a lamb, a cow, a few cows, or even some birds! The very nature of early religion is that everything escalated because, in your anxiety to please the gods, you kept having to offer *more*. What's the most valuable thing you could offer the gods to show them how serious you were about earning their favor? A child, of course. Can you see how child sacrifice lurks on the edges of the Old Testament? It's where religion took you to the place where you'd offer that which was most valuable to you.

Now, on to the Abraham story.

When God tells Abraham to offer his son, he isn't shocked, because, *"early the next morning Abraham got up and loaded his donkey."*

Abraham gets right to it. He doesn't argue, he doesn't protest, he doesn't drag his feet. He clearly knows what to do, and so he does it, of course. That's how Abraham understood that religion worked. The gods demanded that which was most valuable to you. If you didn't give it, you'd pay the price. That's what the world was like at that time.

So Abraham sets out, and, *"he reaches the place on the third day."*

He and his son travel for three days. It is three days in which his son is as good as dead. When they get to the mountain, what does Abraham say to the servants? He says to them, *"Stay here with the donkey while the boy and I go over there. We will worship and then we will come back to you."*

What? Abraham is going to offer his son, right? That's what the story is about, correct? God tells Abraham to offer his son, and he does so—or at least proves that he would do so—that's the point, isn't it?

But what Abraham says to the servants is that he's going to go offer his son, and then come back with his son. Clearly there is something else going on in this story, just below the surface. The story is subverting itself, begging you to see something far more significant going on.

As they walk up the mountain, Isaac asks Abraham where the sacrifice will come from. In the standard reading of the story, he's going to his death *because his dad loves God so much.* But we've already seen Abraham tip his hat that something else is up. So we're not buying that angle.

What is Abraham's answer? *God himself will provide.*

How clever! It's a non-answer answer. Abraham is in on the joke, or whatever it is that you'd call it.

Then Abraham gets ready to offer his son, but he doesn't because God stops him and then he offers a ram instead. End of story.

Except that it isn't the end.

An angel shows up and says that Abraham is going to be blessed and, *"through your offspring all nations on Earth will be blessed..."*

So, back to our original question: What kind of God would ask a man to sacrifice his son?

Now, an answer: Not this one.

The other gods may demand your firstborn, but not this God.

So if God doesn't want Abraham to offer his son, why the charade?

Several responses:

First, the drama is the point. Abraham knows what to do when he's told to offer his son because this is always where religion heads toward. So at first, this God appears to be like all the other gods. The story, at first, seems to be like the other stories about gods who are never satisfied. The first audience for this story would have heard this before, and it would have been familiar. But then it's not. The story takes a shocking turn which comes out of nowhere. This God disrupts the familiarity of the story by interrupting the sacrifice. Picture an early audience gasping. What? This God *stopped* the sacrifice? Huh? The gods don't do that!

Second, the God in this story *provides*. Worship and sacrifice was about you giving to the *gods*. Yet *this* story is about *this* God giving to *Abraham*. A God who gives? Who provides?

Third, this isn't a story about what Abraham does for God, it's a story about what God does for Abraham. Mind blowing. New. Ground breaking. A story about a God who doesn't demand anything, but gives and blesses.

Fourth, Abraham is told that God is just getting started, and that this God is going to bless Abraham with such love and favor that through Abraham everyone on Earth is going to also be blessed. This God isn't angry or demanding or unleashing wrath. This God has intentions to bless everyone. Abraham is invited to trust, have faith, believe, and to live in these promises.

Can you see how many game changing ideas are in this one story? Can you see why people told this story? Can you see why it endured? Can you think of any other stories about a son who was as good as dead for three days, but then lived in such a way that the story about him confronted the conventional wisdom of the day, and the gods are angry and demanding with the insistence that God blesses and gives and provides?

All that's left for us to do is to know and trust in our God who is really like that…and so much more.

Exo. 20:1-17
1 Cor. 1:22-25
John 2:13-25

"The foolishness of God is wiser than human wisdom."

In the lines just preceding today's second reading, Paul writes to the people of Corinth: "The message about the Cross is foolishness to those who are perishing, but to us who are being saved it is the power of God." Here's a story from midtown Atlanta from the early, early nineties about Jesus turning over lots more than just temple tables. Actually, the story is not finished!

The first time that I met Juelz and Calvin, it was on a steamy summer morning, twenty-three years ago. I was standing at the back door of a former winter night shelter, which had been useful as far as it went. But volunteers kept saying, "Is this all we are, and all we have to offer?," "Five months out of twelve?," "Two hots and a cot?," "Or a NO DRUGS sign with an informal pharmacy humming every night in the restroom?"

For ten years, the All Saints' Winter Night Shelter had been lifesaving for men on the streets, as well as life-transforming for some volunteers. One person whom I know quit her fancy job at forty and then went to medical school. There were huge insights and moving encounters, but they were always in passing, literally like ships in the night. In the morning, everybody went back to their very separate universes—the volunteers to cars and homes and jobs and families, and the "guys" to the streets. So, we would ponder, "Is this all we are, and all that we have to offer?"

One night, a man was killed in the ticket line waiting to get into our shelter. The church came to a decision. There has got to be a more healing way, a deeper truth, and a more inclusive life.

This is what led me to standing at the back door of the shelter, now grandly and hopefully called "Covenant Community," and looking across the potholes to see two skinny men. One of them was kind of menacing-looking. They were picking their way across the cracked asphalt and eye-ing me with wary expressions. I am from Mississippi, and we wrote the book on chit-chatting, so I said in a little Mississippi chit-chatty voice, "Hey!!" and just started babbling.

Juelz, the scary-looking guy later said, "I was dumb-founded. I was scared to death. Here was a woman—weird priest collar on and all I wanted to do was get past you, and you asked me my name and when I told you, your reply was 'I heard about you and we're glad you are here.'" I can kind of see why Juelz was perplexed. I don't think anybody had been very glad to see Juelz in a long time. I later learned that his wife had banned him from their home for the sake of their children.

Anyway, they told me their names— Juelz and Calvin. Juelz was the tough guy from Harlem, and Calvin was a local, mocha-creamy kid who looked like butter would not melt in his mouth. It turns out that a lot of other stuff had indeed melted in his mouth, and up his nose, etc., etc.

Calvin smiled wanly. They had come straight over from a stint in the county detox center, and were still looking pretty rough. I assumed that they were best friends—you know, like Butch Cassidy and the Sundance Kid. I learned years later that they had never met, and at first glance, they didn't even like each other! Juelz's face looked like thunder, while Calvin's face stayed closed and I kept on babbling my welcome. It was in this manner that they walked in through the door of the 'Covenant Community,' which was neither covenanted, nor community—at least not yet.

Calvin and Juelz were the first residents, and I was the priest on the 'transition team.' Foolishness of the Cross. Totally.

None of the three of us had any earthly idea what we were getting into, and neither did anybody else. One of the co-chairs from the Church committee was a beautiful twenty-five year old, whose day job was translating 'computer-ese' into English, and the other co-chair was an elegant and very persnickety man, the retired head of the Library School at Emory University. The unlikeliness of any possible success of this duo can be summed up by their nicknames: "The Nazi and the Bleeding Heart." Foolishness of the Cross. Truly.

The Board of Directors was the usual white Church volunteer suspects. One sent me her doodles from our first meeting:

> I have no idea what I'm doing here... It's too much for this group who know practically nothing about drugs (or maybe they do), but certainly not about rehabilitation... Money???... Parishioners are still ticked off about closing the shelter... Not sure what I can contribute... Some of these ideas are nuts!... So, so many homeless, so many addicted... Think small. One person at a time.

Later, another wrote to me, "Covenant Community was conceived and birthed through the power of innocence." Truer words were never spoken. For instance, our first board decision was to hire a Clinical Director whose resume, it turned out, was correct in only two of these three words: Recovering Drug Addict—"recovering" being the non-operative word. Crazy as it sounds; Dr. B. did a great job . . . until he didn't. Foolishness of the Cross. I still shake my head in wonder.

At the time, schlumpy, shy, middle-aged board member, Martha D., said she would like to be the "Recreation Director." Among other events, she arranged a retreat to the beach for the board and the residents, as well as a whitewater rafting trip. These were stunning successes. In the process of all of this, Martha D. became an urban bicycling pioneer in her own time. Foolishness of the Cross. Ridiculous.

Now, over seven hundred men have lived in the community nestled next to the Church—only fourteen at a time—each one slinking in, eyes looking dead, their movements slow, and their speech unsure. Some stay. The ones who do stay get in the rhythm and the liturgy of the community. There is lots of back and forth with the Church—friendships, duties, and good quid pro quo kinds of routines. Both Covenant Community and All Saints live the time honored table-turning twelve step wisdom—*those whom have received begin to give.* How foolish is that?

Cal—why he became our first star. He grew up in a family of ministers, and he was gracious to even the most difficult people, making speeches around the city and counseling a number of parish families struggling with an addicted family member. This is the deepest foolishness of the Cross that we have learned. Once you take down the categorical walls between 'us' and 'them,' everyone pretty much has the same stuff going on.

We put Calvin on staff, and he was the light of the Covenant Community. All I can say is to not do that to people. Don't turn them into idols because idols break. Calvin crawled way back down in the hole for seven or eight years. Then, somehow—I don't know the story—but somehow he saw the light again, through the grace of wounded healers including several Covenant Community alumni who never ever gave up on him, just like Jesus doesn't give up on anybody. Cal is back in life now. He's not an idol—just a good guy, with a job, a wife, kids, and friends. Really, the message of the Cross is foolishness, isn't it? But to those who are being saved, why, it is the power of God! All of these years at Covenanted Community have convinced me that the power of the Cross keeps on getting recycled.

Juelz is the longtime Program Director of Covenant Community, and is twenty-three years clean and sober. He still has a face like thunder until the sun shines through. This was the case years and years ago, when he and his wife Desiree reclaimed their marriage and renewed their vows in front of their family and the Community. I was the priest, crying like a baby, my nose running and tears streaming down my face, and the late afternoon light glimmered through the stained glass windows of our Church. It is truly OUR Church now. Foolishness of the Cross all over the place.

Juelz is fighting crazy cancer right now, but he doesn't want to dwell on that. He is a powerful man, and right now he is learning the power of vulnerability. As he recently wrote, "Every once and awhile I need to be reminded that I should stop trying to apply for a position that has never had an opening." And he is busy thanking God for his kids, his grandkids, and his Addict Tribe, the blind who could not see but now they know they are blind and so can see. What a foolish, foolish, foolish cross-shaped life Juelz has led, does lead, and will lead even into eternity.

And so it goes. The tables keep getting turned over—person by person when the buying and selling of numbness becomes the thrill of being really alive!! The message of the Cross keeps on being so foolish, and so powerful—the power of God to those who are being saved. Truly ridiculous. Wondrous. Eternal. But I bet you know that, too.

4ᵀᴴ SUNDAY IN LENT

FR. JAMES MARTIN, SJ

---

2 CHRON. 36:14-16, 19-23

EPH. 2:4-10

JOHN 3:14-21

"For God so loved the world that he gave his only son…"

It's probably impossible for a Christian not to know the second verse of our Gospel reading today: "For God so loved the world that he gave his only son, so that everyone believes may not perish, but may have eternal life."

And if they didn't know that verse before Tim Tebow, they certainly know it now. Everyone probably knows it! Tim Tebow, whom you know about unless you've been living under a rock, or a rock without cable, is the Denver Broncos quarterback whose public displays of religiosity attracted a great deal of media attention. He also had written John 3:16 under the black patch of paint underneath his eyes, used to cut the glare.

Those of you with longer memories will remember that in many football games of long ago, there was often a man who used to hold up a sign in the end zone behind the goalposts; his sign had that same verse in big, bold letters and numbers: John 3:16. It probably sent more than a few curious fans to their Bibles over the years.

It's a beautiful verse about belief in Jesus. It tells us that those who believe in Jesus will have eternal life. Of course, that's only part of the story. One has to not only *believe* in Jesus, one also has to follow him.

Recently, I was on retreat at a Trappist monastery with a friend. As you may know, they have what is called "reading at table." Since the meals are taken in silence, they play an audio book over a loudspeaker. It not only masks the sound of everyone chewing their food and clinking their silverware, but it also provides good spiritual nourishment. This is similar to what the monks themselves do, who live in silence. They have "reading at table," as well, although it is done by one of the monks.

In any event, the book in question was written by the Franciscan spiritual master, Richard Rohr, and was called *Breathing Underwater*. It looks at how the 12-Step Program intersects with the Gospel. It's really quite wonderful. In one arresting passage, he reminded readers that Jesus never says, "Worship me." But he does say "Follow me." In other words, it's not enough to simply worship Jesus as the Son of God, or believe in Jesus as the Son of God. One has to follow up that belief with *action*. So yes, anyone who believes in Jesus will have eternal life. But part of that belief is practice, by following Jesus

But back to that phrase from John. It's not only about belief. It's about something else. It's about something that God *does*. God loved the world. Too often, Christianity is presented in a way that makes it sound as if the story of Jesus is about God having to be pacified, or having to be persuaded to forgive. And, often, we carry around within us an image of an angry, unforgiving God and a loving forgiving Jesus. But here is a text that tells us that God is the one that started it all. God sends his son, even aware that his son will have to suffer. And why does God send his son? Because God loves us.

God is not someone who sends Jesus in order that Jesus might be punished, or so that our sins will be wiped out. God is not the angry monarch, seeking vengeance or retribution for our sins. No, God is more like the father in the Parable of the Prodigal Son, who is not happy until his wandering children have come home. God is love. That is the essence of the being of God.

There is a beautiful meditation from St. Ignatius's *Spiritual Exercises*, which speaks about the Trinity looking down on the world, in love and compassion. The Trinity sees all of humanity: "some at peace, some at war, some weeping and others laughing; some healthy, and others sick; some being born, and others dying." It's a beautiful meditation of care. And the Trinity decides to send the Second Person, Jesus, out of love. All of this is motivated by God's love.

Finally, notice the *scope* of God's love. It does not say that God loves *Israel* so much he needed to send his only begotten son. It doesn't say that God loved the *apostles and disciples and followers of Jesus* so much that he sent his only begotten son. It says that God loved the *world*. That's an easy thing to forget when we sometimes are tempted to see the Church as being against the world. That's quite common these days.

But God loves the world. How could he not? He created it. And if you doubt that, remember that one of the key documents of the Second Vatican Council was not called "The Church against the Modern World." Or, "The Church *above* the Modern World." But rather, it is called "The Church in the Modern World."

So when you're tempted to think of God as an angry, unforgiving, vengeful judge just remember this passage.

And remember who loves you.

5TH SUNDAY OF LENT

REV. DAVID A. DAVIS

JER. 31:31-34
HEB. 5:7-9
JOHN 12:20-33

"Sir, we wish to see Jesus."

The first congregation I served had a sanctuary that seated about two-hundred people. There was a lot of wood in the room; the pews, the pulpit, the railing in the chancel. It was all a beautiful light-colored oak. There were two aisles which divided the room into thirds with no center aisle. In good early-American Protestant Presbyterian fashion, the modest pulpit was in the center and elevated slightly. With the lack of a center aisle, the people in the pew sat in that sight line directly in front of the pulpit. It is an historical, architectural point: the congregation is there for worship, and the pulpit is front and center. The congregation was seated in a way so that the sermon and the Gospel proclaimed are given spatial priority.

A very small plaque was on the back of the pulpit in in my first congregation. Only the preacher could see this, and it was inscribed with a Bible verse. "Sir, we wish to see Jesus." There was no chapter or verse listed. It was left to the preacher or any guests to find the reference. "Sir, we wish to see Jesus." It is a message from the congregation to their pastor: "Through your preaching, we wish to see Jesus." Each and every Sunday, in every season, the intent of Gospel proclamation is to present Christ Jesus to the gathering community, the hearers of the Word. Not surprisingly, that plaque is not unique to one beautiful and modest sanctuary in Southern New Jersey. The message appears to preachers in pulpits in Churches all over! One will never know how many, but in countless congregations in sanctuaries all over, the concealed message from congregation to pastor is tucked in some way, somehow: "Sir, we wish to see Jesus."

"We wish to see Jesus." John 12:21. In the Gospel account, the request to see Jesus comes from some Greeks who came to Philip. Philip went and shared their plea with Andrew. Together, Andrew and Philip went and told Jesus. With all due respect to the preaching tradition that undergirds the embedded message in so many Churches and, frankly, defines my life as a Presbyterian pastor, the answer Jesus offers to Andrew and Philip has little, if anything, to do with preaching. Here in the 12th chapter of John's Gospel, Jesus responds by telling once again about his own death and resurrection: "The hour has come for the Son of Man to be glorified...a grain of wheat falls into the earth and dies.... And I, when I am lifted up from the Earth, will draw all people to myself." In other words, to those inquiring Greek worshippers, if you want to see Jesus, now is the time in the Gospel narrative to watch very closely!

In addition to predicting his Death and Resurrection, Jesus also offers some familiar teaching which strikes a familiar chord for those who have ears to hear. "Those who love their life lose it, and those who hate their life in this world will keep it for eternal life. Whoever serves me must follow me, and where I am, there will my servant be also. Whoever serves me, the Father will honor." For the experienced hearers of the Word, a familiar tune keeps playing in the ear and in the heart. "Whoever wants to be first, must be last of all.... Whoever wants to be the greatest among you, must be a servant of all...the first shall be last...the greatest shall be the servants." If you want to see Jesus, yes, pay attention to his Death and Resurrection. If you want to see Jesus, yes, experience the Gospel proclaimed in the words of a preacher. But never forget, if you want to see Jesus, look to see where the Gospel is being proclaimed around you in lives of servanthood. If you want to see Jesus, don't forget to look there!

You remember in Luke's Gospel when Jesus stood up to read in the synagogue and unrolled the scroll of Isaiah? Jesus read about the "Spirit of the Lord being upon me," and "bringing good news to the poor," and "proclaiming release to the captives," and "recovery of sight to the blind," and "the oppressed going free". Then Jesus rolled up the scroll, sat down, and said, "Today this Scripture is being fulfilled in your hearing." If you want to see Jesus, look to lives of servanthood.

Cadillac aired a commercial during the Winter Olympics that kind of took your breath away when you saw it. It starts with a man looking into the camera and saying "Why do we work so hard? For what? For this?" He then looks to the infinity pool at his house and asks "for stuff?" The man goes on to comment on other countries that take the whole month of August off and he cites the American value of hard work that offers such reward. He names some American achievements and some American achievers. As he unplugs the electric luxury car, he says, "You work hard. You create your own luck. You've got to believe anything is possible." Then at the end of the commercial he says, "As for all the stuff, that's the upside of only taking two weeks off."

With all due respect to a good old-fashioned work ethic, and with no criticism intended for a healthy patriotic spirt, and with an appropriate acknowledgement of all that the American car industry represents…from strictly a theological perspective, and when asking the most basic of questions, like "What is being touted as important here?", and affirming a least common denominator among us about what it means to be human, and pointing to a purpose in life…when looking at the commercial from the perspective of Lent, after it takes your breath away, it ought to make you a bit sick to your stomach. If you want to see Jesus, you don't look to the stuff, you look to servanthood.

In February 2014, *The New Yorker* published an essay by Adam Gopnik entitled "Bigger than Phil: When Did Faith Start to Fade?" The piece traces the intellectual history of atheism. Interestingly, in a piece which tries desperately to pass intellectual muster (there were sentences I had to read three and four times), the title comes from a line in a Mel Brooks movie. With a bit of a snarky flare, the author describes conceptions of God at various moments in the essay as: the God of the Gaps who fills the bill for whatever humanity can't explain, Jehovah as little Tinker Bell who lives only if you say the name enough, God as a dinner guest legendary for his wit who spends the meal mumbling with his mouth full, God as an omnipotent little man in the sky making moral rules and watching human actions with paranoiac intensity. In the end, Gopnik cops to an atheism akin to Karl Marx, and arguing that "relatively peaceful and prosperous societies…tend to have a declining belief in a deity." That as "incomes go up, steeples come down."

Upon further review, what strikes me about the essay is that the author reserves his strongest disdain not for believers who are looking to argue that mystery still exists in science, or those who want to hold out for an existential higher purpose or ground of being for humanity, or even for those who suggest there must still be someone, something, out there at the end of the rainbow of the ultimate answerless question. What clearly irks this particular atheist the most is any suggestion that there is a God who cares about how you and I treat people; the ones we love, the ones we don't know, the stranger, our enemies, that there is a God who calls us to a life of servanthood. As he puts it, "an omnipotent little man in the sky making moral rules and watching human actions with paranoic intensity!"

Paranoic intensity; that sounds a bit dramatic to me. But a God who cares about human interaction? I'll take that every time.

Don't forget to look at the lives of servanthood all around you— if you want to see Jesus.

PALM SUNDAY

PATRICK J. WENRICK

Mark 11:1-10
Isa. 50:4-7
Phil. 2:6-11
Mark 14:1-15:47

"Hosanna in the highest!"

It is so easy to "hear" the voices of the city dwellers as they greeted their expected king as he rode on a colt into the large metropolis known as Jerusalem. Amidst all the excitement and shouts of "Hosanna," I wonder if anyone could "hear" what was going on within the person riding on the colt? What was Jesus feeling? What was he sensing? Was he as joy-filled and happy as those shouting and laying down palm fronds as he passed? Or was something else going on inside this preacher who healed the blind, raised the dead, and who taught with authority? Perhaps this experience was bitter-sweet as he knew, deep down, that he was letting go of a life that took him into people's lives and hearts and where he often stepped outside the box to heal the sick, forgive the sinner, and free the captive. Could Jesus be wondering, as he entered Jerusalem, "Do they still not understand where God is to be found?"

To experience Jesus entering Jerusalem on this Palm Sunday, we might ask ourselves, "What are we hearing?" In our day-to-day life are we listening to the mind and heart of Jesus as evidenced in those engaged in the process of "letting go?" Perhaps they are our neighbors who have been in the same house for years, or to whom we have been a part of their lives and the lives of their children as they grew up and moved out on their own? Yet, now they are facing their senior years and it is painful to maintain the upkeep of the house, let alone their health. They are forced to "let go," not only of a house, but also a home of memories and a secure way of life in order to embrace the unknown in small living conditions amongst people who are mere strangers. Are we attentive to their anguish, their pain, or are we just about throwing a party and bringing gifts as marks of farewell and best wishes? This not only blocks the call of hurt and pain in our neighbors heart, but in our own heart. .

There are those in prisons, hospitals, hospices, and in our own churches and homes who have the heart of Jesus as he rides that colt into the city of Jerusalem. Do we have "ears to hear" what is not being said vocally, but what lies in the deep recesses of their hearts; of our own hearts? One thing is for sure, if we don't take the time to be quiet with ourselves and listen to how God speaks in our lives and hearts, there is no way we will be attentive to Jesus as he speaks in the hearts of others, even those who live under the same roof.

The Scriptures tell us that throughout Jesus's life he often went off to a quiet place to pray. He would definitely take the time to be in relationship with his Father. This relationship is what gave him the courage to step outside the box of society's expectations, and those of the religious leaders of his time. This relationship empowered Jesus to hear what was really going on with the beggar by the pool, or the woman caught in adultery and about to be stoned. It gave him the compassion and courage to say to the righteous crowd "who among you is without sin cast the first stone," or to the blind beggar by the pool "do you want to be healed?"

We live in an age where the art of communicating with another is going through a drastic revolution. We have Facebook, Twitter, and texting. There are high-quality headphones and ear buds which deliver superb sound. These commodities have brought our world closer together, or so it seems. Yet, I cannot help but think that these things can also be all-consuming in that we pay more attention to the words of the text than we do the steering wheel of our vehicle traveling on the road. We become addicted to the chat or to the music so that we cannot let go in order to experience silence, or even to hear the words of a person talking to us so that we may experience the God of mercy and compassion in our hearts, or the need in the hearts of others.

What is it that we need to "let go" of in order to hear the heart of Christ? Is it an attachment to a place, a behavior, an object, or an attitude? Can we let go of it by first developing a relationship with the Father that will help us to let go? Can we then be free to hear Christ as the one who speaks to us at table, or the neighbor on the street, the homeless person, or spouse, or child? Can we hear Jesus utter the words, "Do this in memory of Me," or " Father forgive them," or "Into your hands I commend my spirit" as it is spoken from the lives of people with whom we live, work, and worship?

> The only survivor of a shipwreck was washed up on a small, unin-
> habited island. He prayed feverishly for God to rescue him, and
> every day he scanned the horizon for help, but none seemed forth-
> coming. Exhausted, he eventually managed to build a little hut out
> of driftwood to protect him from the elements, and to store his few
> possessions. But then one day, after scavenging for food, he arrived
> home to find his little hut in flames, the smoke rolling up to the sky.
> The worst had happened; everything was lost. He was stunned with
> grief and anger. "God, how could you do this to me!" he cried. Early
> the next day, however, he was awakened by the sound of a ship that
> was approaching the island. It had come to rescue him. "How did
> you know I was here?" asked the weary man of his rescuers. "We
> saw your smoke signal," they replied.

It is easy to become discouraged when we hold onto what was instead of listening to what might be. God is at work in our lives even in the midst of pain and suffering. Remember this the next time your hut is burning to the ground—it just may be a smoke signal that summons God's grace.

- AUTHOR UNKNOWN

HOLY THURSDAY

FR. GREG BOYLE, SJ

EXO. 12:1-8, 11-14
1 COR. 11:23-26
JOHN 13:1-15

"I have given you a model to follow."

"*Do you understand what I've* just done to you?" Jesus asks, after washing his disciples' feet. From that day forward, the Church has washed the feet of 12 men on Holy Thursday. That is, of course, until Pope Francis celebrated Holy Thursday, not in a Basilica, but in a jail… washing the feet of prisoners…men, women, and Muslims.

St. Francis of Assisi admonishes us with this: "Don't imitate Jesus. Follow in his footsteps." Jesus doesn't want a fan club ("I have all your records. I go to every concert.") You won't find a single "worship me" in the Gospel. But you'll find a ton of "Follow me."

"Do you understand what I've just done to you?" We either simply imitate the action—(the feet of twelve men), or we domesticate the message: "Serve others." Don't get me wrong. I like BOTH service AND clean feet. But what Jesus does is more than service, and deeper than mimicry.

In washing all the dirt-covered "dedos" of his friends, Jesus achieves this remarkable and intimate connection with his followers. With a humility that erases the daylight separating them, Jesus draws them into a tenderness—"loving them to the end"—so that they can follow in his footsteps. "Only connect," E.M Forster writes, and this can only happen in humility.

"If you're humble, you'll never stumble," Robert, a homie who works at Homeboy Industries, often says…and I've adopted it as my own calming mantra. Humility keeps you more interested in being interested, than in being interesting. It keeps "Hubris," humility's opposite, at a safe distance. Humility says, "I need healing." Hubris says, "I am the healer."

Miguel walked into my office after a year of working at Homeboy Industries. He had graduated from our school, and was now taking night courses at a local community college, At 19 years-old, he was a tattooed gang member who began work with us right after release from a detention facility. He had something on his mind. "I discovered something today," he begins. "I discovered that…you're my father. Yeah…it's nice to have a father."

I was startled by this. "Wow," I told him, "You made my whole damn day right there. I would have thought I had won the Lottery if God had handed me a son like you!" But it begged the question. "And YOUR father?"

Miguel waves his hand as a dismissal. "Aw…he was never there for me. Haven't seen him in like ten years."

You can tell when a homie reaches for a snapshot from the family album he'd rather keep closed. "He broke my arm once." He proceeds then to tell me that his father came home from work one day and rushed past Miguel and his kid brother playing in the living room, and entered his bedroom, closing the door behind him. The father emerged minutes later in a rage. "Who stole my batteries?" Well, little Miguel had a toy requiring two batteries. He rummaged through his Dad's drawers and found them. "I did," Miguel squeaked timidly, raising his hand.

Now Miguel begins to quietly sob, and it takes a moment for him to finish the story. Miguel's father walked straight up to him, grabbed his arm…and snapped it in two. Miguel cries all the more in the telling. Then he says to me, "I was six years old…Yeah…It's nice…finally…to have a father."

And the daylight separating us—"Service provider…service recipient" is erased…leaving only a connection born of awe at what the poor have to carry. The humble connection has its roots not in "reaching" people, but in "receiving" them. And in the receiving, we all get returned to ourselves. Only then can we follow in the footsteps of Jesus.

I flew to Washington, DC to speak to a Congressional Sub-Committee on gangs. I brought Louis and Joe with me. They were older "vatos" who did a variety of things at Homeboy. After our testimony, we went to the Holocaust Museum. I encouraged Joe and Louis to walk around the place alone, and at their own pace…wanting to maximize the experience for them. We met in the foyer at our agreed upon time and the two of them were deeply moved. While debriefing in the lobby, we noticed a desk set up off to the side. A man in his 80's sat behind it, reading a book. There was an empty chair in front, as if to invite you to sit in it. There was a sign on the desk: "Holocaust Survivor."

"Wow," Joe says, "What would we say to someone who has suffered so much?" Louis, because he is fearless, dives in, "Well, I'm gonna go talk to him." We tell him to meet us in the gift shop later.

Louis tells us later that the man's name is Jacob. He was 13 when he went to Auschwitz. Both parents were killed there. Two sisters were exe-cuted in front of his eyes. A niece and nephew were also murdered. Louis listened as Jacob shared his story. When Jacob finished, Louis pulled out his business card and handed it to him. "I work at Homeboy Indus-tries. It's the largest gang intervention, rehab and re-entry program in the world. I hope…that if you're ever in LA, you'll come visit us."

Jacob studied the card. "I'm 35 years old…and half my life, I've been locked up." Jacob scoffed a bit. "American prisons," rolling his eyes, " You have your own room. You sleep on a mattress. You have a pillow. We slept on wooden planks. If you spoke in line, they'd pull you out, and beat you nearly to death."

Louis listened intently, then told him, "Yeah…I was beaten a gang 'a times in County Jail. Once…they beat me so bad…I looked like the Elephant Man. Then they threw me naked into a cell, and I slept on a metal sheet."

It was at this moment that I intervened. "Let me see if I got this right, Louis. You were comparing your experience…to a Holocaust survivor?" His response was sure and clear-eyed. "No. I wasn't comparing. There is no comparison between his experience, and what I've been through." And now, his eyes moisten but his resolve doesn't waver. "No. I wasn't… competing…with him." A tear ran down his cheek. "I was…connecting with him."

"Do you understand what I have just done to you?" Only connect. A discipleship, intimate and humble, which seeks not to "reach people" but to "receive them." No daylight…only following in footsteps.

GOOD FRIDAY

DEACON GREG KANDRA

Isa. 52:13-53:12

Heb. 4:14-16; 5:7-9

John 18:1-19:42

"It is finished."

About 15 years ago, my wife and I made a pilgrimage to the Holy Land. There, in the Old City of Jerusalem, we walked the Via Dolorosa, the Way of the Cross, passing shops and souvenir vendors selling cards and olive wood crosses. We prayed at the stations, and we encountered many of the sites mentioned in this Gospel reading.

But one site in particular stands out in my memory. It is the Church of the Holy Sepulcher—the site of Christ's Passion, Death and Resurrection.

It is ancient, and hard to navigate. Upon entering, your guide leads you to a dark and smoky chapel, where candles burn and monks pray, and incense fills the air. You approach a small place beneath a marble altar, a spot only a few inches wide. You bend down and see a dark hole in the stone floor. Nervously, fearfully, you crouch down, reach your hand into the opening and touch a piece of rock—rock worn smooth by almost 20 centuries of hands groping in the dark. The hands of peasants and kings, of saints and servants, all drawn to this very church to do what you are about to do.

And in that moment, you touch one of the most important places in all of human history.

This is the earth that held the cross.

You are touching Calvary.

And for just a moment, the centuries fall away. Here is where the blood fell and women wept. There, just a few inches away, is where Mary stood watch, with John at her side. Nearby were all the others: the centurion, the thief, the guards. Here is where Christ cried out, "I thirst." Here is where he whispered, "It is finished." You're only steps away from where the earth cracked open.

You withdraw your hand from the dark opening and stagger to your feet. The sensation is disorienting. You finally understand that here, at this obscure place, is where everything changed.

Most historians and archaeologists agree that this spot is, in fact, the actual site of the crucifixion. To visit Calvary today is to encounter the place where history's greatest sacrifice was offered—where the Lamb of God was slaughtered, where the Prince of Peace stretched out his arms for the salvation of the world.

This day, in this church, we strive to do what pilgrims have done in Jerusalem for generations: We seek to connect with the mystery of the Passion—this great and unparalleled act of love.

And yes: we seek, somehow, to touch Calvary. We experience it anew. We hear once more the account of Christ's Passion and Death. We realize how much he gave, and why.

But if we are honest, we realize something else: that Calvary is not just one place, at one moment in time.

Calvary is everywhere. It is any place where the Body of Christ is scourged, stripped, broken, pierced.

There is the Calvary of war and bigotry, of persecution and poverty.

There is the Calvary that dwells within every human heart, whenever we turn toward sin and turn our backs on Christ.

The world is haunted by Calvaries.

But by God's grace, Calvary isn't the end of the story.

The great artist, James Tissot, once painted an image of the Blessed Mother that remains one of the most haunting images I've ever seen. It's called "The Holy Virgin in Old Age." It shows Mary at Calvary, many years after her son's Passion, kneeling before the place which held the cross; she is gazing into the Earth while deep in prayer.

It was at that very spot that her son had said, "It is finished." Then, his earthly life ended.

But the Christian story was just beginning.

Twenty centuries later, that very place remains a silent witness to what was—and a testament to what would be.

In Jerusalem, when you go to visit the site of the Crucifixion today, as you approach that sacred spot you are struck by something unexpected.

You realize: there is only one way to touch Calvary.

You have to go on your knees.

And: there is only way to move on.

That is by rising.

In this way, the modern pilgrim discovers something as true today as it was two thousand years ago. Here is the overarching message of these Holy days—a lesson that holy spot in that ancient church teaches every person who draws near.

The journey to Calvary ends…by rising.

EASTER SEASON

EASTER VIGIL

MSGR. MICHAEL DOYLE

GEN. 1:1-2:2, 22:1-18 EXOD. 14:15-15:1 ISA. 54:5-14, 55:1-11 BAR. 3:9-15, 32-4:4 EZEK. 36:16-28 ROM. 6:3-11 MK 16:1-7	*"In the beginning, God created…"*

It is a demanding task for any priest or deacon to preach a homily at the Easter Vigil because it is a lengthy service. I thank you for your attention to a marathon of readings which start with these daunting opening words: "In the beginning, God created the Heavens and Earth." (Gen 1) You might wonder: "When will this end?" It was George Burns who said: "The secret of a good sermon is to have a good beginning, and a good ending, and to keep the two as close as possible." The closing reading tonight was surely a good one, as Mark tells of an angel addressing fearful women at the tomb of Jesus by saying again the words which Gabriel said to Mary of Nazareth: "Do not be afraid." Then to another Mary and her friends: "You are looking for Jesus of Nazareth who was crucified. He is not here." They knew that. Then they heard the best three words ever uttered on the planet: *"He is Risen."* No event in human history matches the moment when Jesus rose from the dead. What a moment when his dead heart stirred in the cavity of his chest, the cavity of a rock, the cavity of all creation!

The first and last readings were not close on the pages of the Bible, or in the milestones of history, but they are connected in the depth of meaning contained within them. They both are profound beginnings. Both proclaim new light to the world. The first in the sun and the moon and the stars, but these rays do not penetrate the darkness in the human heart. The light of the Resurrection penetrates every level of darkness in Creation.

The darkness of death has been, along eons of time, an abiding ache in the human heart. For all of time, men and women have wept when eyelids lowered and froze on the bright faces that shone with light and love. The final curtain on every stage has been a curtain of clay, ashes, and decay. The human heart has groped for meaning along the beaten and unbeaten paths of human history. People were in the dark. But, new stars appeared in the darkness, men and women of wisdom, endowed by God to be torches of truth for them.

On this night of the Easter Vigil, when we wait for the dawn, we, as a family of the same faith and story, listen again to the hints of hope which shone along the way that our ancestors walked. Revelation from God was wind in the sails of our voyage. We came to know Abraham. His story is stunning. Tested at the ultimate point of his wit's end, he did not flinch in his obedience to God and became an anchor post of faithfulness in the journey of faith. Then there's Moses and the Exodus, when God gave new clarity to the purpose of the human journey. This Vigil provides the long, up and down, story of our Salvation. In Exodus 15, God says to Moses: "Tell the Israelites to go forward." Then he, at the command of God, split the sea for them and on they go. The story goes on, too.

The Vigil is like a big anniversary of old and young, when stories are told of good times and hard times. A good sense of belonging permeates our gathering. We heard from Isaiah, a much-loved star in the story. He is speaking of God when he writes: "For a brief moment, I abandoned you, but with great tenderness, I will take you back." Also, "In justice shall you be established, where destruction cannot come near you." Then Baruch chimes in with: "Follow God's law and receive wisdom. Walk by her light toward splendor." Ezekiel, another star, has refreshing words for us: "I will sprinkle clear water upon you to cleanse you from all your impurities. I will give you a new heart…you shall be my people, and I will be your God." (Ez. 36) But no words can compare with the three words in Mark's Gospel: "He is Risen." These words are worth more than all the words in the world. In the back of millions of churches, priests or deacons fumble with fire trying to express a spark in the dark, or more importantly, life in a corpse. Darkness, atmospheric darkness is hard to find in the developed world. But we know that all the darkness in the world cannot extinguish the smallest candle.

Easter is a huge challenge in celebration, but what we do in churches is a faithful effort going back to the eleventh century.

I suppose there is still a stone in the way to the truest realization of the Resurrection. All four Evangelists tell us of the stone, which the woman feared was in the way, yet it was not. Matthew records that "as the first day of the week was dawning, Mary Magdalene, and the other Mary, came to the tomb, and behold there was a great earthquake, for an angel of the Lord descended from Heaven, approached, rolled back the stone and sat upon it." (Matt 28:1-2) Imagine that! As if to say: "There, go look!"

We should not let any obstacle stop us. Jesus did not need to have the stone moved. When his dead heart moved, he could move anything, and he did. It wasn't the shifted stone that started Mary Magdalene's belief in the Resurrection. It took just one word from Jesus: "Mary." Immediately, her heart lit up with joy and total belief. Oh, Lord Jesus, move the stones in our hearts! Speak our names and call us to total faith in the Resurrection. Let it be a realization that stuns us into new ways of saying things, new ways of acting, and new ways of living.

In Sacred Heart Church in Camden, New Jersey there is an annual great human effort and a great hope in God that the realization of the Resurrection may be deepened. First of all, the Vigil has begun at 4:30 am for the past 40 years. Darkness does not have to be manufactured. The many readings are done in a "tomb," a basement of complete darkness except for faint fire exit lights. At the words of the Gospel: He is Risen," a match lights a fast fire of slim twigs and old palm in a hibachi on a table. The Paschal candle is lit with a blazing twig from the fire, and four "holy women" with four candles carry a flame to every candle in the place and good news to every ear: "Christ is Risen!" The Paschal candle is hoisted high above the candles of the congregation. A beautiful scroll flows forward as the words of the Exultet are sung from it. Water is poured with great sound, and the blessing of it with great words. The Paschal candle is plunged into the water, invoking the power of the Holy Spirit. Catechumens are baptized, confirmed, robed in white, and called to stand with candle and cross held high, to proclaim "Christ is Risen" three times to which everyone responds: "Indeed He is Risen!" Then the congregation, led by the Paschal candle, walks out of the "tomb" with bells and candles and incense into a morning of risen light. The procession winds its way back and enters the church, enters a glorious scene of joy, to share the Easter Eucharist.

At the end, the wondrous Call to Christian Love, as found in the Russian Church, is proclaimed. Here is part of it: "It is the day of Passover! Let us be enlightened with the solemn feast. Let us embrace one another! Let us say my brother (or my sister) even to those who hate us. Let us forgive all things for the sake of the Resurrection! In this way we will bear witness that Christ is Risen from the dead.

We truly celebrate Resurrection when love rises above hate or indifference.

EASTER SUNDAY

FR. RICHARD ROHR, OFM

Acts 10:34, 37-43
Col. 3:1-4
1 Cor. 5:6-8
John 20:1-9

"Think of what is above, not of what is on Earth."

Don't you often wonder why so much of human life seems so futile, so tragic, so short, or so sad? If Christ has risen, and we speak so much of being risen with Christ, then why do most people experience their life as tragic more than triumphant? Why is there non-stop war? Why are there so many people unjustly imprisoned? Why are the poor oppressed? Why, even in Christian nations, is there a long history of deceit and injustice? Why do so few marriages last, even among those of us who say that we believe? Why are there so many children born with disabilities? Why do we destroy so many of our relationships? Why?

What are you up to, God? Why is there so much suffering if Christ has risen? It really doesn't make any logical sense. Is the Resurrection something that just happened once in Jesus's body, but not in ours? Or not in human history? When and where and how is this resurrection thing really happening? Is it only after death? Is it only in the next world? My guess is that it is both now and later, and *just enough now* to promise you an also infinite forever.

The Resurrection of Christ is telling us that in the Great Story Line of History, in the mind of God as it were, the Final Judgment has already happened, and it's nothing that we need to be afraid of. Instead, the arc of history is moving toward resurrection. God's Final Judgment is that God will have the last word, that there are no dead-ends, that our lives and human history is not going to end in a sad and tragic list of human crucifixions and natural disasters. When we look at life in its daily moments, this is almost always hard to see. We can only see in small frames. Yet over and over again, here and there, more than we suspect, a kind of cosmic hope breaks through for those who are willing to see and willing to cooperate with this universal mystery of Resurrection. I am never sure if the promise of resurrection creates an intuitive hope in us, or if people who grasp onto hope can also believe in resurrection. All I know is that both are the work of the Holy Spirit within us.

In this part of the world, Easter coincides with Spring-time. I hope that you're noticing the leaves and the flowers being reborn after months of winter. I went out this April morning to watch the sunrise which I was told would rise at 6:30 a.m. But on the west side of the Sandia Mountain Range where I live, it takes a little longer for the sun to make an appearance. I found myself waiting, and waiting. But sure enough, at the very moment of 7:00 a.m., the sun again, as it always inevitably does, peeked over the mountains.

I thought, "You know, this is not so much like a sunrise as a groundswell coming from the earth." It was coming from the world in which you and I live. It was coming, not from the top, but from the bottom. It was saying, "Even all of this which looks muddy and material, even all of this which looks so ordinary and dying will be reborn." Sunrises and springtime cannot be stopped, even when winter holds us with its desperate grip. Maybe this is why ancient people almost worshiped the seasons, and why they themselves became spiritual teachers.

This is the Feast Day of Hope. As the poet e.e.cummings puts it, "I who have died am alive again today, and this is the sun's birthday; this is the birth day of life and love and wings: and of the gay great happening il-limitably earth." Jesus is the stand in for everybody. He gives history a personal, a historical, and a cosmic hope. His one life tells us where it is all heading. He is the microcosm of the whole divine and human cosmos!

This is the feast that says God will have the last word and that whatever we crucify, whatever we tragically destroy, God will undo with his eter-nal love and forgiveness. This feast affirms that God's Final Judgment is Resurrection, that God will turn all that remains, all the destruction and hurt and punishment, into beauty. The word on that usually blank white banner that we see the Risen Christ carrying in Christian art is simple and clear: LOVE IS STRONGER THAN DEATH! God's love will always win! That's what it means to be God.

Without such hope why would you keep living and believing when you see that everything passes on and passes away? Everything is here and gone, here and gone, here and gone. If you haven't noticed that yet, just wait a while. Everything passes. This becomes overwhelming for most people as they get older, and it is often just denied because it is so pain-ful. Without such cosmic hope, we all become cynics. Yet the Christian promise is that God will replace everything with his immeasurable and infinite *life*. Jesus is the standing promise that this is the case.

What the Resurrection is saying, more than anything else, is that love is stronger than death. Jesus walked through both life and death with love, which becomes an infinite life, a participation in God himself. Surprise of surprises! This cannot be proven logically or rationally, and yet this is the mystery that we now stake our life—and our death—on: *nothing dies forever, and all that has died in love will be reborn in an even larger love.*

So, to be a Christian, brothers and sisters, is to be inevitably and forever a person of hope. You cannot stay in your depression. You cannot stay in your darkness because it's only for a time. No feeling is final. It will not last. God in Christ is saying, "This is what will last—my life and my love will always and forever have the final word."

ACTS 4:32-35
1 JOHN 5:1-6
JOHN 20:19-31

"Whose sins you forgive are forgiven."

It was during the summer of 1925 that a poor and uneducated 19-year-old fled her parents and begged to join a convent in Poland; three years later, her dream became reality. Soon after, between 1931 and 1938, the Risen Christ made a number of appearances to Sister Mary Faustina of the Blessed Sacrament. The various messages that Christ gave to Faustina during that time were eventually published in her book, *Diary: Divine Mercy in My Soul*. One of the many conversations she recounts in her book is a direct request from Christ that a Feast of Divine Mercy be established on the first Sunday after Easter, so that all people would take refuge in Christ's mercy.

The first Divine Mercy Sunday was celebrated in April 1935, but it would not be until 2000 when Pope John Paul II canonized her as Saint Faustina and gave this Sunday its official designation. Interestingly, it was five years later that Pope John Paul II died on the Vigil of Divine Mercy Sunday.

It is surmised that this Sunday was chosen to celebrate Christ's universal mercy because the readings of this day always deal with the mercy of Christ. Today's Gospel from John is the famous passage of Thomas' doubt in the Risen Lord, for he had not been present when Christ first appeared to his fellow disciples. Frankly, I think he gets a bum rap, because none of his fellow disciples believed Christ rose from the dead until they saw him, too! But it was the Sunday after Christ rose from the dead that we find all the disciples still hiding behind locked doors. Once again, Jesus appears, but this time Thomas *is* present—Thomas—who like his fellow disciples needed to see in order to believe in the Risen Lord. As we know—as soon as Thomas sees, just as when the disciples saw, just as when Mary Magdala saw—they believed that Jesus was the Christ.

But it seems clear that it wasn't enough to just see and believe. It wasn't good enough for the followers to hole up in the Upper Room day and night, and tell each other that they believe. Jesus was looking for them to do more, and thus was calling them to be sent forth—just as his Father had sent him. They needed to get out from behind the locked doors of their lives, and to continue to do what Jesus did—teach, heal and forgive. But now, things were a bit different when they would go to the temple and teach, as did Jesus. This difference is tied to a particular line that we hear each year in the Passion story, and it has significant meaning.

Remember what happened the moment Jesus died? The sanctuary veil of the temple was torn in half, from top to bottom. Now keep in mind that this was not your everyday living room curtain. This temple veil was 4-inches-thick with a height of almost 70 feet, weighed 4 tons and required 300 priests to carry it in place. The purpose of this curtain was to separate and define the 'holy' from the 'unholy.' The Latin word for 'temple' is 'fanum,' and everything outside the temple veil was called 'profanum'—thus the derivative of our word 'profane.' There was no longer separation of holy and unholy with the tearing of this veil; there was no more 'profane.' Rather, everything was now 'fanum,' or the 'holy,' and the 'temple.' Christ's crucifixion and death on the cross ended the division of who was deemed by man to be 'holy' and 'right,' and who was 'in' and who was 'out.' For it is in the death and resurrection of Jesus the Christ that the disciples *and* each of us are sent forth to call *all* people to God. One only has to focus on the core of today's Gospel to know that we are all called to do this!

When Christ appeared to Thomas and all the disciples that were gathered in the Upper Room, he did not ask for retribution toward his persecutors.

He did not call for a "just war" on his oppressors...

He did not ask them to start a new religion...

He didn't ask them to write a book of Canon Law...

He didn't ask them to go out and build cathedrals and basilica's...

And Christ certainly did not ask them to go out and decide who was worthy and who was not...

Rather, the Risen Christ sent the disciples forth from the Upper Room with the gift and graces of the Holy Spirit, and asked them to do one thing. He said:

> *Whose sins you forgive are forgiven them, and*
> *Whose sins you retain are retained.*

He asked them to go forth and forgive others, just as he had done. This direction and empowerment was given to all of his disciples, and to all of his followers, not just the apostles. The Risen Christ reminds us that we are *all* called to forgive, and we are called to forgive all. We are called to forgive our spouses, our children, our parents, our co-workers, our priests, our deacons, our Church, our institutions, our government, and even those who violate us.

But probably the most important and the most difficult person to forgive is ourselves. Very few of us want to go there—but that is what Jesus emphasized and taught. No matter what we have done, God loves us and forgives us with unconditional love and unending mercy. This was what he told his disciples and it is the same message repeated to Saint Mary Fautsina. You can almost picture Christ shaking his head after 1,900 years and saying, 'They missed my point! Let me try it again!' when he told Faustina, "Every soul who believes and trusts in my mercy will have it."

Christ tells us through today's Gospel that those trespasses and debts which we are willing to let go of, the ones in which we forgive in ourselves and others, *are* forgiven. They are released from being a part of us; while those that we hold onto and bind within ourselves will erode our well-being, thereby blocking relationships with others and with God.

This whole concept of seeing and believing, which we heard in John's Gospel, is based on the fact that in order for forgiveness to take place we must be able to see God in others, and see God in ourselves and also be open to forgive. That is what he called his disciples to do, and that is what you and I are called to do.

So, on this Divine Mercy Sunday, may we ask for and trust in God's mercy, and give that mercy to others.

May we, filled with the graces of the Holy Spirit, step outside of our personal locked doors and have the strength to forgive all.

During this Easter Season, may we open our eyes to see God in others and within ourselves, so that through this newly-gained insight we, too, may believe and have life in God's holy name.

3RD SUNDAY OF EASTER

FR. PAUL A. HOLMES, STD

Acts 3:13-15, 17-19
1 John 2:1-5
Luke 24:35-48

"You are witnesses of these things."

W*hy doesn't every Catholic attend* Mass each Sunday?

Several years ago, New York's Cardinal Dolan was asked this question and he said that, instead of throwing up our hands and lamenting how nearly two-thirds of Catholics stay home on Sunday mornings, we should look at the parishes where there actually has been an *increase* in attendance. He said, "When we look at such churches, we find a joy-filled priest, someone who preaches the truth and provides a warm, hospitable and *joyful* welcome."

"Joy," he said, "is contagious." And we'd see even more men becoming priests if those who are already ordained could somehow become famous for the joy that they feel.

There's something *to* that observation, I think. And it's especially true during this season of Easter. There's so much to be *joy*-filled *about*. And I'm hoping that some of the joy that I feel somehow rubs off on some of you today.

The Scriptures today speak to us about Heaven—even though the word is never mentioned. And what St. Luke describes in his Gospel should have us thinking about Heaven. He, and the other Gospel writers, spend a good deal of time, and a great deal of effort, making sure we know that the Risen Lord *has a real body*.

Last week, the Risen Jesus made a beeline for Doubting Thomas and invited him to put his fingers into the nail holes that were left in his hands—not *just* so that Thomas would know that it was really Jesus—but to let Thomas know that Jesus, even in his risen state, still had a *body*.

And, of course, the disciples on the Road to Emmaus recognized Jesus not just in the *breaking* of the Bread, but (presumably because they saw) Jesus *eating* the bread he broke. Once again, to let them know that the Resurrection doesn't do away with the *body*.

And today, Jesus asks for—and then eats—some baked fish.

All of this touching, and talking, and eating has but one purpose: to remind us, always, that when Jesus rose from the dead, his new life included the body he'd had all along.

But the Scriptures aren't meant to let us know only about *Jesus's* risen body. They're meant to let us know that *this* is what *our* risen bodies will be like, too!

Too many people—too many Catholics mistakenly believe that, when we die, we become like angels. Well, I'm here to tell you that there are *more than enough* angels in Heaven—they don't need more! Too many Christians believe that, when we die and go to Heaven, we'll just be "spiritual" beings. That, somehow, we'll be separated from our bodies and become just "disembodied" souls.

Our faith tells us something completely different. Our faith tells us that, without my body, I'm not *me! There's no such thing as "me" without my body.*

All these Resurrection appearances by Jesus are supposed to be potent reminders to Christians that all the movies we've seen about life after death—that, somehow, we're just "spirits" forever separated from our bodies—are just a lot of hooey!

This is why I'm filled with joy this morning!

When I preach that Jesus loves me, I mean he loves the "me" that you see in this pulpit. And when I preach that Jesus loves you, I mean he loves the "you" that I see sitting in the pews. And when I preach that we'll all see one another in Heaven one day, it'll be the "we" that we already know, and love.

I'm filled with joy because, in Heaven, I'll see my Mom and Dad and be able to hug them, and they'll be able to hug me back. I'll be able to kiss them, and they'll be able to kiss me back.

And I'm filled with joy this morning because in Heaven, I'll be able to eat!

I'm filled with joy every Sunday because I get to preach *good* news! Our life here on Earth isn't for nothing. The relationships I've had here on Earth will continue in Heaven.

Maybe people have stopped coming to church on Sunday because the rest of us have stopped believing in Heaven—because there's no *joy* in our churches.

So I ask you: Could you *please* tell everyone out there that there's at least one very happy priest who's tickled to death about what's waiting for us in Heaven! And that he's at this parish every Sunday!

4ᵀᴴ SUNDAY OF EASTER

MARY ELIZABETH SPERRY

Acts 4:8-12
1 John 3:1-2
John 10:11-18

"I am the good shepherd."

We live in a world of standards and guidelines. No matter the area of life—from eating, to working out, to teaching, or to factory work—someone has established guidelines or standards to help you do it 'right.'

Many of these standards have greatly improved our lives. Without them, our food and water would be less safe, children could labor inhuman hours in dangerous workplaces, and environmentally-caused illnesses would be even more common. Yet, some other standards are dangerous. People who hold themselves to unrealistic standards of beauty may suffer from eating disorders or other psychological difficulties. If we hold ourselves to worldly standards of success, we may be encouraged to neglect other important elements of our lives, including faith and family; we may even judge harshly those who do not meet these standards, and wonder what they did 'wrong.'

The readings today remind us that, in his living, in dying, and rising, Christ changed everything, setting new standards for those who bear his name. As Christians, we are called to live by standards that the world does not know, standards which often make no sense to those who do not know Jesus.

The core of the standard which Jesus established is simple to understand, yet very difficult to live: we are called to love others as Christ has loved us.

Christ loves us with a love that is sacrificial. On the cross, he laid down his life for us. But even before that, he laid down his life each and every day as he served the people, ministering to their needs, sharing the Good News with them, healing the sick, treating them with compassion and dignity. He was the Good Shepherd, who laid down his life for his sheep.

In the same way, we are called to live and love sacrificially. In the future, which has not yet been revealed, we will be judged not by how well we meet the world's standards, but by our willingness to emulate Christ's sacrificial love by laying down our lives for others.

The standard set by Christ may seem like nonsense to the world. After all, the world looks at what we achieve and possess, not at what we give. It lauds the rich and powerful, not the poor and humble. To the world, a shepherd who abandons his sheep in the face of danger makes perfect sense—he's only looking out for number one, saving himself with no concern for others. After all, the pay isn't worth his life. But Jesus is not that sort of shepherd. Instead of running away, Jesus sacrifices himself for the sheep, placing their needs and welfare above his own.

Why did Jesus lay down his life for us? It is because we are made in the image and likeness of God, and "may be called the children of God." God loves us so much that he sent his Son to live and to die as one of us. Jesus went to his death willingly, choosing to lay down his life for us.

We are called to hear the voice of our Shepherd, who calls us by name, and to show the same self-sacrificing love to those around us. In doing so, we follow the example of Peter and John, who healed the crippled man at the temple gate. Rather than walking past him as though he did not exist, Peter and John treated him with the dignity and love due to a child of God. They gave this man what they had—healing him in the name of Jesus Christ.

Caring for those rejected or ignored by the world will not help us get ahead, or bring us any worldly benefit. In fact, it may raise questions or even opposition, as it did for Peter and John. Called before the council to defend their actions, Peter used the opportunity to preach the Good News of Jesus Christ, in whose name all may be saved.

If the world does not know Christ, it will not understand or validate our loving actions. But we must act with love anyway. Through our actions, as well as our words, we preach the truth of the loving God who laid down his life so that we might live.

Our love cannot be limited to those who "belong to our fold." Instead, our love must be all-encompassing. We must reach out to others, giving of ourselves—from our abundance and even from our want. We cannot love only those who seem familiar, or worthy, or easily lovable. We must lay down our lives—and our pursuit of success by the world's standards—on behalf of those most in need of love. Through our loving actions, those outside the fold may come to know the Good Shepherd, who works not for pay, but for love of his sheep.

5TH SUNDAY OF EASTER

DEACON WILLIAM T. DITEWIG, PhD

ACTS 9:26-31

1 JOHN 3:18-24

JOHN 15:1-8

"I am the true vine."

Poor *Paul. He must have* been a hard man to be friends with. From everything we know about him in Scripture, he was a fiery man, passionate about his beliefs and impatient with those who disagreed with him. He never backed down from an argument, and he certainly was not your average newly-hatched Christian! As Saul, he was on fire to destroy Christians everywhere and anywhere that he could find them. He was present and holding people's cloaks as they stoned St. Stephen to death, making Stephen the first martyr of the New Covenant. Then, "still breathing murderous threats against the Lord's disciples, went to the high priest and asked him for letters to the synagogues in Damascus" to give him the authority to arrest any persons who were disciples of Christ, and to bring them to Jerusalem for their own martyrdom.

Then on the road to Damascus to carry out his plans, Saul has a blinding encounter with the Risen Christ. In an instant, his life is transformed. He stumbles blindly on to Damascus, where the Lord has prepared Ananias to welcome Saul, to baptize him and to restore his sight. Now the neophyte Paul, like many other newly-initiated people, is filled with enthusiasm and passion to proclaim Christ to all who would listen. The passionate Christian-hater was, in short order, transformed into an even more passionate proclaimer of Christ. Flush with zeal, he "soon began to proclaim in the synagogues that Jesus was the Son of God."

Is it any wonder that people had trouble believing this lightning conversion? At first, the Christians in Damascus were skeptical of their new brother, fearing that this might be some kind of trap to lure them to their own martyrdom. Then, after he seemed to break into that community, his fellow Jews, who felt that he had now broken with them in following Christ, plotted to kill him! His fellow Christians, perhaps with not a little sense of relief, but also to save Paul's life, help him escape and return to Jerusalem. Here's where we pick up today's story.

Now in Jerusalem, Paul encounters the same skepticism and fear from the Christian community. Only when Barnabas gives testimony about Paul's conversion and his preaching in Damascus, do they begin to relent. We are told that he again takes up preaching openly, and uses his own unique gifts and training to debate with the Greek-speaking community in Jerusalem. They wound up having the same response as the folks in Damascus: they tried to kill him! Once again, the Christian community thought it best that Paul move on, and they helped him get safely on his way back to his hometown of Tarsus. There, scholars tell us, Paul remained relatively sedate, focused on being a simple disciple of Christ, not taking up his apostolic mission again until some years later.

What does all this have to do with us today?

As we journey through this Easter Season, reflecting on the impact of Christ's ministry, suffering, death and resurrection, we find ourselves facing the question: *What now?* Christ has won the victory over sin and death, so what do I, as a disciple of Christ, do now? We find the answer in Christ's command to "go and make disciples, baptizing them in the name of the Father, and of the Son, and of the Holy Spirit." We exist to evangelize; it's that simple. We exist to do what Paul did after his own conversion: go about and proclaim that Jesus the Christ is the Messiah, the Son of the living God.

Our readings tell us something else, as well. Before we can evangelize properly we must be grafted onto the Vine that is Christ. In order to be fruitful in proclaiming the Lord, we can never be separated from the Lord or from each other. The image of Christ as the Vine, and we as the branches, expresses such a profound truth. Grafted together into the Christ, we live his Resurrected life, the same life which we extend to others. We celebrate that communion we share with each other in Christ in the very Eucharist that we share here today.

But our Scriptures show us that this process of preparing and grafting new branches onto the Vine is not without its own challenges. The Church is not some kind of "pie-in-the-sky" utopia in which everything is sweetness and light, or a place in which we no longer encounter challenges and dangers. Paul, eventually revered as the great Apostle to the Gentiles, struggled mightily to overcome his past and to carry out his Christ-given mission. Throughout his letters he not only claims his discipleship, but also his apostleship, despite his murderous past. He endured shipwreck, imprisonment, rejection and martyrdom in his quest to proclaim the Risen Christ to the world. Some Christians, even St. Peter, often struggled with him. Yet through it all, they remained in communion with each other, grafted strongly onto the Vine of Christ.

How do we live out our own Baptismal call to be "priest, prophet and king" to those around us? Are we open to our own "Damascus moment" of conversion to Christ? Do we eagerly embrace a life of proclaiming Christ to others, regardless of where we are and how people might receive us or the message? On the other hand, are we open to hearing the Word from unexpected witnesses? How would we react to a new Catholic whom had previously been rabidly anti-Catholic, yet was now proclaiming Christ to us?

Would we accept that person into our company, or would we be happy to help that person find a different community?! Through it all, with our various personalities, strengths and weaknesses, how do we remain strongly grafted on the Vine of Christ?

How would we receive Paul into our parish community today?

Acts 10:25-26, 34-35, 44-48

1 John 4:7-10

John 15:9-17

"Remain in my love."

Have you ever heard someone say, "I *used* to go to church, but I'm not welcome now."? These words, and variations of them, may be spoken in anger, sadness, or resignation, but most always are spoken in hurt. Hearing them breaks my heart.

What church doesn't welcome or like God's people? God longs to draw everyone into an intimate relationship, as members of the mystical Body of Christ. All three of today's readings orient us towards God's invitation toward all people, offered in love, and made manifest through our own participation and action.

First, we hear about Cornelius, a Roman citizen, who prostrates himself before Peter. Without hesitation, Peter tells him to get up, reminding Cornelius that he, too, is human, and not divine. We are all human, and Jesus—who is Divinity enfleshed, came to draw us into deeper relationship with God through one another. Peter tells Cornelius that God shows no partiality, and that every nation which "fears him and acts uprightly" is "acceptable" to God. At this point, the Holy Spirit "fell upon all who were listening to the Word." Such an event was shocking to the "circumcised" who were amazed by God's generosity, and amazed by God's welcome toward those that they considered to be outsiders.

This makes me wonder why God's generous welcome remains such a constant source of astonishment to many people. Shouldn't it be obvious 2000 years later? Yet here we are, perpetually stunned by God's love. What are we—whether lay, vowed, or ordained ministers—called to do? Leave people prostrate before us? Leave them angry, hurt, and separated from the Body of Christ? Or do we imitate Peter—who declared his own humanity, and who offered the healing power of God's love?

God's love, as expressed in and through Jesus Christ born as human in the world, indeed continues to startle us. At the upcoming Feast of the Ascension, we will be reminded not to keep "looking up at the sky." We can't simply stare and wonder where God went. We must go out and raise others up with love, and not be shocked by it!

Jesus's love, moving in the Holy Spirit, is the current that charges us with the power to go out and raise others up. This love in action, as demonstrated by Peter today, continually raises others. Imagine God's love in action as a film of falling dominoes, run in reverse! Think about the dynamism of the Spirit as each of us rises up, then raising others up as a result of the power of Christ's love.

Our second reading, from the First Letter of John, and also John's Gospel, both reinforce the power of this love in action. God loves us first, and all else is response from us. It can be a challenge to remember that, because we like to think that we are the masters of our own destiny. But we always move in response to God's love in action, which is animated by the Spirit and embodied in the Risen Christ. Jesus tells us that we must love one another; it is not a suggestion—it is a command. If we are to follow Jesus, we have no choice but to comply. Yet, don't we all struggle, both with loving and with bringing others into that love?

"This is my command," says Jesus, "love one another." "Remain in my love," comes earlier in the Gospel of John, as we read today. Another utterance tells us to "love one another," this time coupled with "as I have loved you." Did you hear the words, "you are my friends"? Jesus adds that he "no longer calls us slaves." Jesus says, "It was not you who chose me, but I who chose you," establishing all that we do is done in response to God's empowering love.

How are we to "remain in" Jesus's love? In *The Joy of the Gospel*, Pope Francis points out that "Christians have a duty to proclaim the Gospel without excluding anyone." We remain by including others! What else can we do with our brothers and sisters who feel unworthy or unwelcome, as they experience a "not-quite-good-enough" response from church? This is what has been appropriated, intentionally or not, through the practice of exclusion instead of welcome and mercy. .

What are we to do? How can we change things that seem so much bigger than we are? Here are three ways in which we might try.

First, let us truly try to love one another. Talk is cheap; we all know how hard this is. Let us see if we can find ways to view others with the eyes of the heart, in the same way that God sees us. This does not mean you have to become best friends with your enemies, but perhaps we can soften our own hearts to love them in some fashion. How does this help someone else who feels left out? Leave that in God's hands. The dynamism of the Spirit does something because softer hearts are inclined to love. God initiates all; so if there is one person, or group, that you have a problem with, try to let it go with love. Where we might see someone with dislike or suspicion, God sees only love. Together, let us pray to surrender to that love; we may be surprised with the results!

Secondly, let another person love you. We all know people that we keep at arm's length, or even push away. We may feel too busy, not sure of their intentions. Maybe it is someone you keep at less than arms' length, but whom you have not really "let in" to your heart. Ask God for help, and see what happens by letting them love you first. Remember that Jesus' command is lived out fully when we love one another. Are you willing to try?

Third, let God love you. What? Yes, let God love you… *as you are*. We all put on a mask or persona for the world, even for those close to us. We don't want to disappoint those we love, especially God. It may seem easier to cover up and not reveal parts of ourselves to others, but God sees and knows all, even if we imagine or pray that God doesn't. Take the bandage off the wound of your heart, and let God's love in. See what healing happens. Like Peter, we are human, but we can love. Be patient and do what you can; God will do the rest.

These three kinds of attempts of loving and being loved are how Jesus transforms the world, and how we can lift others up in that love. We are all transformed through this love! At some time or another, we may all be stranded at the gate or worse yet, we may walk away from it. Can we be like ripples in a pond, with the love of God unleashed in the Risen Christ? Go change the world, and be changed by the power of God. Go forth in love!

ACTS 1:15-17, 20-26
1 JOHN 4:11-16
JOHN 17:11-19

"So I sent them into the world."

It can be tempting to ask for the cup we are given to be taken away, to leave the daily cross behind, to flee the world (*fuga mundi*), as the desert monks and nuns sought to do.

It can be comforting to imagine oneself so committed to the Christian life and to following God's will, that participating in society and associating with others is something to be despised.

It can be simpler to set off alone, apart from distractions and pressures, distant from the needs and wants and demands of others.

But Jesus makes it clear in today's Gospel that God wants none of this.

Like the Lord, we are called not to be *"of* the world," but to remain *"in* the world," as the common religious expression goes. This tension can be difficult to sustain, and far-too-often, well-meaning women and men of faith find themselves falling toward one extreme or another: either frightfully fleeing, or fully embracing *the world.*

Jesus came into the world, lived in the world, engaged with all people in the world, ate and drank, laughed and loved in the world. Yet, he was not part of what so many in his own time thought that being in the world meant. The world, as St. Paul writes at the beginning of his First Letter to the Corinthians, is shorthand for speaking about a logic and wisdom that is purely of human making. It is a way of viewing people and creation according to the standards established by those who hold and seek to maintain power and social status, and those who likewise desire to be the ones in power with social status to help sustain this vision.

Whereas, the *world* says some people are unlovable, some actions are unforgiveable, and some are more important and have greater value than others. Amen, amen, God in Christ Jesus says to us that all people must love as they have been loved, all must forgive as they have been forgiven, and in the eyes of God everyone has an intrinsic and inalienable dignity and value. To be *of the world* is to embrace a creed of human logic and order; to be *in the world* is to profess faith in a God that turns those standards upside down.

Jesus's prayer to the Father in chapter seventeen of John's Gospel follows shortly after Jesus's instructions to his disciples in chapter fifteen in which we too are told that Jesus desires that we remain in his love just as he has remained in the Father's love. If we love as we have been loved, our joy will be complete. This prayer to the Father is something of a follow-up to what we have already been told, a reaffirmation that to follow in the footprints of Christ will necessarily be challenging, and is also a reassurance that God will protect us on that journey.

But this prayer to the Father also reveals something about what it means to live in the present time, the time of cosmic Advent, the time of *already* and *not-yet*.

There are many examples throughout Christian history of people who model for us the at-times difficult, yet important, living of this tension. Two of my favorite models of Christian discipleship, one medieval and one modern, illustrate two different, yet insightful, ways to follow Christ *in the world* while recognizing that we do not belong to the value system and logic *of the world*. These are Francis of Assisi and Thomas Merton.

After what is typically described as his "initial conversion," Francis of Assisi went off to live a quiet life of prayer and service. He never intended to found a religious community, nor did he have any sense of the grand experiment in Christian living that would come to bear his name. Instead, he thought that he had to withdraw and be alone with God—just as so many faced with the tension of living *in* the world without succumbing to being *of* the world similarly do. However, God had other plans for him. In short order, Francis came to discover that one could never be a Christian *alone* and *apart*, but only always in relationship with others. In time, Francis, and those who began to follow his way of living the Gospel, embraced a life of itinerant mendicancy or begging, deliberately seeking to live with and among the people of villages and cities, the rich and poor alike.

Unlike many of the women and men religious of his time who embraced the logic of *fuga mundi*, receding into the cloisters of monastic life, Francis and his followers took to the streets and marketplaces, meeting folks *in the world* and preaching to them—in word and deed—about how the Gospel calls us to shift our values so that we no longer simply live as those *of the world*. The call was one of adjusting expectations and values to reflect what God has modeled for us in Christ.

Another model of living this tension, albeit from the opposite side of the spectrum of religious life, is the twentieth-century monk and writer, Thomas Merton. At first glance it would appear that Merton embraced the *fuga mundi* attitude in living a monastic vocation, seemingly leaving the world to enter the cloister. However, this is not exactly how things played out. Merton recognized that he could not simply disengage with the broader world. Instead, through his books, his thousands of correspondences, and one-on-one meetings with visitors to the Abbey of Gethsemani, Merton remained actively engaged *in the world*, while being a prophetic voice that was clearly not *of the world*. Merton was an active participant on the timely subjects of peace and nonviolence, civil rights and social justice, church reform, and religious renewal. Long after his death, he continues to inspire many. He demonstrated that even the monastic life, which seems so much on the surface like an abandoning of the world, is really another form of living the Gospel in the world.

While not all women and men are called to live a life of professed religious vows like Francis and Merton, each of us stands in the place of Matthias in today's First Reading from the Acts of the Apostles. At that time it was a matter of replacing Judas, today it's a matter of continuing the apostolic tradition of discipleship. Our baptism calls us to each step forward and accept the call to be prophets in our own times and places. The way this plays out, the manner in which we can most directly show forth the compassionate face of God, is to "love one another." (1 John 4:11) In loving one another, we not only make God's presence known, but we, too, experience the love of God in us. For, as our Second Reading concludes: "God is love, and those who abide in love abide in God, and God abides in them."

ASCENSION OF THE LORD

MSGR. MICHAEL DOYLE

Acts 1:1-11
Eph. 4:1-13
Mark 16:15-20

"They went forth and preached everywhere."

I will begin by asking God's forgiveness for all of the inadequate homilies that I have given on the Feast of the Ascension within the past 53 years. Not one of them ever ascended beyond the level of mediocrity. To tell the truth, nor do I have a memory of ever hearing anything memorable on this subject from the pew. This topic is literally above my head, indeed above the clouds for most of us. So, my take on this attempt is: I will fail…nicely.

It is always a comfort to think that there is a connection, an intimacy of spirit, between the tongue of the homilist at the podium and the ear of the listener in the pew. Later in the Mass, the priest at the altar will proclaim four words in the imperative mood: "Lift up your hearts!" And the sharing congregation will loudly assert: "We have." What a delightful response, so pleasing to God! "We have lifted them (our own hearts) up to the Lord."

We all know that "Up" is generally a good word. Things are looking up. The daffodils are up. Not great with prices for the buyer, however. *Up* is the name of a charming movie with liftoff, travel, distance and magnificent music by Michael Giacchino. But, at an infinitely higher level, "up" is connected to the story of the Ascension.

In Acts 1:9, we read that the disciples gathered and Jesus said to them: "You will receive power when the Holy Spirit comes upon you and you will be my witnesses throughout Judea, Jerusalem, and Samaria, and to the ends of the Earth." When he said this (his last words to humanity on the level of the Earth), the passage says, "as they were looking on, he was lifted up and a cloud took him from their sight. While they were looking intently at the sky as he was going, suddenly two persons dressed in white garments stood beside them and said: 'This Jesus who has been taken up from you into Heaven will return in the same way.' After Jesus had told his disciples to stay in the City, they returned to Jerusalem from the Mount, called Olivet, which is near Jerusalem, a Sabbath day's journey" (two-thirds of a mile).

Mark and Luke, too, ended their Gospels with the Ascension on a hopeful note. Mark: "The Lord Jesus, after he spoke to them (his disciples) was taken up into Heaven and took his seat at the right hand of God. But they went forth and preached everywhere." But not before the Spirit came upon them. Luke says: "He was taken up to Heaven," but adds that afterwards, "they returned to Jerusalem with great joy."

At the site of the Ascension, which is the Mount of Olives, about 2,700 feet at its highest, Jesus left his dear friends with loving instructions and with the most reassuring promise in the world: "I am sending the promise of my Father." So, "stay in the city (Jerusalem) until you are clothed with power from on high." It was surely a happy ending, loaded with great hope and joy.

More than 30 years before, angels were at hand for the annunciation of his conception and more delightfully for the annunciation of his birth in Bethlehem. Isn't it amazing that only about six miles separate Bethlehem, the place where Jesus was born and first touched the Earth, and the Mount of Olives, the place where he stood on higher ground for his Ascension, his Glorious graduation into Heaven? The Ascension is literally out of this world. It is surely a summit scene in the history of Creation, and up there in the lineup of magnificent events in the Gospel story of Salvation. It is one of the seven peak levels of the Incarnation: Conception, Nativity, Baptism, Transfiguration, Death, Resurrection and Ascension The highest point one can attain, says Nikos Kazantzakis in *Zorba the Greek*, is not Knowledge, Virtue, Goodness, or Victory, but something even greater, even more heroic...*Sacred Awe*. Those two words form the best human response to the Ascension.

It is astonishing to think that in the vast space of the universe, the Son of God, at his Ascension, was standing with bare feet on a circle of planet Earth that was, interestingly enough, no more than two feet in diameter. We know today that the technologically visible universe (only a piece of it) is a region of twenty-eight billion light years in diameter. Light travels at a speed of one hundred and eighty thousand miles per second. That is far too fast for the human mind to ever catch up with it! But that human mind can go to the Gospel of St. John and read: *"In the beginning was the Word, and the Word was with God, and the Word was God. All things came to be through God and without God, nothing came to be...and the Word was made Flesh"* and walked on the dusty paths of the Earth (John 1).

In the extraordinary painting of the Ascension by Salvador Dali (1958), the powerful Resurrected body of Jesus is going from us like a diver, diving upwards into the vastness of vastness—or maybe the Divine launch, or the liftoff of all Creation in Christ. But the soil of the Earth is on the soles of his feet. They were not washed. Maybe he is taking the mark of the dusty paths he walked. He is taking us all. Amusing to me are these few lines, entitled "A Wee Bit of Dirt."

What am I doing!
I said to myself
As I dutifully dug
In the grooves of my boots
At the end of a good holiday
I wanted my soles to be clean.
No! Heavens Above!
Not of Ireland's clay!
That I picked on the way
As I walked on the land that I love.

The Ascension, like the Death and Resurrection of Christ is, with all that is associated with it, a profound and dynamic culmination of the Incarnation of God in the world, because as Jesus states: "It is better for you that I go. For if I do not go, the Advocate will not come to you. But if I go, I will send him to you." (John 16: 7) So the Ascension is an enormous reality. In the Rosary, we call it a mystery, a *mysterium*, transcendent truth, deeper than all the wells in the world. It is not some sacred seesaw at play: if I go up, you come down. No, it is the glorious flow of the infinite energy of the most Holy Trinity expressed in the awesome dynamism of the Incarnation. We bow our heads.

After three years of agonizing experience on this small planet, Jesus entered into a tussle with evil to the death. It was death on the cross. It was betrayal, desertion, humiliation, and devastating ingratitude. It was execution in front of his mother. But a bad Friday turned out to be Good Friday. He arose and ascended in his Earth-made body into the infinite peace of Heaven. "Into the place of peace," says John Henry Newman, "which is all in all. He is in the very abyss of peace ... (he is in) the ineffable tranquility of the Divine Essence. He has entered his rest. That is our home, here we are on pilgrimage and Christ calls us to his many mansions which he has prepared."

In the collect prayer, today we say: "Gladden us with holy joys, almighty God, and make us rejoice with devout thanksgiving! Amen."

PENTECOST VIGIL

ROB BELL

GEN. 11:1-9
ROM. 8:22-27
JOHN 7:37-39

"*That is why it was called Babel.*"

*T*oday we hear the story of the tower of Babel. It is one in which the people decide they're going to build a tower that reaches to Heaven, *"so that we may make a name for ourselves and not be scattered over the face of the whole Earth."*

But God comes and inspects what they're doing and decides that if they can do this, *"nothing they plan to do will be impossible for them."*

And so God decides, *"Come, let us go down and confuse their language so they will not understand each other."*

End of story.

Now, I'm assuming by now that you approach a story like this looking for details, hints, anything to help you better understand what was going on at this time in history so that you can answer those compelling questions that you'd ask about anything in the Bible. Namely, why would people find this story important and worth passing on?

And here lies the answer:

First, who built Babel? If we go back one chapter, we read that:

"Cush was the father of Nimrod, who became a mighty warrior on the Earth. He was a mighty hunter before the LORD...The first centers of kingdom were Babylon (also known as Babel), Uruk, Akkad..."

What else do we know about Nimrod? The name Nimrod comes from the Hebrew root word *rebel*. And why does this matter?

Well, by the time you get to the story about the tower of Babel, what we know is that it's being built by a very, very violent and powerful warrior who is also building lots of other cities, and that his name is connected with the idea of rebelling. This is called *empire building*. It's what happens when someone, or a group of people, use military might and economic dominance to crush anything-and-anyone in the way of their plans.

Are there any other details we may have missed in our earlier readings of this story?

Yes. What was it exactly that they said to each other about how they were building the tower? They said to each other, *"Come, let's make bricks and bake them thoroughly."* They used brick instead of stone, and tar for mortar.

These details are huge. They used brick instead of stone. Have you tried to build something tall out of stone? It's next to impossible. Why? Because stones are of all different shapes and sizes, and they're hard to stack on top of each other. It's a total hassle.

But this is a story about bricks. Someone invented the brick. You can make bricks the same size and shape; you can make bricks to exact specifications for whatever it is you are trying to build, such as a tower.

If you'd been building things with stone for, like, forever, and then you started using bricks, what thoughts would you immediately have?

Perhaps your thoughts would be along the lines of how amazing the bricks are by allowing us to make all kinds of buildings possible that were not possible before. So, just how big could we make something with these new bricks?

But in the story it isn't just bricks that they're building with; they're also using tar for mortar. Mortar is like cement, which helps the bricks stick together.

What's another name for these details about the brick and mortar? Technology! This is a story about, among other things, technology. Someone invented something new: brick and mortar—which allowed people to make and do things they hadn't been able to do before.

What does all of this have to do with Nimrod? This is a story about what happens when a powerful warrior who's building an empire gets his hands on new technology and then begins to use it to set himself up as a god while crushing everyone and everything in his path.

And what does that tell us about the world in which the author of this story was living? This was a new phenomenon. People were spreading and scattering and settling in new places, and some were gaining more and more power and influence which affected everybody else. (Whenever you hear someone say that corporations and banks on Wall Street have gotten too powerful, then you are hearing echoes of the same sentiment, thousands of years later!) This story reflects a growing awareness and concern that there is a higher good for humanity than the strong dominating the weak, the powerful crushing the powerless, or the proud raising themselves up to godlike status.

Imagine building little walls out of stone your entire life and then making a trip to Babel and seeing people beginning to work on a tower made of bricks. It may have been awe-inspiring, but we can also assume that it would have been *terrifying*. If somebody can do *that*, what else can they do? Or to put more of an edge on it *what couldn't they do?* Imagine if other countries had nuclear bombs, but your country didn't. And imagine what it would be like to not have nuclear bombs, but to know that one of those countries that did have nuclear bombs had actually used their nuclear bombs in recent history, dropping those bombs on actual cities that people lived in. It is terrifying.

What does this story tell us about what it means to be human? We have tremendous power and ability as humans. We can invent things, build things, dream things up, and then make them. It's extraordinary, and it's to be celebrated and enjoyed! Just think of HD Flatscreen, Chipotle, Almond Surfboards, anything made by Apple, Clark's Desert Boots, Rickenbacker guitars... I could go on, and so could you. We also have the tremendous capacity to use our energies, minds, power and abilities to further our own purposes and greed and empire building at the expense of those around us, making the world less and less a peaceful home where everyone is thriving.

So, perhaps the real power of the story is the haunting warning that it brings when we make it all about ourselves, our accumulations, our egos, our power, or our desire to rule. When we become too full of ourselves, too obsessed with our own importance, too fixated on elevating ourselves to the top of the tower that we're building (and we all know that towers come in all shapes and sizes), God has endless, clever, and unexpected ways of scrambling our efforts, thwarting our plans, and sometimes even *confusing our language so we...babel*.

ORDINARY TIME

---

1 Sam 3:3-10, 19 1 Cor. 6:13-15, 17-20 John 1:35-42	*"Speak, for your servant is listening."*

*G*od's call of Samuel. It is a call not unlike other calls in the Bible: the call of Moses, the call of Abraham, the call of Elijah, the call of Isaiah, and the call of Jeremiah. This is a call story and you will hear plenty of that "here am I" language. Samuel was the son of Hannah and Elkanah. You will remember how Hannah, distraught in her barrenness, presented herself in the temple to pray. Hannah prayed and wept, and wept and prayed, so much so that the old codger priest Eli accused her of being drunk. But the Lord remembered Hannah. She gave birth to Samuel. As the Bible tells it, she lent him back to the Lord, for as long he lived.

In contrast, Eli's household was not quite exuding such piety and devotion. Here's the quote from I Samuel 2:12: *"Now the sons of Eli were scoundrels; they had no regard for the Lord..."* Who knew it was such a Biblical word, "scoundrel?" Eli was very old and he heard what his sons were doing. Eli had also found out along the way that the Lord wasn't very pleased with the state of things. There wasn't much secret to the matter of Eli's house and the Lord's discontent. Eli was living and serving in that very broken, crumbling house.

Samuel was serving God under the tutelage of Eli, as a result of having been lent back to the Lord by his parents. His residency program is summed up in v.19: *As Samuel grew up, the Lord was with him, and let none of his words fall to the ground.* None of his words fell to the ground. Now, whose words would we be talking about? None of his words fell to the ground. The Lord was with Samuel so that none of the Lord's words ever fell to ground? Or the Lord was with Samuel and the Lord made sure that none of Samuel's words ever hit the ground? *As Samuel grew up, the Lord was with him, and let none of his words fall to the ground.* Whose words would they be? There's a bit of pronoun ambiguity here. Granted, I may be the only one intrigued by pronoun ambiguity. The translators and commentators certainly don't waffle much. It's the Lord making sure that the Lord's words don't fall. The clarity is not a whole lot better in the Hebrew. There's this blur in the text; the Lord's word, Samuel's word.

It is both the challenge and the wonder of the prophetic tradition; the gift and mystery of the Gospel proclaimed. It's the Word of God experienced in the blur of our hearing and speaking, and the Word of the Lord in what the Apostle Paul would call "the foolishness of our preaching." Yet, the Word of God is so distinctly 'other' when it comes to this or that human voice. The Word of God is never equated one to one with human words. You don't just point to this preacher or that prophet. It depends, too, on that inward illumination of the Holy Spirit amid the blur of our hearing and speaking the Word; the Lord's Word; Samuel's Word; our hearing of the Word. The pronoun ambiguity is a bit theological.

Here in one chapter, we've gone from *the Word of the Lord was rare in those days; visions were not widespread.* We've gone from the Word silenced to the Lord's Word made so fresh in and through Samuel, that the words never fall to the ground. The Lord did not let any of Samuel's words fall to the ground and Samuel did not let any of the Lord's words fall to the ground. Whose words would that be? (Samuel? The Lord?) The answer, of course, is yes.

The one doing the catching? Catching those words? I remember serving as an acolyte when I was young in my Presbyterian Church in Pittsburgh. Acolytes would light the candles every Sunday. While I was worried about candles, my Catholic friends were learning the ropes of being an altar boy. I remember them telling me about the job of making sure that the priest wouldn't drop any of the Hosts because the Body of Christ there in the bread should not hit the ground. In trying to understand Samuel and the Word among many words, there's a sacramental image at work in catching those words. Hearers of the Word keep it from falling to the ground.

Tradition would affirm that in keeping those words from the ground, God is in fact, being faithful to the promise. As the prophecy is fulfilled and as the history of God's people unfolds, the words never fall to the ground. Ultimately, the message of the prophet, the leading of the Old Testament judge, or the sermon from the preacher are all completely and utterly dependent upon the One who is steadfast, whose Word abides forever, the One who is the same today, yesterday, and tomorrow. Yahweh is the Divine Word-catcher right then and there in Samuel's life and ministry. The house of Eli falls. Eli's sons perish. Israel is defeated in battle. The Philistines capture the Ark. *The Lord was with him, and let none of his words fall to the ground.* The Lord did what the Lord said.

It's an affirmation of the very providence of God. On some days, frankly, such an affirmation is no small thing. There is a belief down deep that God is, in fact, still at work, still faithful to the promise, still steadfast and full of mercy, and that our lives and our world are still completely cradled in the care of God. As the Psalmist proclaims "you hem me in, behind and before, you lay your hand upon me." Some days, that affirmation goes a long way toward comfort, hope and the future. God won't let God's word fall empty to the ground!

But catching words, it's more than that. It requires sitting back and simply allowing God to all the catching, and then sitting back and offering commentary on the state of God's Word-catching. It means watching current events and then offering opinions about God's activity in the world. It's safer, I guess, to sit back and point out one's perceptions about God, history, and life while others, rather than bearing the Gospel into the world with all of the bumps and bruises of life, go about some of their own catching of words, as it were.

Amidst that blur in our understanding, that mix of our hearing and speaking of the Word of the Lord, and amidst the pronoun ambiguity of an Old Testament narrative, there's a place for you and me. Somewhere in that sacramental image of scurrying around and making sure that no Word falls, somewhere in the scrambling of a faith-life, in the dance of discipleship, the grace-filled moments of discipleship, in the selfless, sacrificial call to servanthood that only comes in response to the Word, somewhere in our experience of the Word of the Lord—we ought to be making sure God's word doesn't just fall to the ground.

I remember a trip to the National Civil Rights Museum in Memphis, which is attached to the Lorraine Motel where Dr. King was shot. I was a part of a small group of Presbyterians whom were receiving a private tour. Since the arrangements had been made, the museum's schedule had changed a bit. It seemed that early that afternoon Oprah Winfrey was coming to receive an award. Our guide was put in the position of having to rush us through. At one moment, we were standing in front of a mock-up of the podium in front of the Lincoln Memorial and we were listening to Dr. King's "I have A Dream" speech. The poor young woman had to usher us away, far from catching any of the words; she couldn't even let us listen. The message of justice, empowerment, equality, non-violence, and anti-poverty do not quite make it on a quick trip through a museum. My colleagues and I were longing to hear more of Dr. King's voice.

When we celebrate and remember Rev. Dr. King, part of the tragedy is the loss of his voice, and the loss of his words amidst God's Word. It's one thing to listen to that dream from the march on Washington, but it's another thing to try to wrap your mind around what Dr. King would have to say about war, torture, immigration, the death penalty, Muslim/Christian/Jewish relations, justice, empowerment, equality or non-violence, here and now!

Dr. King was a preacher. As for you and I, we believe in God's Living Word, a Kingdom Word, a Word of the Kingdom which shall come on Earth as it is in Heaven, God's Living Word, a testimony to God's future, the Lord's promise, a witness to the Word made Flesh, a Word that overflows with Gospel truth, and God's Living Word. It is that blur that comes between our speaking and our hearing, that work of the Spirit where one doesn't just stand before a display, but one participates with the proclamation of your life. There is that Living Word, which is God's Word and the Word of the Lord; you and I have to, by God's grace, keep it from falling to the ground. In order for that to happen, everyone is going to have to catch some words.

3ʳᵈ SUNDAY IN ORDINARY TIME

ROB BELL

JONAH 3:1-5,10
1 COR. 7:29-31
MARK 1:14-20

"The word of the Lord came to Jonah."

---

*T*he *Assyrians were mean, nasty,* brutish, violent, and oppressive. This made life miserable for the Israelites year after year after year. It's during this era in history that a story emerged about an Israelite named Jonah. And according to this particular story, Jonah's God tells him to take a message *to the great city of Nineveh.*

And Nineveh was in…Assyria.

Assyria? Our worst enemy? Those hated infidels who have made life for our people a living hell time and time again? You want me to go into the center of the beast and do something good for them? Seriously?

Jonah wants nothing of this, and so he heads to the nearest port, jumps on a ship, and sails in the opposite direction!

Of course he does. You'd get in a boat, too!

Often this story is told in such a way that Jonah's disobedience is the point of the first part, along the lines of '*See what happens when we don't do what God tells us to do?*' But how do you imagine the first audiences would have reacted to this story when Jonah won't go to Nineveh? They hated the Assyrians. Would they have focused on his disobedience, or would they have cheered him on because they could totally relate?

So he gets on the boat, a storm comes up and there's a discussion among the crew about the cause of the storm. They determine that he's the problem, and so they throw him overboard. Then he's swallowed by a big fish. He prays in the belly of the fish, and then after the fish spits him out he finally goes to Nineveh. The Ninevites are fantastically receptive to his message, and then the story ends with him so depressed that he wants to kill himself because of a *gourd*.

There's so much in the sheer strangeness of this story.

You would assume that a story told by Israelites about Assyrians would stick to fairly straightforward categories of good and bad, right and wrong, righteous and evil.

But the Israelite in this story, the one who supposedly follows God, actually runs in the opposite direction away from God. The word that's used is *flee*. Jonah *flees*. He then ends up on a boat full of "pagan/heathen" sailors who *pray*.

While they're praying for the storm to stop, Jonah doesn't pray at all. Instead, Jonah *sleeps*.

The pagan, heathen sailors ask all sorts of questions trying to figure out why this storm has come upon them, only to discover that Jonah is the problem, which is something that Jonah knew all along.

Then, when he finally does get to Nineveh, after he's resisted God again and again, these horrible, mean, nasty Assyrians turn out to be open to God's message. They are so open that the king orders, "...*Let man and beast be covered in sackcloth.*"

Sackcloth was what you wore when you were crying out to God, when you were acutely aware of your sins, and when you were asking for God's mercy. The king orders everybody to repent and wear sackcloth—including the animals!

We're familiar in the modern world with frameworks which portray things in dualistic terms: there are the good people, and then there are the bad people; there is the right thing to do, while there is also the wrong thing to do; there are the people who need saving, and then there are the people who do the saving.

But in this story, the categories are all scrambled. The supposedly righteous Israelite is defiant and lazy, while the supposedly evil and wicked heathens are receptive and open to God's message for them.

And then in the end, after Jonah has had a change of heart and he's seen this massive, miraculous change of heart in the Ninevites right before his eyes, he's so upset by it that he wants to die.

He says to God, "*I knew that you are a gracious and compassionate God, slow to anger and abounding in love, a God who relents from sending calamity.*"

And then he adds, "*Now LORD, take away my life, for it is better for me to die than to live.*"

What a bizarre story! This is a story in which none of the characters do what you'd expect them to do. Which raises the questions: So why did this story survive? Why did people find this story important, or worth telling and preserving? What does it tell us about how they understand who they are, or how they felt about God?

There are several possible answers.

First, this story is about a man; but it's also about a nation. Jonah doesn't want to go to Nineveh because the Assyrians had treated the Israelites so horribly. The story asks this question: *Can Jonah forgive the Assyrians?* But the real question is: *Can Israel forgive the Assyrians?*

Jonah is angry at the end; he is angry that God has been so kind to them.

But, of course, Jonah is angry.

When you haven't forgiven someone who has wronged you and then something good happens to them—when they are blessed or shown mercy, or experience favor—it can be infuriating. This leads us to a larger theme in the Bible: According to the story that's been unfolding up until Jonah gets on a boat, Israel had a calling from early in its history to be a light to the world, to show the world the redeeming love of God.

It's a calling that they haven't lived up to.

There's a question, then, that lurks in the story of Jonah.

Can you forgive your worst enemy and still be a channel through which God's redeeming love can flow to them?

It's a question for Jonah because it's also the question for Israel.

This is why the book of Jonah doesn't end with a conclusion or a judgment, or details about what Jonah does next.

The book ends with a question, a question which God has for Jonah: *Should I not be concerned about that great city?*

It's a question for the Jonah character in the story. But at a far more significant level, it's also a question that the author is asking the audience, an audience whom we can only assume would have had many, many personal reasons to answer "No."

For the people who first heard this story, it would have been intended to have a provocative, unsettling effect. What about the Assyrians? Well, the Assyrians were like a huge, gaping open wound for the Israelites. Bless the Assyrians?

This story is extremely subversive because it insists that your enemy may be more open to God's redeeming love than you are.

That's why the book ends not with a conclusion, but instead, with a question. It is a question that God has for Jonah, and also a question which God has for the Israelites:

Should I not have concern for the great city of Nineveh?

This story demands what is called *non-dual awareness.* Many people see the world in dualistic terms, or terms in which there are the good people and the bad people, the sinners and the saints, or us and them—a world in which people stay true to the labels and categories in which we've placed them.

But this story wants none of that. It blasts our biases and labels to pieces with the declaration that God is on everyone's side, extending grace and compassion to everyone—especially those we have most strongly decided are not on God's side.

Religious people have been very good over the years at seeing themselves as US, while the people that aren't a part of their group are viewed as THEM. But in this story, the dude who sees himself as *us* is furious because of how chummy *God* and *them* have become. He's so furious that he'd rather die than live with the tension.

This is really a story that has the capacity and potential to confront and disrupt us with God's love—the kind of love that can actually transform us into more mature and courageous people.

The kind of people who even love their enemies.

4TH SUNDAY IN ORDINARY TIME

FR. DANIEL P. HORAN, OFM

DEUT. 18:15-20

1 COR. 7:32-35

MARK 1:21-28

"I should like you to be free of anxieties."

They left everything behind; that's how powerful his words were.

In the section immediately before this passage that we hear in today's Gospel, Jesus calls the first disciples to follow him. They were simple fishermen, whose lives were probably rather plain and routine. These first followers would not have been the most likely to drop everything and follow this unknown wandering teacher at his invitation. Yet they did. The power of Jesus's words comes through in today's reading.

Mark's account of the beginning of Jesus's ministry consistently returns to the power of Jesus's words. These words have the power to make people walk away from their whole worlds to follow him; they have the power to cast out demons, and they have the power to heal and forgive.

One of the interesting things about the power of words (or lack thereof) is the trust that is required for them to bear legitimacy. Put another way, we must *believe* in what is said in order for the words to have true power. If someone comes to you and tells you something that you don't believe or find ridiculous, what power do those words have over you? However, when one believes the words which are being communicated, things can change and we can change.

In today's First Reading from the Book of Deuteronomy, we hear God proclaiming to the people that, "I will raise up for them a prophet like [Moses] from among their people; I will put my words in the mouth of the prophet, who shall speak to them everything that I command." While we can rightly assume that the words of God's prophet are true by virtue of their source in God, not everybody will *believe*. This is why God then adds: "Anyone who does not heed the words that the prophet shall speak in my name, I myself will hold accountable." It can be easy to be blown away by the impressive actions or deeds of Jesus casting out demons or healing. This is, of course, what gets the people in Capernaum talking about this carpenter's son from Nazareth. But what is more difficult is to follow God's instruction to the people in our First Reading, to heed the words of the prophet, which requires our participation as well as our openness to the Spirit, our trust, and our belief.

Passivity has little place in the life of discipleship. Too often we want to be shown and have everything handed to us like those who encountered Jesus in his own time. I am reminded of another passage in Scripture where belief in the words of Jesus was lacking, but the desire for more direct evidence was strong:

> *Then some of the scribes and Pharisees said to him, "Teacher, we wish to see a sign from you." But he answered them, "An evil and adulterous generation asks for a sign, but no sign will be given to it except the sign of the prophet Jonah. For just as Jonah was three days and three nights in the belly of the sea monster, so for three days and three nights the Son of Man will be in the heart of the Earth. The people of Nineveh will rise up at the judgment with this generation and condemn it, because they repented at the proclamation of Jonah, and see, something greater than Jonah is here!"*

> (MATTHEW 12:38-41)

This is a perennial theme in the Gospels: Jesus announces the Reign of God and proclaims the Good News, yet few believe; few make the effort, and few allow themselves to be open to the work of the Spirit in their lives. Jesus's foreshadowing of his death and resurrection implicates all of us who come afterward. His point draws on the irony of Jonah the prophet, who himself did not heed the words of God but fled instead. The Ninevites, in whom Jonah had no faith, were immediately converted to penance by their openness to the words of God. They are the ones who, like the Good Samaritan or the prodigal Father, counter-intuitively reveal to the would-be follower of Christ what it means to embrace the teachings of Jesus.

Where do we fall in this cast of Biblical characters? Are we only amazed and open to Jesus when things are done for us, easily and without our faith and belief? Are we like the Pharisees and those who demand of Jesus some tangible signs to suit one's curiosity or assuage one's doubts? Or are we like the first disciples who drop everything at the words of God, as did the Ninevites who are likewise moved to conversion?

My guess is that, if you are like me, we are far-too-often on the side of the Pharisees and others in the crowds hanging around Jesus. We are interested, intrigued even, but we still aren't ready to commit. We want yet another sign, another promise, another guarantee, another recommendation, some other assurance that this guy is for real. Why is this the case? I think that St. Paul hits the nail on the head with the passage from 1 Corinthians in our Second Reading today. We are simply too anxious about all the wrong things.

There is a way to read Paul's words as a critique of married life, but that's not really the case here. Instead, Paul is concerned with exhorting new and would-be Christians to reorganize their priorities and see the world for what it really is. How much energy and effort are wasted worrying about the wrong things in life? Marriage is used as but one illustration of how even good things can be taken as occasions for distraction and misplaced energy. Not all married women and men are "anxious about the affairs of the world," or experience that "their interests are divided." But many do, and many can find all sorts of reasons to be distracted by the wrong things. Just as this may be the case for married couples, it is also the case with those in consecrated religious life. Those who are vowed religious can easily become distracted by the internal community politics, by who is more important, by who is living more authentically, by all sorts of things that create in us a sense of anxiety about unimportant matters. When this happens, whether to spouses or religious or anyone else, we no longer heed the word of God because we're too busy about other things.

Today's readings offer us the opportunity to reflect on how we do or do not respond to the words of God in Jesus Christ, or the prophets that came before him. Are we simply curious bystanders, or do we embrace our baptismal vocations as disciples of the Lord? Are we with the Pharisees and onlookers, or are we like those first disciples and Ninevites? Are we ready to believe, to heed the words of God, and to live as women and men of the Good News in our world, or are we anxious about too many other things?

5TH SUNDAY IN ORDINARY TIME

MSGR. WALTER NOLAN

JOB 7:1-4, 6-7
1 COR. 9:16-19, 22-23
MARK 1:29-39

"He drove out many demons."

There's an ad on television that ends up saying, "Whatever happened to the middle man?" Well, I don't know what happened to the middle man any more than I guess you do. But I do know what happened to the "They" in the Gospel. Simon's mother-in-law lay in bed and "They" told him about her. At sunset, "They" brought to him all that were sick or possessed with demons. The "They" became "us", which is you and I. It is you and I who are invited to be cured and healed. It is you and I, "Us", who invite others to come, and to be cured and healed. After Mass today we'll bless those who wish to be blessed with the Blessing of St. Blaise. We say at that blessing: "Through the intercession of Saint Blaise, Bishop and Martyr, may you be cured of every ailment of the throat and all other ailments." I think I would be bold enough to say to you that I would almost want to change the words 'may you be cured' to 'may you be healed'—that you may be *healed* of any ailment. I think that the cure is very important, but I happen to believe that healing is more important. What is important is not only the cure, but that inner healing, that inner transformation which makes us true followers of Jesus.

In order to understand, we must look back to the beginning of Mark's Gospel. If you are a fan of football, then you know that it is the quarterback who calls the signals. He will call out numbers or colors, or tap his helmet, or move his leg a certain way, and it all means something. The quarterback for Mark's Gospel is Mark himself. At the very beginning he gives us the signals—he clearly calls them out. One! Ten! Eleven! Or, as we read more simply—Chapter one, verses ten and eleven. Right at the beginning of his Gospel, he tells us of the Baptism of Jesus. At the Baptism of Jesus Mark says that Jesus had come up out of the water and he saw the Heavens opened and the Spirit descend upon him like a dove; then a voice from the Heavens said, "This is my beloved Son with whom I am well pleased." Mark calls out the signals which tell us that healing is going to be taking place in the Gospel. He calls the signal that no longer is there a separation between Heaven and Earth, but rather, God wants to be part of our human needs. He is telling us that there is a new creation and because the voice from the sky said, "This is my Son," he's telling us that this new creation is the Son of God and that his Son will bring Salvation, which in Greek really means 'healing' and 'justice.'

The cure is different from healing, and I think that healing is what is really important. Swami Ramdas, a spiritual writer, suffered a very debilitating stroke in 1997. He made the following distinction by stating, "while cures aim at returning our bodies to what they were in the past, healing uses what is present to move us more deeply into 'soul awareness' and in some cases physical improvement. Although I have not been cured of the physical effects of my stroke, I have certainly undergone profound healings of mind and heart." Healing can happen, even without the cure.

Michael Lerner, who works with people diagnosed with cancer, if faced with a diagnosis of cancer, said, "I would pay a great deal of attention to the inner healing process that I hope a cancer diagnosis would trigger in me. I would give careful thought to the meaning of my life, what I had to let go and what I wanted to keep."

Jesus cures. His cures are the sign of the Kingdom of God. His cures are the invitation for us to go deeper. His cures invite us to healing. We interpret these signs as God's loving response to our own human needs. But the interpretation is meant for healing, to change our minds, and to initiate new ways of being with one another. I guess the proper response to healing is repentance, to change our mind, and to change our behavior. To remain dazzled by the miracle is not the point at all, yet sometimes even in the New Testament they were dazzled by the miracles. In today's Gospel, the cure and the healing took effect in the mother-in-law of Simon. Not only was she cured of the fever, but then she got up and did God's will, which led to service. The touch of Jesus became the transfusion—his life flowing into her life. When we receive Eucharist, it is a transfusion of Christ's life flowing into our life. Not so much for the cure, but to bring about the healing. God's service to Simon's mother-in-law became her service to others. The cure can provide physical relief, but the healing connects us to the deepest center of ourselves. It is through this center that we touch God, and we touch our neighbors.

Healing may or may not result in a cure, but what is important is that healing comes from the cure. Do you recall the story of the ten lepers? They all were cured. But only one came back to give thanks, and perhaps only one, I think, was really healed. The others were off someplace jumping for joy. The one who came back saw the personal transformation in his life to the love of God. The one who came back would take Mark's words:

> The Lord our God is Lord alone. You shall love the Lord with all of your heart, your soul, your mind and your strength. You shall love your neighbor as you love yourself.

Right after the prediction of his Passion, Jesus told the crowd and his disciples, "Whoever wishes to come after me must deny himself and take up his cross, and follow me." Jesus wants us to be followers. He never asked us to be fans. A fan gets excited about the miracle. The fan wants the cure, but not the healing. I guess it's the fans of the world who cheer at the Super Bowl when their team wins. Do you notice how fans boo really easily when something goes wrong, or when the Hail Mary pass doesn't work? Jesus doesn't want this. The followers, you and I, will soon have our throats blessed today after Mass. But I hope when we have our throats blessed that we also realize that we're asking for the inner healing of God's love.

We followers share the prophecy of Ezekiel, a prophecy of healing. Listen to the words:

> *I will give you a new heart and place a new spirit within you. Taken from your bodies, the stony heart and given you natural hearts. I will put my spirit within you and make you live by my statutes, careful to observe my decrees. We shall live in the land I gave my fathers. You shall be my people and I will be your God.*

It is in living Ezekiel's prophecy that we are healed. God *is* Love. No one has anything to fear from a God who is Love. When we accept this gift, then we are truly healed.

6TH SUNDAY IN ORDINARY TIME

FR. WILLIAM J. BYRON, SJ

LEV. 13: 1-2, 44-46
1 COR. 10: 31-11, 1
MARK 1: 40-45

"I do will it, be made clean."

Today's Gospel story raises an interesting question—the question of the willingness of the Lord to respond to our needs. Somewhere deep inside our doubting selves there is a strange hesitation, a lurking suspicion concerning the willingness of the Lord to respond to our requests, to reach out and meet our needs. This is not self-doubt that I'm referring to; it is a doubt we entertain regarding the willingness of God to care for us. In effect, it is a doubt regarding God's love for us. Today's Gospel invites you to make an act of faith in God's love for you.

Put yourself in the place of the leper you meet in today's Gospel. He is obviously in need. He wants to be cured of his leprosy. He approaches Jesus, with a request, "kneeling down [he] begged him and said: 'If you wish you can make me clean.' Moved with pity, [Jesus] stretched out his hand, touched him, and said to him: I do will it, be made clean."

If you want to, you can cure me. Of course I want to. Be cured. There's a concise summary of this exchange, of this encounter. Repeat it in your mind's eye. See the response of Jesus. Hear the words. Note the immediacy of the response: Of course, I'm willing to cure you. I want to cure you. I've been waiting for you to ask. Why would you even hesitate?

Yes, there is a certain hesitation on the part of the person in need, but there is also a certain humility accompanied by the courage to take the initiative in approaching Jesus. If you don't put yourself within his reach, he cannot reach out and touch you. If you don't speak out, he can't hear you.

When you look at your situation only from your side, all you can see is hesitation and doubt compounded, perhaps, by the temptation toward self-denigration and the unfortunate conviction of your own unworthiness as a result of your yielding to that temptation. But look at it from God's side and what do you see? You see in this Gospel story that Jesus was "moved with pity." Meditate for a moment on the divine pity. Realize that pity is preexistent to the request in this story; pity is a precondition on God's side as you approach him. God pities you before you even realize your need for pity. And your need for pity confers upon you a certain worthiness to receive the help you need from God.

O Lord, I am not worthy, we so often say. Of course, we are not worthy, but our unworthiness is no obstacle to the movement of divine pity in our direction. In a broad swoop of "of-course-I-will-it" pity, the Lord is ready to come to you in any need.

You may be saying to yourself now—and I am fully aware of it at this moment—that God does not always respond visibly, immediately, and forcefully to your call for help. You pray and nothing happens. You ask and hear nothing in reply. Your leprosy gets worse; your need goes unattended. Does that mean God's not there, there is no God? No. Does it mean that God is not listening, that God is inattentive to you and your needs? No. Well, what does it mean? It means that God has a plan for you and your salvation that will work out on God's own timetable. It means that God wants nothing but the best for you and the best is yet to come. It means that an act of faith is required of you—faith in God's existence, faith in

God's love for you, faith in the presence of the divine pity ready to be released in your regard according to the will of God.

There is a beautiful prayer in every Mass that the priest used to recite (silently, according to the rubrics) just before receiving Communion. The priest addresses Jesus, who is present there on the altar, and says in the old version before the reform of the Roman Missal: "Lord Jesus Christ, Son of the living God, who, by the will of the Father and the work of the Holy Spirit, through your death brought life to the world. . ." This prayer goes on to ask that through the reception of the body and blood of Christ the priest may be freed from his sins and from every evil, kept faithful to the teaching of Jesus, and never permitted to be separated from him.

I want you to savor those words "by the will of the Father and the work of the Holy Spirit." They point to both the "plan" (the will of the Father) and the "engine room" (the work of the Holy Spirit) for the delivery of the gift of your salvation. God's will is present in the world. The Holy Spirit is at work in the world. Your job is to connect, as best you can, your will with the will of the Father. Your challenge is to see with the eye of faith that the Spirit is indeed at work in your world and to pray that the "work of the Spirit" may be made manifest in you and in your corner of the world.

So this brings us back to where we began, to the assertion that I made at the beginning of this homily: Today's Gospel, I suggested, invites you to make an act of faith in God's love for you. Even though your leprosy may not yet be cured, even though your declared need may not yet be met, God's love for you is real and his Holy Spirit is at work in your world on your behalf, he is with you and present to you in ways you simply cannot see. All you can do is believe.

And, by the way, you might consider giving God a word of thanks today for gifts unseen and unnoticed. You might begin by thanking the Lord for responding so spontaneously and generously centuries ago when this poor leper stepped up and asked for help. It is never too late to say thanks. Thank the Lord who gave that help. Ask that same Lord to remember you and, by the will of the Father and the work of the Holy Spirit, to permit you, on God's own mysterious timetable, to participate in a generous share of the divine pity.

IsA. 43:18-19, 21-22, 24-25

2 CoR. 1:18-22

MARK 2:1-12

"Rise, pick up your mat, and go home."

As is common knowledge, over the years some folk have been known to have had brushes with the authorities on their way home from social occasions.

One man tells of his experience. "Last night," he says, "on New Year's Eve, I was out partying with some friends and had a few too many beers and some rather nice wine. Knowing full well that I may have been slightly over the limit, I did something I've never done before. I took a bus home. I arrived home safely and without incident—which was a real surprise, as I have never driven a bus before and am not sure where I got this one."

It's the old setup and twist gag—which is my introduction to this familiar gospel story of the paralyzed man let down through the rooftop. My contention is that there are surprising hidden twists and turns that we might miss in this story—but they can reveal a lot about ourselves and our spiritual journey. So let's take a look.

To begin with, visualize the scene. The storyteller, Mark, opens it with a large crowd of people in the house and spilling out into the street. Think Christmas Eve: the church was packed. We had to send people to the hall. People couldn't get into the church.

So it was in Mark's story: there were so many people that they were blocking access to Jesus. And right away this gospel detail evokes a twist, a telling metaphor, as we think of how at times the Church with its rigid rules and regulations, its obstinate spirit, its bureaucratic mindset, has blocked access to Jesus; how the bad example of some Christians, the proud withholding of forgiveness and compassion, the disdain and pride of so-called good people, the hypocrisy of the religious have all blocked access to a merciful and healing Lord. That crowd blocking Jesus from "outsiders," a hidden image in this gospel, uncomfortably mirrors our behavior.

Another twist: there is a taken-for-granted subtext to the gospel story, namely that people in Jesus' time firmly believed that illness and bad fortune were related to sin. This or that person was physically, socially, or mentally afflicted because they or their parents committed some sin, and the affliction was God's punishment. In other words, they deserved what they got, and so the people in that house had little sympathy and much disdain for the man lowered on the mat.

The gospel subversively reminds us that this attitude is still with us in the people, for example, who say that the homeless person asking for a handout deserves to be ostracized from our company because he has chosen to be lazy and live off the system. Some do this, but in these days of high unemployment and foreclosures, decent people are, for the first time in their lives, going to food shelters, and it's not so easy to make that judgment.

Some people say that the out of control alcoholic or drug addict deserves to be denied financial help or housing because it's his or her chosen way of life—in spite of what we know about the fierceness and power of alcohol and drugs and how hard it is to deal with them—and how fortuitous it is that AA, for example, has taken a different view. The gay man deserves to be abused because he has chosen a sinful lifestyle, and the righteous God is right to afflict him with AIDS for his immoral behavior. But then one thinks of the great tennis pro Arthur Ashe: a virtuous man, father, Christian, athlete, who was infected by the AIDS virus in a blood transfusion and died at the age of forty-one.

His bright and charming little daughter was six at the time. In a poignant letter to that little girl, a letter full of hope and the most tender love, Arthur Ashe assured her that he would be with her all the days of her life after his death. He encouraged her to cultivate a deep, personal relationship with God, suggesting that a good way to do this would be to continue in the practice of her mother's Catholic religion. What do you do with Arthur Ashe and innocent babies born with AIDS if God is bent on revenge?

Recently one blogger wrote that clearly God sent the horrible death from cancer to the late Christopher Hitchens because he was an atheist and deserved to die.

The gospel story upends all this and tells us that God is bigger than our judgments: Jesus did not disdain the so-called sinful paralyzed man, but quickly offered him healing both of spirit and body. Maybe the message is that pain is not a penalty but an opportunity.

Next, let's note the detail of Jesus' command: *stand up*, he ordered the man, and carry your mat home. The Stand Up, the preeminent Easter symbol, reminds us that we are constantly in the process of dying and rising. Life is a pilgrimage of ups and downs, and Jesus is there to lift us up. As for taking home the mat—what carried the man in, he carries out—this is possibly meant to be a reminder of the man's former life, like a scar that shows where he was healed, a reminder of the amazing grace that touched him. Or perhaps the keeping of the mat was meant to be a kind of "show and tell," an occasion, many times, to proclaim the good news of Jesus, to evangelize.

Finally, let's not forget the four determined friends: there would be no forgiveness, no cure, without them. That's what friends are for. The message here is loud and clear: we need each other. We depend on each other. We must reach out and, by deed and witness, bring people to Jesus.

So, this fabulous and vivid gospel story has lots of drama—including, I might add, the practical, as when, in a bible study group, in reference to the four friends breaking through the rooftop and sending debris all over the place, a man wanted to know who was going to pay for it all. He was an insurance man.

But there it is: blocking access to Jesus, playing God in our judgments, true friendship, evangelizing—it's all there in twelve verses: a colorful gospel with provocative twists.

Reprinted from Once Upon a Gospel: Inspiring Homilies and Insightful Reflections *by William J. Bausch,* ©2008. *Twenty-Third Publications. Used with permission. All rights reserved.*

Hos. 2:16, 17, 21-22
2 Cor. 3:1-6
Mark 2:18-22

"You yourselves are our letter, written on our hearts."

I picked up a novel that had been life-altering when I read it in college. I loved the heroine, who was ugly, tenacious and courageous. She had awakened something within me. At the time, I had been a young woman, becoming aware that so much of our culture measured a woman's worth by her niceness and looks (or lack thereof), and the protagonist enraptured me with her gritty looks and manner.

When I picked up a cheap copy of the same book recently, I struggled to get through it. It was not because I knew the plot. I hadn't remembered the story all that well. I simply grew critical of the language and wondered why the words didn't move me in the same way. The book hadn't changed, but I had. Even more precisely, I think the words had changed me so much that it just didn't have the same influence over me.

The experience reminded me of the power of words. Paper can be flat and lifeless. We can skim through a book with half-hearted attention, trying to stay awake, like a college student reading for a required class. We count down pages and hope that it will end quickly.

Or, we can let the words dance on the page, with rhythm and vitality. They sparkle with meaning and alter us, becoming a part of our lives and spirits. We amend the way that we think and live after reading them. We understand people differently. They transform the way we interact with our neighbors.

As we turn to Second Corinthians, it is good to pause and acknowledge the great chasm between when this letter was written, and now. People did not have the sort of access to paper, ink, and literacy that we do, so it is difficult to apprehend the meaning of this text in our world of hyper-publishing, when every thought can become broadcasted to thousands. Words have become so abundant that they have become cheap, proliferating from our fingertips with rapid speed as we peck at our smartphone keyboards. At one time people spoke thoughtlessly and now they can type without much thought, as well.

But some things stay the same. For instance, there is a clear, perceptible difference between the flat word and the living word. There is a distinction between the letters that sit on a page, and the ones that pull on our shirtsleeves and urge us to be better people. Words transform us and today's scripture passage points out a couple of the ways that they alter us—through recommendations, the law, and the Spirit.

At the heart of this passage is the subject of letters of recommendation, a concept we certainly understand. When a credible person writes that another person or group can be trusted, a sort of power is transferred. We see this happening with resumé recommendations, academic degrees, book endorsements, or product ratings. To get a recommendation from the right person can be life-altering. Perhaps the Christians in Corinth felt they needed the determination of reliability and trustworthiness.

Then there is the transformative power of the law. Jewish people huddled into synagogues so that they could unfurl the scrolls and read the Scriptures which had been passed down from generation to generation, leaning in as the syllables were uttered or sung. They read the law that connected to every aspect of a person's life, from verdicts in murder cases to how to cook dinner.

Though recommendations and laws had life-altering power, the author points at a much greater power that letters can wield. This power is the word of the Spirit, when words became embodied in the fleshy hearts of Christians.

A transition is happening here in Corinth. We can perceive the way that they are interacting with the Law a bit differently; the author is letting us know that there is a distinction between a flat set of rules and regulations and a loving people who work out their Salvation with a sweaty brow. The Word of God has taken on flesh in this Christian community in Corinth, and through them, we understand that there is a difference between writing down laws and living love.

That is what the Gospel is all about. In some real way, it is not about the words that sit on a page. It is not about recommendations or laws, but it is about that embodied, messy, fleshy living that becomes good news. It is when we feed the hungry, shelter the homeless, visit the sick, and care for the orphans that we embody new promises and new relationships. We are bearers of the law of love.

Let us go out with this hope: that we can be the Spirit-animated Word of Christ, that our actions might give life to all those whom we meet. To the glory of God our Creator, God our Liberator, and God our Sustainer.

Amen.

MICHELLE FRANCL-DONNAY

DEUT. 5:12-15
2 COR. 4:6-11
MARK 2:23-3:6

"Stretch out your hand."

*I*t is said that in the fourth century, Simeon the Stylite, spent more than thirty years living on top of a fifty-foot high pillar on the edge of the Syrian Desert, confined to a platform that was three feet on each side. He was driven up the column, not so much by his desire to get closer to God, though that surely played a part, but to get further from the crowds who clamored for his advice and disturbed his prayers. Yet, they still came, from Constantinople and Antioch, emperors, archbishops and farmers alike, clambered up a ladder to have a word with the saintly Simeon, until finally his brother monks built a double wall around the pillar to keep the curious at bay.

There are weeks where my calendar makes a pillar in the desert, guarded by high rock walls and a solid community. It seems like a great idea. I imagine the items on my to-do list jumping up and down, yelling for my attention, surrounding me on all sides, scrambling to find a ladder to climb up to the top of the list. It's tempting to try to quiet the demand-ing crowd by plunging into the list first thing, crossing off this task, or answering that request. But the tasks keep coming up the ladder.

A few years ago I started writing "pray" at the top of my daily to-do list, to be sure I didn't fail to start my day with God, no matter how chaotic life was. I confess I also put it there so I could cross it off, so I could feel productive, even in prayer.   -

God? Great! Help? Thanks. Bye. Amen.

And I check off God for the morning.

The Catechism of the Catholic Church reminds us that "prayer ought to animate us at every moment…we cannot pray 'at all times' if we do not pray at specific times." [2697] My habit of scheduling prayer on my calendar is not a bad thing; it's a jumping off point, not just for my day, but for the formation of my prayer life. Writing about living with a religious rule, with its ordered times of prayer, Richard Rohr, OFM observed that it kept "my feet to the fire long enough for the Gospel to become fire, and my feet to become feet."

My daily reminder to pray holds my feet to the fire, too, until I can pick up the day's work and walk. Until I can, as fourth century Doctor of the Church Gregory Nazianzus advised, remember Christ more often than I draw breath. Of late, I've started to wonder if I should stop crossing it off and simply let it stand at the head of my list, to be more aware of God's presence as God "guides the beginning of my work, directs its progress, and brings it to successful completion" as Thomas Aquinas's prayer before study so beautifully captures.

Prayer is not inherently productive, however. "Being useless and silent in the presence of our God belongs to the core of all prayer," wrote Henri Nouwen. Can we waste time with God, even in the face of urgent tasks? Can we practice simply letting God look at us? Saying nothing. Doing nothing.

The Sabbath holds our feet to the fire in this regard. Today's first reading from Deuteronomy exhorts us firmly to be unproductive at least one day out of the seven. Do no work. Let no one work in your stead, not even your animals. Let the world lay fallow for a day and see what happens when you are useless and silent in the presence of God.

Mark's Gospel offers us one image for what might happen when we give ourselves over to Sabbath time. The Pharisees are fussing about the precise limits of the rules, while Jesus is letting the disciples flout the rules—fresh ears of wheat are not edible, they were not picking up a snack on the way—and all the while a man with a withered hand sits in the synagogue. Silent and useless.

"Stretch out your hand," commands Jesus. And the hand is whole again, perfect. I gaze upon you, says God, and you are healed. Did the man notice the very moment he was once again made whole, when the bones knit and his muscles responded with strength? How not? But did the person next to him?

Sunday is not the day we flip the week's calendar over, not merely a day we are obliged to go to Mass to make a return to the Lord for what we have been given. It is not about the rules. The Sabbath is for noticing—for noticing that God is present, for noticing that we have been healed, for noticing that our neighbor has been healed.

The Sabbath is a reminder to sit unproductively, and be alert to what happens when Light shines forth from darkness and God beholds us. Stretch out your hands, and see that what has been crushed has been made whole in Christ's dying and Rising.

10TH SUNDAY IN ORDINARY TIME

REV. PENNY A. NASH

GEN. 3:9-15
2 COR. 4:13-5:1
MARK 3:20-35

> *"Whoever does God's will is my brother and sister and mother."*

*T*his is one of the stranger stories in the Gospel of Mark (and that is saying something!). Jesus is apparently healing people right and left and left and right, so that the word begins to get out not only that an untold number of people are being healed (hallelujah!), but that the healer, this guy named Jesus who came from Nazareth of all places, is acting very strangely (uh-oh!). There are so many people gathered, and there is so much to be done, that there isn't even time to stop and eat. There is so much healing that needs to be done, and apparently Jesus is so focused on healing everyone he comes near, that he is perceived as being in a frenzy. He is not just working at a frenzied pace; he himself is in a frenzy.

This frenzied behavior disturbs the people. They begin to say that Jesus is not in his right mind. Then the scribes come along and announce that Jesus must be possessed by the Evil One to be acting this way. What else could it be?

And so the word gets out to his family, and, alarmed, they decide they had better come get Jesus and take him home.

Everyone believes Jesus is crazy.

I find it interesting that what the people, the scribes, and even Jesus's family focus on is his behavior and not the fruits of his work. People are healed, right and left and left and right! But the response by everyone else (presumably, those who were healed don't have a problem with this) narrows down to this: Jesus is in a frenzy. There's something weird about him. There's something wrong with him. He's out of his mind. He is doing the work of the devil. Somebody needs to come and get him.

Nobody asks this question: "Who is going to help these people? Jesus has been working overtime so that he might bring them back to wholeness."

Nope. All these people are brought to wholeness, but the focus is on the sanity of the healer. Who in their right mind would do what Jesus does, or do it with so much passion and compassion? Who would be so selfless and giving? Who would care so much for those whom others don't have time for? Who would nearly go berserk in order to make others whole?

And so he must be crazy. And his family hears about it and comes to take him away.

Yet, the question remains: "Who is going to help the people Jesus came to help?" Nobody in this story seems concerned with that at all.

The irony is, of course, that while the people and the scribes and Jesus's own family are trying to ferret out a motivation for Jesus's behavior, they end up with "mental illness" for an answer instead of "God's overwhelming compassion and desire for healing, wholeness, and reconciliation among God's people."

Now, why is it that God is so passionate about those whom others ignore, either by choice or because they simply don't know how to respond? Is it BECAUSE they are unaware that God cares so much? Is it because of the circumstances of those who are ignored (poverty, addiction, lack of status, and yes, mental illness) that God wants so desperately to make them whole?

Well, like mental illness, God is mystery. On my best days, I am content to believe that God made us, and God loves us, and God wants us to be whole. If that's crazy, then fine by me.

I don't want to make light of mental illness. Nor do I want to make light of the real anxiety that many of us have when trying to comprehend such broad topics as mental illness, poverty or chronic health issues. We often ignore these issues because we don't believe we are equipped to even cope with, much less actually help, people who are in dire straits. Dealing with these things on a daily basis for even a little while will be exhausting. We don't mean to be callous, we just feel inadequate.

And so, God created community. We don't have to solve these huge problems alone. We don't have to take care of everyone ourselves. We do these things together as family or friends or neighbors or members of society. God wants healing and wholeness in a big way and we want to want what God wants.

But first, we have to be able to see those whom others ignore; we have to see them and remember that they are God's beloved. We have to believe that God wants them to be whole, and that we can contribute to their well-being as a community of God's beloved; then we step out in faith and in love.

We have to ask this question every day: who will care for those in such dire straits, those for whom wholeness seems so elusive? Jesus was crazy about them. Perhaps we should be, too.

11TH SUNDAY IN ORDINARY TIME

FR. RICHARD ROHR, OFM

EZEK. 17:22-24
2 COR. 5:6-10
MARK 4:26-34

"The Kingdom of God is like a mustard seed."

Recently, while in Romania, I was blessed to give a retreat to jail chaplains from all over Europe. As always, when I give these kinds of conferences or retreats, those who attend teach me much more than I teach them. I shared with these chaplains my own experience of being a jail chaplain in Albuquerque, New Mexico, for 14 years. On this Father's Day I want to tell you one special thing that I told them.

I bought boxes and boxes and boxes of cards each year when Mother's Day approached, because everyone wanted to send a card to Madrecita. The first year, I thought I'd also be prepared for Father's Day, so I pre-ordered a whole case of Father's Day cards. But I couldn't give them away. No one wanted to send a card to their father. That is very often why they were in jail!

When I told this story to the Europeans, many just nodded their heads. Most could not think of an example of any jailed man or woman who had a good father. This very lack of fathering and lack of love from an older and wiser man had instilled within many young people anger toward the world, toward all authority, and toward all father-figures—because they didn't have a father at all, or more often a good father. We often fear what we don't have, and as a result we mistrust and reject without even knowing it. For example, if your first father abandoned you, you would expect every other man to do the same. And since the best defense is a good offense, you often pre-emptively force all men in authority to reject you. Jean Vanier, the holy founder of the L'Arche communities once told me personally that you can presume most people carry two wounds, one in regard to their sexuality and another in regard to their relationship to authority. I find that to be profoundly true in my experience.

It was even hard to get the inmates to trust any "Father" God because they were pretty sure he would reject them, too. Again and again I had to tell them that God was unconditional love, but they had not programming whereby to understand that. It drew a blank stare. I told them that God, just like the father in the story of the Prodigal Son, was always running toward them. They had no ears, no mind, no heart to understand this, to believe, or to comprehend it. Men, they assumed, were always brutal, absent, cold, alcoholic, abusive, distant—anything but love.

Brothers and sisters, how did we get to such a place? How did we get to such a place that the man of the species expects so little of himself, and gives so little of himself to the world? And largely fears and attacks the world? If "daddy" is dangerous, absent, or bad, it is an unsafe home and an unsafe universe. All I can do is either retreat (drugs, alcohol, etc.) or attack.

In today's Gospel we have a most extraordinary image of what Jesus expects his work to produce and achieve, and it's a rather surprising metaphor. This is presented in contrast to the first reading from Ezekiel, in which God says, "I will choose a branch from the top of the tree, and I will plant it on top of a mountain, and it will grow into a great tree." Jesus says just the opposite: "I'm going to pick a little tiny mustard seed, the smallest of all the seeds…. We will scatter the seed on the Earth, and we'll hardly notice that it's growing. It grows all of itself."

What an image of how change happens, how growth happens, and how love happens! You see, it's not in doing great, big, heroic things, but in doing little things with love and joy, little things like being a good daddy on an ordinary day when no one notices.

These European jail chaplains felt so insignificant in the Church. They weren't pastors of big parishes. They weren't noticed by the bishop. All they did, day after day, was go to the jail and sit in people's cells, and hear their stories. They tried to be the good father that these men and women never had. They didn't look or feel too glorious. But notice that Jesus's parables of the Kingdom are intentionally non-glorious. They're not big. They're not organizational or institutional images. Jesus doesn't talk about creating a huge building. He doesn't talk about running an institution from Rome. He just talks about little people doing little things that are hardly noticed. And they change the world. Little by little, they yield the harvest.

That's the story of most of our lives. Most of us in this Church are little people. We're not heroic or big. Our names are not in the papers. It's about little things done with love. At the end of time we will look back and see that these are the mustard seeds which changed the world. Maybe it doesn't look like 'Church work.' You're just contributing to your neighborhood. Maybe it doesn't look like 'holy things.' You're just smiling at the check-out girl at K-Mart. It all looks so ordinary, so natural. It doesn't look religious at all. It's just a little mustard seed—that quietly grows and spreads this love, this healing, this joy, this caring—that is the Risen Christ.

Brothers and sisters, this "mustard seen conspiracy" has little to do with formal or clerical ministry. Many of us who stand here in these fancy vestments doing formal ministry, but sometimes we don't do it with love or joy or caring. And I wonder if it bears much fruit? But it is the little things that you have the power to do every day in your ordinary, simple lives which changes the world. It doesn't look like Church at all, but Jesus is saying here that this is the real and deepest meaning of Church. I think that in the end, we're all going to be very surprised as to how church happens. Remember, Jesus first and most simple image of his presence in the world was nothing more than "two or three" (Matthew 18:20) gathered in his spirit—the spirit of the Son of a totally loving Father.

12TH SUNDAY IN ORDINARY TIME

MARGARET BLACKIE, PhD

JOB 38:1, 8-11
2 COR. 5:14-17
MARK 4:35-41

"And the wind ceased, and there was a great calm."

The second reading today calls us to transformation. "So whoever is in Christ is a new creation: the old things have passed away; behold, new things have come."

So what is this 'transformation?' We are called to live for Christ. But what does that mean? Living a life of faith is so much more than agreeing to a set of assertions about the nature of God. If it is to have meaning, then it must change us in a fundamental way. But what might that change be?

Anyone who is actively seeking God in some way is already taking a step in the right direction. There are a good many of us on the road, but few of us have gotten there. We may have begun to glimpse the possibility of the transformation which we are called toward, but far too few of us have fully-immersed ourselves into the invitation extended by the Risen Christ. Instead, we remain captive to our fears. The Gospel today gives us a vivid image of the power of fear. The raging storm, the boat taking on water-there is real, tangible, physical danger. And Jesus is asleep.

We all encounter such situations in our own lives from time to time: the diagnosis of a serious illness; being made redundant; the failure of a marriage; the collapse of a business; or perhaps even the accumulation of many small, but not trivial, stresses. The threat of drowning in our own fears, grief, and raw emotion can, at times, feel overwhelming. It can feel as though Jesus is asleep.

In the Gospel, the disciples are able to wake Jesus up. He calms the storm and then all is well. How often do we desire that we could just shake Jesus awake? If only he would take this from me; if only he would calm this storm, all would be well. My faith would be strong and I would never doubt again.

But notice what happens at the end of the passage. The disciples ask, "Who then is this whom even wind and sea obey?" You would think that after witnessing this—having had their lives in profound danger, and the danger being removed by the action of Jesus—that they would have a strong and unshakeable faith. But this is not the case. They have asked similar questions earlier in Mark's Gospel, and they repeat them again later on.

So what are we to do when storms threaten to tear apart the very fabric of our lives? All I can say with certainty is that Jesus is not asleep. He is paying attention, but the storms rarely get resolved quite so simply. I pray for the storm to pass. I pray for the grace to weather the storm.

Praying for the grace is a shorthand term which I use to describe a process that I have learned to use. It begins with acknowledging the presence of the storm. Then I find it helpful to focus on Jesus's question: *Why are you afraid?* I begin to mentally explore the situation. *What is the thing that is truly paralyzing me? What do I fear? What do I dread?* Then I ask for the grace to be released from that fear.

We are so used to living in a world which actively generates fear and we often forget that fear is profoundly problematic. Fear is probably the greatest barrier to our transformation. We cannot move forward in faith until we have learned how to sit with our fear, to recognize it, to name it, and pray for the grace to be released from fear.

We think that our faith will be cemented when we are rescued from our storms. The problem is that we forget our pain too quickly. In the long term our faith is best served by learning to navigate our difficulties in conversation with Jesus. Engaging with the tough questions—*why are you afraid?*

If we dare to start asking those questions, we begin to discover that true freedom is possible in this world. We begin to discover that true freedom is not a mythical place beyond the reach of the trials, tribulations and tragedies of our world. Rather, true freedom comes when we are able to navigate our way through these things without being capsized. It can take us to a place where we can suffer terrible losses, without totally losing ourselves or without losing companionship with God.

Every time that I have been paralyzed by life circumstances and have prayed for grace, I have found that the storm does indeed abate. Sometimes this happens because the exterior circumstances shift in an unexpected way, but more often than not, because something in me shifts.

Perhaps take some time to consider where you are in your life today? Is there a storm raging? Is the wind just a little stronger than you would like? Take a moment to sit next to Jesus and let him ask—what are you afraid of? What do you fear? Talk to him a little about that, and then ask for whatever grace it is that you most need.

13ᵀᴴ SUNDAY IN ORDINARY TIME

REV. JOEL BLUNK

Wıs. 1:13-15,
2:23-24

2 Cor. 8:7, 9, 13-15

Mark 5:21-43

"You see how the crowd is pressing upon you?"

A middle school girl told this "knock-knock" joke while hosting a variety show fundraiser sponsored by her church youth group:

Knock, knock.

Who's there?

Interrupting cow.

Interrupting co...

MOOOO!

Then, being new to the stage, she interrupted us again to ask innocently, "Do you get it? Do you get it?"

We all know what it's like to be interrupted. Jesus certainly knew. The way Mark tells the story of how Jesus handled interruptions helps us to better understand what matters to him, and also to appreciate his availability to those in need.

In my early years as a pastor, I had a conversation with my father in which I still recall. I was having a hard time keeping up with the demands of sermon preparation, meetings, pastoral visitation and all that was expected of me. The phone was constantly ringing, and people were stopping by unannounced; this was before the onslaught of email and cellphones! "There are so many interruptions," I complained, "I can't get anything done!"

My father, also a pastor at the time, calmly interrupted to say, "Joel, never forget, the interruptions *are* the ministry."

That conversation changed everything. Although interruptions can still be a challenge, I see them differently now.

Mark makes it clear that Jesus was interrupted regularly and often, and it is no stretch to say, by and large, interruptions created the context and the opportunities for his ministry. Rather than putting people off, or ignoring their problems, or asking them to make an appointment, Jesus responds in the moment in loving and inclusive ways.

In the very first chapter of Mark, we see Jesus in a remote place, by himself, at prayer early in the morning. Simon and others interrupt him to say, "Everyone is searching for you." Jesus interrupts the prayer time and goes immediately with them to tend to the crowd. (Mark 1:35-39)

Later, while preaching, Jesus is approached by a leper, a man thought to be dangerously unhealthy because of a skin disease. The man kneels before Jesus, saying, "If you choose, you can make me clean." Jesus stops what he is doing, stretches out his hand and touches him, saying, "I do choose. Be made clean." (Mark 1:40-41) The man interrupts Jesus; but Jesus, by touching the untouchable, interrupts that man's isolation and begins his restoration to community.

Next comes a more familiar incident. While teaching to a full house, a man with paralysis is lowered on a stretcher through a hole in the ceiling. When Jesus sees the faith of the man's friends, he says to the man, "Son, your sins are forgiven. Pick up your mat and walk." (Mark 2:1-5) His friends interrupted Jesus; but Jesus also interrupts normal social behavior by calling the man "son," recognizing that the faith of his friends has already interrupted the isolation of his paralysis and given him legs upon which to stand.

And so it goes, again and again, in Mark's telling of Jesus's ministry.

In the Gospel text for today, Jesus is interrupted twice. And in both instances, without hesitation, Jesus drops what he is doing to respond.

First, Jairus, a man of position, wealth and influence, comes to Jesus, and falls at Jesus's feet, and begs him to come and save his daughter who is near death. Jesus responds.

Then, as they are on the way to Jairus's home, a woman stops Jesus in his tracks. Unlike Jairus, who is part of the elite, this woman is a nobody. She is marginalized because she is a woman in a male- dominated culture, and because she had been hemorrhaging for twelve years, making her ritually "unclean" and unfit for relationships of any kind, except with other women. She is an outcast, probably a pauper, and essentially unseen in that culture. No wonder she reaches out to Jesus in secret! But Jesus stops on the spot. He acknowledges her. His journey to care for Jairus's daughter will wait as he gives this woman his undivided attention.

In neither of these cases does Jesus hesitate. He drops what he's doing to be part of their interruption, and God's interruption in their lives.

It is interesting to note, however, that it is not so much to perform a "healing" that Jesus allows these interruptions. Instead, it is to be the first to recognize what God is doing with the woman on the road, and then again with Jairus's daughter.

The Greek word translated "make well" in Jairus's request and "made you well" in Jesus's words to the woman are usually translated as "save" in other places. Here, in Mark's reporting, it means more than a simple cure to a physical ailment, though that seems to be what Jairus and the woman were both seeking. They each longed for a cure, Jairus for his daughter's sickness, and the woman for her hemorrhaging.

What Jesus recognizes and announces in both cases is something deeper. The woman's life is restored and her reintegration into community has begun, and she can now be valued again for who she is. In Jairus's case, we don't know exactly what happens, but we do know that his daughter gets up from the bed when everyone thought she was dead! She, too, is restored to her family relationship. Both are saved, in the fullest sense of the word, beyond just cures and healings.

Faith—a trusting openness—plays a key role.

When Jairus arrives home with Jesus, everyone is weeping. He is told that it is too late. But he remains steadfast and hopeful in what is to be. It is all the more remarkable that Jairus trusts Jesus when there is growing opposition and plotting among Jairus's colleagues to have Jesus killed (Mark 3:6); he trusts Jesus when others gathered at the house laugh in derision. God's healing, redeeming, restoring, and saving come to full expression with faith like that.

Likewise, the woman trusts to the point of knowing that all she needs to do is get next to Jesus, touch the hem of his garment, and her life will take a different turn. It's this very act which stops Jesus in his tracks—interrupts him! He knows something has happened, and that it is a result of this woman's receptivity to God's saving ways. That is an interruption for her, a saving and salving interruption.

Then, Jesus speaks to her, not by name but as "daughter," an address of kinship. "You are part of my family," he is saying in effect. "And your faith has made you well." In reaching out, you are restored to relationship. Saved. Your interruption with me has become God's interruption to the loneliness, vulnerability and sadness of these past years. This is a new beginning.

There's an invitation in here for us, too. We, like Jairus and the woman, are encouraged to know that Jesus is who Jesus appears to be. These stories are our encouragement not to lose heart when other voices challenge or deny by telling us that we're wrong and it's just no use, or encouraging us to simply give up and close the door.

The healing and wholeness which Jesus offers doesn't insure that every ailment or suffering will end immediately, or that we won't die, or that everything will turn out just the way we want it all of the time. But it does affirm that even death is not the end of the story. It's another interruption, an opportunity for God to do what God has shown us in Jesus Christ.

EZEK. 2:2-5
2 COR. 12:7-10
MARK 6:1-6

"He was amazed at their lack of faith."

*A*ll week long, *I've been* thinking I have a problem with this Gospel.

Mark tells us that Jesus couldn't perform any miracles in Nazareth—*because of a lack of faith.* Well, for the past thirty years, I've had a problem with this Gospel. I've not been able to understand this "lack of faith" thing.

I keep saying to myself: *Hey, Jesus was God! Surely his divine power was more powerful than his neighbors' lack of faith.*

After all: If we turn the dial back to just a few Sundays ago—we've got Jesus sleeping in a boat, and when a storm comes up, his disciples are terrified and wake him up to *do* something. And we hear Jesus himself say to them, "What's the matter with all of you? Don't you have any *faith?*"

But in that case, Jesus was able to answer their prayers—he was able to rebuke the wind and calm the waves—even though his own disciples lacked sufficient *faith.* In other words, *their* lack of faith didn't put a crimp in Jesus' style. Their lack of faith wasn't a sufficient obstacle to his power to save *them.*

So, what's going on in Nazareth?

I've often found myself preaching that there's no right or wrong way to pray. That God takes us as we are. And we shouldn't feel guilty when it seems that our prayers have gone unanswered, as if it's *our* fault, as if it's *our* level of faith, as if it's *our* lack of proper piety that forced God to say "No" to us.

It's critical, I think, in our relationship with the Lord, that we *let* him have the power that is his. We want to control so much, that we foolishly believe, sometimes, that we can control God, too.

And all I've preached for the last quarter-century is: *Give up!* Give up trying to wrestle control away from God. Give up trying to go "toe to toe" with him, believing that *our* prayer, *our* piety, our *goodness*, or our *faith*, is so powerful that God has to give in to it.

So: What's going on in Nazareth?

Maybe Jesus couldn't perform any miracles in his hometown—not because their faith in *him* was insufficient. Maybe it was because their faith in *themselves* was too great. They believed that *they* were in control: That their *image* of Jesus was somehow greater than whom Jesus really was; that their *estimation* of his power was greater than how powerful Jesus really was; that their *view* of the world was in some way more accurate than Jesus's view of the world—*and that was the problem!*

Jesus doesn't force himself on others—not on his neighbors, and certainly not on us. Jesus doesn't hurl miracles at those who don't want them—not at his own relatives, and certainly not at us.

But that's not what usually bugs us about God.

You and I aren't like the people of Nazareth at all, are we? We think to ourselves, "Hey, I've *got* faith. I believe. I come to Mass on Sunday. So: Send me my miracle!" You and I *want* God to hurl his miracles at us! You and I *want* God to force himself on us, don't we!

Well . . . maybe not.

What if the miracle that *God* wants to perform isn't the miracle that *we* want God to perform? What if God wants to perform a *holiness* miracle— you know, somehow getting us to stop sinning, to stop gossiping, to be more generous, more patient, more loving? What if *God* wants to stir us into holy action—not so that *our* lives will be better, but so that the lives of *others* will be better?

Maybe we really *don't* want God to be God. Not if it means we have to give a tenth of our gross income to the poor. Not if it means having to go hungry ourselves so that those who are starving might have food, or shelter, or clothes. We want God to be God—but not if it means having to give up one bit of the control we enjoy right now.

Maybe our faith in *Jesus* is just fine. It's the faith that we put in *ourselves* that's the problem: Maybe I have to give up; maybe I have to give in; maybe I have to let God be who *God* is in order to let *me* be who *I'm* supposed to be!

The next time you and I are praying for a miracle, let's remember that we probably have enough faith in God. And that, maybe, we have just a little too much faith in *ourselves*. Too much control. Too much of "I know what I need, so please fork it over"—and not enough of "Lord, help me to *know* what I need." We might pray, instead, "Lord, I don't want to be 'hard of face' or 'obstinate of heart.' Just get me to understand, and believe, truly believe, that 'in my weakness I am strong' and that 'your grace is enough for me.' Do with me what you will."

Now, *that's* faith!

That's the kind of faith that produces miracles! Maybe not the miracles *we're* looking for, but the miracles *God* wants to perform!

15TH SUNDAY IN ORDINARY TIME

FR. JAMES J. GREENFIELD, OSFS

AMOS 7:12-15
EPH. 1:3-14
MARK 6:7-13

"Jesus summoned the Twelve..."

S *ummon and send*—these are Jesus's first actions in the Gospel reading for today. I think they are God's primary actions within our lives. Will we let God summon us, and then send us?

First, let's look at 'summon.' I think it is fair to say that 'summon' is a word that we don't use too much, but perhaps we could benefit from re-familiarizing ourselves with it. Today, 'to summon' someone is to authoritatively call on someone, as in our criminal justice system. If we receive a summons from a judge, then we better go to court, or else! But, 'summon' in its earliest Latin origins means 'to give a hint.'

Mark's Gospel today says that Jesus summoned the Twelve. Perhaps their ministerial call was in responding to the countless hints given by Jesus in his aim of building the Kingdom. After all, isn't that the way we grow in our vocations? We respond to the countless hints presented over the course of our lives; in effect, we answer the question which the poet Mary Oliver poses in *The Summer Day*: "Tell me, what is it you plan to dowith your one wild and precious life?"

A friend recently asked his mother why she chose to marry his father close to 56 years ago. She couldn't remember! I wonder if she couldn't remember because what led her to pick him was so subtle, or because of the countless unmemorable things they did together that made her feel safe, loved, and beautiful. There were no extraordinary fireworks in the sky, just ordinary feelings in the heart—God's hints to her heart.

Do we trust the hints of God's summoning? Or, do we force our way—our own designs of control, wishful thinking, or resentment, and then pave our own path? In our daily lives, where is God summoning us, hinting at where we need to go, what we are called to do, what the next right thing is?

We also see God sending, which is the second action of Jesus today. Jesus sends the Twelve, and only after they are sent do these Twelve become apostles, for the word apostles means "sent forth." We even see the word 'post,' as in 'post office' and 'postal' in the word 'apostle.' As apostles, though, the message is deep within us which God is sending through us. We are carriers of God's Word, and it is interesting to see how those first apostles were sent.

"One ought to reserve an hour a week for receiving letters," Friedrich Nietzsche once wrote, "and afterwards take a bath." Nietzsche called the postman "the agent of rude surprises." He found "an unexpected letter sullied his day and spoiled his work," wrote associate editor James T. Keane, SJ of *American Magazine*. Yes, apostles are sent with a message that may not be received well by others, but nonetheless are called to be living letters of testimony to Jesus Christ. So are we!

Jesus sent them out in pairs. Let's think about that. Did he do that because he knew it was lonely for them? Maybe he was faithful to Genesis: "It is not good to be alone." I wonder how he picked the pairs. There must have been quite a dynamic. Did he pick friends to go with one another? Maybe he paired them up according to talents, in order to balance the teams. Maybe he paired a really good speaker with a really good beggar; an optimist with a pessimist; an introvert with an extrovert, Or a dreamer with a pragmatic doer. Or, maybe he paired up folks who were not getting along so that they would come to believe in the beauty of the message of forgiveness and loving one's neighbor. Imagine if it were us: Jesus would choose the one person whom we need to spend some time with in order to be healed, to forgive or be forgiven, to listen to in a fresh, new way—not just to hear the Gospel, but to experience the Gospel, its love and its power.

However he sent them, we don't know. But we do know that they came back rejoicing, and must have liked the experience. They liked what they learned; they liked what they did; they believed in their mission. What marked their mission was preaching, yes. But, what defined their mission was that they were dependent on nothing other than the person next to them and the faith that they were sent by God. In our sending, are we able to trust and rely on those we have been sent with? Just as the apostles of the Gospel went in pairs with no food, no sack, nor any money in their belts, are we independent of material things and interdependent of each other? After all, this is the way God sends us into our daily lives.

In conclusion, it is important to remember that Church is not something we go *to*, but rather something we are sent *from*—and also the people we live among. It is good to remember that the exit signs we see above the doors in our Churches are for more than complying with safety standards. The word Mass comes from the Latin *ite, missa est* which means 'go, you are sent.'

Yes, 'summon and send'—these are God's primary actions in our lives. Will we let God summon us, and then send us?

JER. 23:1-6
EPH. 2:13-18
MARK 6:30-34

"The apostles gathered together."

There are three things, among many, to notice about the first few lines from this beautiful passage found in the Gospel of Mark.

First of all, after having spent time spreading the Good News, the disciples gathered together to discuss with Jesus all that they had "done and taught." Jesus may have even asked them, "How did things go today?"

Too often, we think that God already knows what we've done and said, and so we conclude that there's no need to bring our lives to God in prayer. But Jesus encourages the disciples to "report" on what happened. The Greek word Mark uses is *apengeilan*, from the same root that forms the word "angel," the one who tells, reports or announces. Jesus asks his friends to report to him what they saw, what they heard, and what they experienced.

God wants to hear about our lives, and wants us to bring our lives to God in prayer. Why? It is because God knows how important it is to share our experiences—both good and bad. It brings us into deeper communion with God; it helps us to feel God's support, and reminds us that we are not doing this alone. Plus, God wants to be a part of our lives, like any friend would; and what friend doesn't want to hear about our daily experiences?

Secondly, notice that Jesus invites the disciples to discuss these things in a group. Mark uses the Greek word *synagontai*: "they are gathered together." (The word "synagogue" comes from the same root.) The communal dimension of the retelling is an important part of the overall experience. These things happened to us—not just to me.

When I was in Galilee last summer, it dawned on me that Jesus could have chosen just one person to help him: Peter (or Andrew, or James, or John, or Mary Magdalene, or any of the individual disciples). Instead, Jesus called a group of people together. Not only because he knew how important individual talents are for the community, but because the group dynamic was itself valuable—for both Jesus and the disciples. We are social beings. As the theologian Jane Redmont has written, there is a reason that all those stories about the Holy Spirit happen in groups.

Thirdly, Jesus invites the disciples, after their work, to "Come away by yourselves to a deserted place and rest a while."

Each part of that invitation is important for our spiritual lives. We need to "come away," that is, to withdraw or retreat from the busyness of our day. We need to do it "by ourselves," that is, with an attitude of solitude (even if it's in a group!) The "deserted place," whether that's your room or a retreat house, is sometimes essential for prayer. The physical setting is important. The word Mark uses is *eremon*: solitary, from which the word "hermit" comes. That's not to say you can't pray anywhere, but sometimes the desert is the best place. Finally, we all need rest—even the disciples. Even Jesus.

So, come away with Jesus to a solitary place, and report to him all that has happened. He wants to know.

17TH SUNDAY IN ORDINARY TIME

JAN RICHARDSON

2 KINGS 4:42-44
EPH 4:1-6
JOHN 6:1-15

"Gather up the fragments left over, so that nothing may be lost."

In one of my earliest memories, I am perhaps five years old. I am standing in my parents' bedroom with a stack of my artwork. Drawings in pencil and crayon, paintings in tempera, watercolor, and finger paint: these are the pieces that my mother has gathered up and saved. The entire collection. And I am systematically tearing up each piece.

The most vivid part of the memory is when my mother walks in. I have torn my way nearly to the bottom of the stack by this point. Horrified to see the pile of shredded paper, Mom asks me why I have done this. "Because they weren't any good!" I tell her, amazed that she can't see this for herself.

I don't know where I got this idea; it didn't come from my family, which valued and supported creativity. Clearly I had a precocious inner critic.

For many years after that, I held onto my belief that an artist was someone who could draw or paint well. Although I made forays into those media from time to time, I still carried with me that inner critic who had blossomed so early in my life. A long time would pass before I began to understand myself as an artist and to connect with and claim that part of my soul.

Just as I was about to graduate from seminary, I started seriously playing with paper and found myself transformed. In the process of cutting and tearing and pasting—those basic skills I had picked up in kindergarten—something magical happened that did not depend on being able to paint or draw. I had found my medium. In the practice of collage, I discovered a path to a place where it became harder to hear the voice of my interior critic.

That path led me to become the artist in residence at a Catholic retreat center, where a Franciscan friar named David opened the door for me to create a ministry that brought together all the pieces of my vocation as an artist, writer, and ordained minister. One day, as I worked with Brother David in the studio, he asked me, "Where did your fascination with paper come from?" My long-forgotten memory of the five-year-old who shredded her artwork suddenly came to the surface. I told David that story. "Perhaps," I said, "becoming a collage artist was my way of putting those pieces back together."

I came to experience paper collage as a spiritual practice and as a metaphor for the creative work that God was doing in my life. In much the same way that I would sit at my drafting table and piece together the scraps to create something new, God was doing this work within me. Through the work of my hands, I began to learn in a tactile, tangible, in-my-bones fashion how God gathers up the pieces of our lives and creates anew with them. The light and the dark, the rough and the smooth, the pieces that draw us with their beauty as well as the ones we would like to throw away: God makes use of every fragment, every shard, every scrap that is part of our story.

I have come to see God as the consummate recycler. In God's economy, nothing is wasted. The broken as well as the beautiful, the torn as well as the whole, the pieces we treasure as well as those we might prefer to toss aside or bury or forget: everything—*everything*—can be used. Transformed. Redeemed.

We see this again and again in the ministry of Jesus, how he always knows what to do with what has been lost, overlooked, left behind. Jesus knows the possibilities contained in the pieces, knows the value that lies within what has been broken and discarded.

Gather up the fragments left over, Jesus tells the disciples one day. With five loaves and two fish belonging to a child, Jesus has just fed five thousand people. It would be easy to suppose the miracle is finished when, as John tells us in his Gospel, the people are satisfied, having eaten as much as they wanted. Jesus, however, is not done.

Gather up the fragments left over, so that nothing may be lost.

It is part of the miracle this day: how Jesus, with such intention, cares for what remains. He sees the abundance that persists, the feast that remains within the fragments. We might think the marvel of the story is that there was enough for everyone. And yet for Jesus, enough does not seem to be enough. He knows the secret of the scraps.

Call it the persistence of wonder, or the stubbornness of the miraculous: how Christ casts his circle around the fragments, will not release his hold on what is broken and in pieces. He bids his followers to gather them up: a sign of the wholeness he can already see, a foretaste of the banquet to come.

Blessing the Fragments

Cup your hands together,
and you will see the shape
this blessing wants to take.
Basket, bowl, vessel:
it cannot help but

hold itself open
to welcome
what comes.

This blessing
knows the secret
of the fragments
that find their way
into its keeping,
the wholeness
that may hide
in what has been
left behind,
the persistence of plenty
where there seemed
only lack.

Look into the hollows
of your hands
and ask
what wants to be
gathered there,
what abundance waits
among the scraps
that come to you,
what feast
will offer itself
from the fragments
that remain.

18ᵀᴴ SUNDAY IN ORDINARY TIME

REV. PENNY A. NASH

Exo. 16:2-4, 12-15	*"He gave them bread from Heaven to eat."*
Eph. 4:17, 20-24	
John 6:24-35	

There's a lot of talk about bread in the readings for this Sunday. From Exodus we hear about the manna from Heaven that God gave to the wandering Israelites in the wilderness; the manna wasn't enough for them, and so God also flooded them with quails. But the Gospel of John takes us further. The people who ate the manna still died, but those who partake of the bread of life, Jesus himself, will live forever. This Gospel is emphatic: Jesus is life, Jesus is the bringer of abundant life, and Jesus is therefore the true Bread come down from Heaven. And that true Bread is available to everybody, not just to a few.

There is food, and then there is spiritual food. But the people get all fixated on bread.

I often struggle with this, myself. Despite the fact that ours is among the richest nations in the world, there are many in our cities and towns and rural areas who are hungry for real food. They do not have enough to eat. They rely on assistance from a variety of (sometimes dwindling) sources for physical sustenance: governmental, religious, and private non-profits. And I often remember the Letter of James in which the author admonishes the church community thus: "If a brother or sister is naked and lacks daily food, and one of you says to them, 'Go in peace; keep warm and eat your fill,' and yet you do not supply their bodily needs, what is the good of that?" (James 2:15-16, NRSV). And so I get fixated on bread.

And yet people are also truly hungry for spiritual food. They crave it, but do not know how or where to get such sustenance. They may have plenty to eat and drink or to wear, a warm dry place to live, a job and all the things people wish for, and yet they are starving because no one has provided them with food for the soul.

And, of course, there are people who lack both, who have neither physical food nor spiritual food.

We don't have to make this a dichotomy. We shouldn't make this a dichotomy. Perhaps one of the reasons why so many people are hungry for spiritual food is because of their experiences with the Church? Perhaps it may be they have heard about the Church—e.g. that the people are always arguing about whether Jesus meant something literally or figuratively, arguing about whether we are supposed to feed people's bodies or feed their souls? Perhaps they have had the experience described in the Letter of James, that they were hungry and they received a smile and a platitude in response?

The Gospel makes it clear that both physical food and spiritual food are intertwined within the life of faith, and that we each need both in order to experience the wholeness which God wants for all of us. The people have eaten the loaves and fish on the mountain, but they still crave something else. When Jesus tells them about the spiritual food that he provides, they ask him for that, too. He knows what they need and he wants to give it all to them. He came that they might have life, and to have it abundantly.

So, they don't have to be fixated on bread. We don't have to be fixated on bread. But this is still difficult. The Gospel is always calling us to trust God, to believe that God loves us and wants to care for us, and that God has created a world overflowing with good things so that we don't have to worry. We are supposed to trust that God will give us the bread for our souls, as well as the bread for our stomachs. But there is always this question: *Where are we going to get this bread?*

A chronically, physically hungry person has a very short horizon. A person who is living in an impoverished state makes decisions based on "right now" because that's all the person can see. And if the focus is simply, out of necessity, on the next meal, then how can one focus on the Heavens and the stars or the majesty of creation, and on relationships and on prayer or on anything? How can one tend to the spiritual when the physical lack is so insistently present? No wonder a hungry person is fixated on bread!

We are called to tend to one another's needs with the understanding that while we desperately need spiritual food, there are many among us who are not going to be able to take in much spiritual nourishment when their bodies are crying out for bread. Jesus fed the multitudes first, and then began to talk about himself as the Bread from Heaven.

There are also those among us who believe that the physical is all that they need. And so they want more and more, and yet they continue to feel empty. The bread is not enough, but they do not know where to get spiritual food. Are we prepared to give that away, too?

It seems to me that we are called to be the hosts of more than one kind of banquet in the world. There is food, and there is spiritual food, and we are called to give it all away as if there is always more than enough because there is more than enough.

Jesus is the gift we are called to share with others so that we all might be brought to wholeness together. Wholeness is neither merely physical, nor spiritual, and neither is faith, and neither is our God.

1 KINGS 19:4-8
EPH. 4:30-5:2
JOHN 6:41-51

"I am the bread of life."

The desert plays a significant role in the lives of many throughout Biblical history. Remember Moses leading the Israelites out of slavery and into the desert where they wandered for 40 years? It seemingly took a long time for the Israelites to be stripped of their false selves and the graven images that they had created. They certainly complained more than once about their plight. God was with them throughout their journey, sustaining them even though the days and nights became wearisome

Jesus, in the New Testament, is baptized by John in the Jordan River. Then, in the Gospel of Mark, Jesus enters the desert prior to the beginning of his public ministry. It is here where he is tempted to live a life of *Sensationalism* (turn these stones into bread), *Security* (throw yourself down from the parapet of the temple and bid angels to rescue you), and *Submission* (all these kingdoms of the world will be yours if Jesus would bow down and worship the evil one). Of course, Jesus is able to resist these ways of attracting others to follow him, and relies solely on his relationship with the Father. It is this relationship from which he draws the strength he needs to do the will of the one who sent him, and to continue with the message to heal, to forgive, to teach, and to preach a Gospel of Unconditional Love—for which the Father has for all, not just for some.

In today's reading from Kings, Jezebel (wife of King Ahab of the Israelites and worshipper of the god Baal) threatens to kill Elijah for killing the false prophets. She threatens to kill him by the sword. In fear for his life, Elijah flees and seeks the safety of the desert. One might say that Elijah has experienced what many today refer to as "burnout." He is over-burdened, and just wants to quit. In the desert, he asks God to take his life. He is exhausted; he has had enough, and wants to die. He sits down under a broom tree in the desert and falls asleep only to awaken to find bread and drink...nourishment for the journey to Mt. Horeb, where he will encounter God's presence in the slight whisper of wind. Once again, God sustains another in the desert by providing food for the journey. It's amazing how even when we feel like we are in a spiritual desert, God is always present; yet, we often need to actually rest in order to be nourished and strengthened.

There are many times in our lives when we become like Elijah. We have become weary of the implications and responsibilities we have accepted, whether it be a home, our place of employment, or just being overwhelmed by our physical suffering and mental anguish that are a common part of life. The lack of forgiveness and holding onto resentments only compounds our weariness, and causes us to become frightened to live a life of trust. Perhaps we are the grown children of parents who demand our attention, while our children clamor for their share of us, as well. We want to flee to a place where there are no tasks, no responsibilities, no suffering. We are afraid that we are going to collapse under the weight of all that rests on our shoulders. We want to escape to that broom tree in the desert, or anyplace that is away from our present reality. We are afraid! Our prayer to God is "take my life...I am exhausted.... I can't do this anymore". This is the point of surrender and acknowledgement of another.

Though Elijah was burned out, showed signs of depression, and wanted to give up, he was never reprimanded by God for showing weakness. In fact, he was given bread and drink to sustain him along his journey. God was with him in his exhaustion and in his wanting to give up. It is at this place of surrender that Elijah is able to allow God to take over. The bread and drink give him the strength to get up and not give up. He is strengthened to climb Mt. Horeb, where he will encounter God in a still, small whisper. Can we recognize God's presence in times of crisis and suffering? Can we see, as Richard Rohr says: "the only way the Lord can call us to greater wisdom is by making the system fall apart? That's called suffering. It's how God shows us that life is bigger than we presently imagine it. Faith allows us deliberately to live in a shaky position so that we have to rely upon Another."

Jesus, in the Gospel today, calls us to experience him as the Bread of Life. Part of this nourishment, this bread and drink, might be taking a good hard look at what we continue to carry from the past. Some refer to it as baggage, as if it weighs us down along the way. This baggage can contribute to our feeling burdened, resentful, and disgusted with life. The nourishment that we need for what weighs us down is the bread and drink of forgiveness. It is forgiveness that will give us the energy to get up and not give up. It is forgiveness that will give us courage in the presence of fear, and will dissipate resentment (recycled old negative feelings), and help us to move towards the Presence of God lighter and freer than ever before.

We need to take the time to go into the desert (a room, a church, a park, a garden, or a beach), and to reflect upon God's Word. Talk to someone... Go beyond the desire to "handle things on our own". Take the time to forgive those who have hurt, betrayed, abandoned, or shamed us. We need to remember that our exhaustion might be caused by our holding onto experiences of hurt and pain from years long past. We sometimes want to say to God, like Elijah, "just take my life," rather than enter the process of forgiving. Many still do not understand that forgiveness is something that we do for ourselves, and is not necessarily for others. We forgive in order to move on with our lives. It doesn't necessarily mean that we will be friends with those who hurt us, but we will be free and energized to continue the journey. We will be free from the resentments which have weighed us down for years, and made us lose sight of our mission and call to follow the Lord. Forgiveness allows us to become what today's second reading so clearly asks of us: Be imitators of God!

20ᵀᴴ SUNDAY IN ORDINARY TIME

FR. PAUL A. HOLMES, STD

Prov. 9:1-6
Eph. 5:15-20
John 6:51-58

"I am the living bread that came down from Heaven."

"*Seeing is believing.*" *This is* common wisdom. If you just show me something, let me see it with my own eyes, *then* I'll believe.

Even in the Scriptures, we have "seeing is believing." Just after Jesus is born in Bethlehem, the Wise Men follow a star to the manger, and we're simply told that when they saw the child, they believed. And—just after the Resurrection, Peter and John race to the tomb. No body; all that's left are the linens they'd wrapped Jesus in. And we're simply told, "They saw, and believed."

At the two most important moments of his life, Jesus's birth and Jesus's Resurrection—the phrase "seeing is believing" takes center stage.

But what did the Wise Men and the Apostles actually *see?* A baby in a manger. Admittedly, pretty strange—because animals are usually eating from a manger. But there's nothing visible to the human eye that should tell them that this baby, this baby lying in a manger, is the King they've been looking for.

And the Apostles? All they see is an empty tomb. There could be lots of reasons it's empty. Nothing there that should move them to believe in the Resurrection.

If you and I had seen the baby lying in a manger. . . . If you and I had seen the empty tomb. . . . Would we have "seen and believed"?

You and I come to Mass each Sunday, I think, "eager" to see, and "eager" to believe. But I don't think we're much like the Wise Men, or like Peter and John—so ready to believe even when what they see doesn't really tell them very much.

What are you and I so eager to see this morning?

I suspect that there may not be very many of us really "eager" to see the Eucharist. Most of us, I think, have gotten a little "used" to the presence of Christ's Body and Blood in our midst.

We modern Catholics, I think, don't need much prodding to believe in the Eucharist. We're much more eager, I think, to see other miracles—miracles that might touch us more poignantly—miracles that might *get* us to really believe in God. That might get us to really believe in his power. His love. His care and concern for us.

"Sure, you've given us your Body and Blood as our food. But what have you done for me lately?"

We're very eager, I think, for God to really show up! Cure some cancer. Get rid of my sister's lymphoma! Let a parishioner of our parish win the lottery. Now, if we saw something like *that*, then we'd believe!

Maybe we're not all that impressed with the miracle of the Eucharist—maybe we're eager for "other," "real" miracles, instead—maybe we keep coming back to church eager for miracles that are much more "showy" and "impressive"—because we don't see what's there for the *seeing*.

Well. . . .

I'm suggesting this morning that we change our tune with God. When I hold up the Host and the Chalice this morning, let's see what's really there. When I hold up the Host and the Chalice this morning, let's see the gift of *eternal life*!

"This is the bread that came down from Heaven. Unlike your ancestors who ate and still died, whoever eats this bread will live forever."

That's pretty impressive, isn't it?

The Wise Men saw a child in the manger—and they believed in a God who so loved the world that he gave us his only Son.

Peter and John saw an empty tomb—and they believed in a God who keeps promises, raising his Son from the dead, just like Jesus said he would.

Let's you and I *see* and *believe*! Let's be *eager* to embrace the miracle that happens right before our eyes every Sunday morning.

And let's pray to be satisfied. Satisfied with just the Body and Blood of our Savior. Satisfied with a miracle that's not all that "showy." Satisfied with the offer of *eternal life*!

21ST SUNDAY IN ORDINARY TIME

MICHELLE FRANCL-DONNAY

JOSH. 24:1-2, 15-18
EPH. 5:21-32
JOHN 6:60-69

"You have the words of eternal life."

"*Choose," urges my mother, as* I peer into the basket the farmer places down in our dim front hallway. The pale grey cartons of eggs are stacked on one side, a sharp contrast to the brightly colored candy on the other. I clutch a nickel in my small hand; do I want purple or red? Is there no green apple? Candy was an infrequent treat in my rural childhood, making it so hard for me to choose.

Forty-some years later I'm sitting in a sun-drenched office overlooking the Atlantic, clutching a cup of tea, listening to my director explain the next step in the Spiritual Exercises of St. Ignatius, the Meditation on Two Standards. "It will be here to see a great plain, comprising the whole region about Jerusalem, where the sovereign Commander-in-Chief of all the good is Christ our Lord," says Ignatius, "and another plain about the region of Babylon, where the chief of the enemy is Lucifer." Lucifer sits on a throne of fire and smoke; Jesus stands in a lowly place. Their standards are flying; the battle lines are drawn. Choose.

For anyone drawn to spend four weeks walking with Christ through the Spiritual Exercises, the bare choice itself isn't hard. It's already been made. As Joshua proclaims in the first reading, "As for me and my household, we will serve the Lord."

Or is it? Many of the disciples walking with Jesus in John's Gospel complained that the choice was tough, *sklerós* it says in the Greek, as something dried up and hard to chew on. "Unless you eat the flesh of the Son of Man and drink his blood, you do not have life within you," Jesus has said to them just before this Gospel opens. Words that scandalized them, words that shook their faith, words that were hard to swallow.

To choose to stand with Christ is a choice that leads to things we are not sure we want to eat, cups we are not sure we can drink. "If you want to get warm you must stand near the fire: if you want to be wet you must get into the water. If you want joy, power, peace, eternal life, you must get close to, or even into, the thing that has them," says C.S. Lewis. "Eat my flesh," says Jesus, "that I might abide in you, and you in me." Choose.

Saint Ignatius invites us to look closely at the camps, to see what we are getting into when we eat of the flesh and drink of the blood of God's Holy One. To choose to carry Christ's standard, says Ignatius, is to welcome poverty—spiritual poverty and perhaps even material poverty. To choose Christ is to prefer rejection over worldly honors. To choose Christ is to elect to stand with the foolish and the useless, to joyfully embrace humility for the sake of the Gospel. Choose. It could be tough.

The difficulty in choosing, for me, lies not in my intention, but in noticing the choices before me in the midst of my daily life. Choices rarely present themselves cleanly, with bright flags flying to identify the camps, and the lines of battle so clearly drawn. Instead, it is a man facing me on the sidewalk, asking for something to eat. Choose. It is the mentally ill woman who wants a ride home from church. Choose.

Saint Ignatius hoped this meditation would give those who made it a concrete understanding of what is fundamentally driving their choices, in our hearts as well as our heads. Can I recognize what is stirring me up in each situation? Is it greed? Is it fear? Or is it love?

Pedro Arrupe, SJ, the former Superior General of the Society of Jesus, said, "Nothing is more practical than finding God, than falling in Love in a quite absolute, final way. What you are in love with, what seizes your imagination, will affect everything. It will decide what will get you out of bed in the morning...what you read...whom you know...Fall in Love, stay in love, and it will decide everything." Where else would we go, Lord?

The Twelve remained with Jesus, not for power, nor out of fear, not because it was a rational decision, but because who they fell in with was Love. And what we love, decides everything.

DEUT. 4:1-2, 6-8
JAMES 1:17-18,
21-22, 27
MARK 7:1-8, 14-15,
21-23

"*Every perfect gift is from above.*"

Is there any perfect gift? Are we even capable of giving one? Be honest. I'm not talking about the Lexus in the driveway with the giant red bow, or the extravagant gold necklace given at an anniversary, or the other myriad set-ups that make up our commercialized fantasies. I'm talking about the act of *giving* the perfect gift.

When I give, I usually do it with an itchy palm, because I want to receive a bit for myself in return. I want the adoration of my husband or daughter. I hope that I picked just the right gift, that I met their desires before they even knew they existed, and that I had enough money.

But it goes beyond me wanting to buy love. This expectation spills into our faithful giving, as well. Whether it's the shiny brass plate on the hospital wall, the comfortable room of the Church that bears our moniker, our name printed on the list of annual donors, or a simple thank you card, we want recognition and gratitude for our generosity. We expect a little bit back in return.

It's how the world works, after all. How many times have we hesitated to ask a favor from a friend? Then we remember, "Oh, yeah. I can ask her. She owes me one."

Even the most altruistic people, committed saints who get up early in the morning in order to serve food to men and women experiencing homelessness, often expect a smile and a "thank you" when dishing out the meal. I have seen the oddity of it. A person sleeps outside, in horrible weather, anxiously huddling over his meager belongings all night. The next morning, he makes his way to the soup kitchen so he can relieve himself and get a bite to eat. He's still a bit irritable when he stands in the long line to get his food. He grunts when it appears on his plate.

Then, the woman dishing out the eggs cannot understand why he is not in a better mood! She stands there, with her dry clothes, with the full knowledge that her own belongings are tucked neatly away behind the locked doors of her home, and she insists that should be thanked for her great selflessness.

Why does this happen? Was the book of James talking about this complicity when it speaks of the perfect gift? We give because it will make us feel good. We donate because it will make us better people. We contribute because we made some cosmic bargain with God. We hold our hand out to others because we want them to think that we're kind. We sacrifice because it will make us a good Christian. Each gift, each act of generosity can be tangled up in this shady web of expected reciprocity. And a perfect gift—one that is free of presumption, quid pro quos, or mutual backscratching—is so difficult to give.

Yet, we keep trying. A perfect gift may be near impossible, but it is an act of worship to keep working at it. It is a reflection of what we have been given when we give to orphans and widows. It is true religion when we care for those who cannot possibly give anything back.

A couple of friends of mine began to wonder what would happen if our spiritual lives and prayers were directly related to acts of faith. What would happen if praise to our Creator included donating time to care for creation? What would happen if confession included actively making amends to the people we wronged? What if Churches not only served Communion in those tiny proportions, but began to feed the hungry right off the Communion table? What would happen if we didn't just tell friends, "I'm praying for you" when they were going through a terrible ordeal, but we actually stopped and gave them something to relieve the situation? What would happen if Christians invested as much time into doing the right things as believing the right things? What would happen if we learned to give a perfect gift? Our world would probably look much different than it does now. Perhaps it would look a little more like "Earth as it is in Heaven" if we actually worked for an Earth that mirrors Heaven.

This is the echoing hope of James. We can give that perfect gift. We can live that undefiled religion. When we become frustrated by sitting back with our big ears trying to hear and say all the things that seem pleasing, then we must roll up our sleeves and become do-ers. We will need to start dedicating our time, energy and talents. We probably won't give any of it perfectly. There is bound to be some self-interest involved in our acts. But we must keep trying, because every good and perfect gift comes from above, and so it is our hope and our longing to keep giving, to be reflections of the One who gave us our very lives.

May we go out to love, to strive, and to give, to the glory of God our Creator, God our Liberator, and God our Sustainer. Amen.

23ᴿᴰ SUNDAY IN ORDINARY TIME

MICHAEL LEACH

ISA. 35:4-7

JAMES 2:1-5

MARK 7:31-37

"Then the lame shall leap like a deer."

Have you ever seen a deer leap over a fence? It stands still, springs, and then floats over the barrier like a butterfly. It's sheer poetry in motion.

The Bible is poetry on a page. Today's reading from Isaiah soars:

> *Then the eyes of the blind shall be opened,*
> *and the ears of the deaf unstopped;*
> *then the lame shall leap like a deer,*
> *and the tongue of the speechless sing for joy.*
> *For waters shall break forth in the wilderness,*
> *and streams in the desert;*
> *the burning sand shall become a pool,*
> *and the thirsty ground springs of water;*
> *the haunt of jackals shall become a swamp,*
> *the grass shall become reeds and rushes.*

You are probably wondering when "then" will be. When will these wonders happen? When you "listen," says St. James—when you stand still before Jesus, who beckons from the other side of a noisy world and which holds us back from opening our ears to hear the good news and sing for joy. In this Gospel story Jesus takes a deaf and mute man away from the crowd, touches him, and whispers, "Be opened!" The man's heart leaps like a deer. He hears life in the desert, and speaks spontaneous words of praise as if he were the thirsty ground bubbling with water. This is what happens when we give up and then give it over to Jesus. We see. We hear. We live.

So often in my life have my ears been deaf to Jesus's voice because of the static in my head. It's not that Jesus isn't speaking to me all the time. It's that I am more interested in the rock and roll of human life than the sound of silence that brings his peace. Jesus told us, "Where your treasure is, there your heart will be also." (Matthew 6: 21) When what I treasure is being somebody or just being liked, or being perfect or just not failing, all I hear is what I think the crowd is thinking about me. But then I listen to the "still small voice," (1 Kings 19: 12) and Jesus transforms my values. I begin to hear and speak what is true and beautiful and good. (Phil 4: 7) I am as free as a deer and my heart beats peace.

Many of the healing moments in my life have come when I have felt all fenced-in by thoughts of guilt or fear. My brain tries to figure a way out but it can't, and then I can't take it any longer and I beg Jesus to help me. "I'm a prisoner of my own thoughts. Take this away from me, Jesus. I don't know what to do or what not to do. I don't want to think about it anymore. Please, give me your thoughts. Give me the right idea. Give me peace. Tell me what I need to know right now."

And for an instant, a drop of rain touches the burning sand in my brain like the spittle Jesus placed on the mute man's tongue, and I hear this whisper: "*I am here for you. I am here for you.*"

So many times have those exact words struck me like Jesus's words to the deaf man. For many years I thought those words meant only that God is here for me. And it does. But later I understood that it also means I am here for God. The first soft voice—"I am here for you"—opens my ears. God is with me, everything is all right! Even though I walk through the shadow of the valley of death, God is here, loving and guiding me. (Psalm 23). The second "I am here for you" opens my heart. I am here for God—to know God and love God and serve God, and also to love my neighbor as myself. I treasure the truth that I am my neighbor, and my neighbor is me; God is in both of us and we are both in God. I listen, I see: I, too, am the poor of the world—the deaf, the mute, the lonely, the humble, the lame, the marginalized, the broken who cries out in faith: "Who is weak, and I am not weak? Who is made to stumble, and I am not inflamed?" (2 Cor: 11: 29) I leap the fence of my psychological prison like a deer, suspended above it in motion, and "then" am one with Jesus and the deaf man and all who shout his name. Today is one of those Sundays when all three readings blend one into the other like stanzas in an epic poem. God is here for us and we are here for God. God heals us, and we go forth and can't stop preaching God's goodness and grace. Sometimes we even use words.

God is Love and Wisdom, here for us, and we are here for God, vessels where love and wisdom pour forth without trying. We speak spontaneously and even say silly things that make people laugh because it is a silly world, and we don't take it seriously any more. Our minds and hearts are free from any thoughts of what should or should not be. And if we fall and forget, God is still here for us.

"Get up from the ground and be not afraid" (Mt 17: 7), calls Jesus from the other side of the fence that isn't even there. "I am here for you. I am with you always. And you are here for me, with me forever." What could be a more perfect poem?

24ᵀᴴ SUNDAY IN ORDINARY TIME

FR. JAMES MARTIN, SJ

Isa. 50:4-9
JAMES 2:14-18
MARK 8:27-35

"Who do people say that I am?"

What a strange question Jesus asks his disciples: "Who do the people say that I am?" Did you ever wonder why he asks this odd question? Is it possible that he doesn't understand who he is? Probably not. In Matthew's Gospel, Jesus has just fed a crowd of four thousand people. Before that, he walked on water. So it's likely that at this point in his ministry, he knows who he is.

So why the question?

Perhaps Jesus had heard the disciples arguing about that very question as they were walking to Caesarea Philippi, which is about 20 miles north of the Sea of Galilee. Maybe he wanted to put an end to all their speculation. Maybe he felt sorry for them: they still didn't get it, despite all that they had seen Jesus say and do.

Perhaps Jesus knew that they wouldn't dare ask him because they thought it might be a taboo subject. Or perhaps, he was just curious about what they thought about what he was doing and saying.

So, he asks.

The disciples gave him what was probably a fair summary of popular opinion at the time. Herod, the first-century ruler of Galilee, thought that Jesus of Nazareth might be John the Baptist come back to life. A number of Jews believed that Elijah's return would herald the coming of the Messiah, which some thought would come soon. And the comparison to a prophet like, say, Jeremiah seemed sensible because of similarities between the prophet and Jesus.

But the disciples are careful to avoid saying what they believe.

So he asks them directly: Who do *you* say that I am?

Only Simon, the fisherman from Galilee, gets it right. You are the Messiah, the "Christos," the Anointed One, he says. And Jesus tells everyone that the conclusion that Peter has come to is not through some intellectual deduction. That is, he's not figuring it out. He is inspired by God to see this. Understanding who Jesus is isn't simply the result of a rational process, it's something more. It's a spiritual gift. It's an "Aha" moment for Simon: something that comes from outside of him. It's an insight that comes from God.

So Jesus now renames his friend, Simon. As you probably know, names were a big deal in the ancient Near East. To know someone's name meant that you had power over them. So in the Book of Exodus, when Moses asks God his name, and says, "Whom shall I say sent me?" God says, "I am who I am." The answer, in other words, is 'none of your business.' And, in the New Testament story of the man possessed by demon, when Jesus asks the demons their name, the demons say, "Our name is Legion, for we are many." The demons have cleverly avoided giving Jesus their name.

But Jesus has authority over Simon, and so he gives him a new name: Peter. In the original Greek, it's "Kephas," or "rock." In Latin, it's "Petrus," or "rock," which is where we get the name Peter. Fr. Dan Harrington, the late New Testament scholar, once told me that he thought that Jesus might have been a little playful here. Peter was a kind of hardheaded guy, and had what Dan often called an "angular" personality. So it's conceivable Jesus is giving him a kind of nickname: "Rocky."

More to the point, Jesus tells the disciples that Peter is now the rock on which Jesus's church is founded. Peter stands at the beginning of the church, and it's at that moment that our experience of church begins. All those discussions we have around the editorial table about the church, all those discussions you have in your parishes about what kind of church we should be, and all those conversations you have in your family about your parish, start from this moment—from Peter's insight about who Jesus is, and Jesus's declaration of who Peter is.

Today, our church is built on Jesus Christ, of course, but also on the legacy of that sinful, holy, flawed, headstrong, passionate, strong-willed, fearful, courageous, loving, short-tempered, faithful, entirely human person: Peter, who now prays for us in Heaven.

But it's also built around something a little more tangible, something easier to see: that is, the Eucharist.

It's a beautiful paradox, isn't it? Our church is founded on a saint who prays for us in Heaven—the most far-off thing you can imagine—and it is also founded on something as simple as bread and wine—the most common thing you can imagine. Yet through the mystery of the Mass the bread and wine become something entirely uncommon: the Body and Blood of the person who stood before Peter all those years ago.

Today, we celebrate those two realities coming together—the church's transcendence and its nearness. The dedication of a church, even a little chapel like ours, reminds us that the People of God need a place to worship together, to celebrate the Eucharist together, and to see themselves as the Body of Christ together. Because we never do anything alone in the church.

And that's the way it's always been. Think about it for a moment. Jesus didn't just pick one disciple, even though he could have! He could have just chosen Peter, or Mary Magdalene, or Thomas to be his assistant. We may be so used to Jesus choosing twelve apostles that we forget that he could have done whatever he wanted—he could have chosen one assistant.

But instead, he chooses a group, he calls them together, not only because he needs companionship and help, but because he knows we do, too. He calls the disciples together and forms them into his church, and invites them to join him at the table, just as he calls us together as church, and around the table, too.

Around the table—in this chapel dedicated to Edmund Campion, a Jesuit Saint who died professing his belief in all these things—we who work together, will be able to worship together. And in that work and worship, we will be better able to answer that question which Jesus posed all those years ago: "Who do you say that I am?"

25TH SUNDAY IN ORDINARY TIME

DEACON JIM KNIPPER

WIS. 2:12, 17-20
JAMES 3:16-4:3
MARK 9:30-37

"Whoever received one child in my name receives me."

Each year this weekend has been designated by the American Bishops as Catechetical Sunday. Bishop Richard Malone, a former Chair of the Committee on Evangelization and Catechesis, once stated: "Catechetical Sunday is a time to celebrate the work of the catechist and renew our gratitude for these faithful men and women who persevere in the labor of passing on the faith."

Catechetical Sunday calls for us to acknowledge the commitment that our teachers have for our students in bringing Christ to life within our parish. But this Sunday is also a time when we need to remember that each one of us is called to catechize. For, just as Jesus the Christ sent forth his disciples at Pentecost to teach—we, too, by virtue of our Baptism, are called to be a people of action—to bring forth Christ to others. We are *all* charged to be catechists.

The word 'catechize' simply means to teach by word of mouth in order to promote a change or transformation. Remember that our early Church was strongly orally based—the stories were passed down from generation to generation by word of mouth. Scripture scholars tell us that Jesus, as far as we know, never wrote any papers or letters. It wasn't until about

20 years after his death that St. Paul began to write his letters, and then another 10 to15 years passed before Mark wrote the first Gospel.

We live in this visual world of video, internet, email, text messages, books and publications where we read, absorb to some degree, and then move on to the next communication. Both catechism in the early Church, and still today, require this verbal storytelling and careful listening; it is one reason why we proclaim the readings—so that the words will be heard… so that the words will teach…so that the words will transform.

This brings us to today's Gospel proclamation from Mark. We find Jesus taking his twelve disciples off on a journey to get away from the crowd so that he can speak to them of his pending Passion, Death and Resurrection. And, not surprisingly, the disciples have no idea what he is talking about, or at the very least do not want to discuss it. Instead, they are busy among themselves arguing who among them will be the greatest. Can you see Jesus shaking his head? You want to feel sorry for the disciples—as they simply do not get it.

But look at what Jesus actually does, as I think it is the key for today's Gospel. Jesus takes a child, wraps his arms around the child, and then places the child in front of them: he then tells his disciples that they must be willing to receive such a child in his name. We find throughout the Gospels, time and time again, Jesus using a child and telling his followers that in order to enter the Kingdom of God that they must be converted and transformed to be like a child. We may think this sounds a bit absurd—for don't we all spend our life "growing up" and moving away from our childhood; yet Christ calls for us to be transformed like a child. *Why a child?* I think this story may shed some light upon this question.

There was a family that had a new baby and upon bringing the new born home the parents were met at the door by the baby's little 4 year-old brother who said, "I want to talk to my baby brother—alone." This somewhat surprised the parents. But they let the 4 year-old in the nursery with the brother and they shut the door…but they put their own ears to the door as they wondered what he was going to say. And apparently this is what the 4 year old said: looking down into the crib he said: "Quick! Tell me who made you! Tell me where you came from! I'm beginning to forget."

While we have no idea the age of the child that Jesus used…my guess is that the child was close to 3—4 years old. For it is those magical years where a child has not moved into that linear, left brain consciousness yet. It is an age where everything is still an enchanted universe… where it is still possible to believe in what you do not see. It is the age where one does not judge…one does not exclude…one does not care about race, creed, color, sexual orientation nor care about power, prestige or possessions. It is the age where it seems everything coheres and yet… we all seem to unlearn it in a way…we simply forget.

And I think this is why Jesus brought forth a child so many times! The disciples were arguing who was the greatest. The tax collectors were reaping their wealth and the Pharisees were determining who was in and who was out—all themes that are repeated today some 2,000 years later. Like the twelve, we usually want to be on top, but Jesus calls us to be happy on the bottom. We want to the boss, be he wants us to be the servant. We want to be grown-up and admired, but he tells us to be like children. We want to achieve a lot, but he says we need to receive a lot. And we want to determine who is worthy—but he says that all are called to this table. Indeed, it does seem that we continue to forget where we came from and what Jesus calls us to do.

And if we open our eyes and pause long enough—children have much to teach all of us. Last month the local papers featured a story about one of the girls who graduated 8th grade from our grammar school. She asked that anyone who had planned to give her a graduation gift to simply gift her a supermarket card so she could help feed some hungry people at a local soup kitchen. From her gifts she raised enough money to purchase 40 chickens for the fledgling soup kitchen's first hot chicken dinner. There is no doubt that this 8th grade student didn't forget the gospel message—and evidently neither did her parents in raising her and neither did her teachers here at St. Paul. But by her charitable actions and service for others she proclaimed God's Word. She catechized those who witnessed her actions and she opened herself and others up to be transformed.

In short we are all called to be like the child—we are all called to serve others—within our communities and beyond. We can celebrate all the sacraments…we can have incredible liturgies and we can educate our children through our school and religious ed programs—but in order for our spiritual life to grow it requires all of us coming together willing to use our God given gifts and putting the gospel into action. It requires not just education (the head) but also transformation (the heart). As it was once said: Faith is much more caught than taught.

So how can we 'catch it' and helps others 'catch it'? Begin by looking within your family—it is your first church—no doubt you may find one who is need of your touch, your words, your comfort…or maybe it is within your workplace or your neighborhood—remember it doesn't have to be big in size and scope—it only took a few chickens to make a difference for that soup kitchen—it is often the little things that lead to transformation.

So as we enter this cool and crisp season of fall…

May we give thanks to all those who catechize and are generous with their time…

May we listen to the proclaimed word and be open to the change it can bring about in us…

May we remember the call of today's gospel—to be like the child who is fully opened in both mind and heart …

And may we always remember who made us—where we came from—and to never forget that we are all called to love and serve the Lord and each other.

26ᵗʰ SUNDAY IN ORDINARY TIME

FR. WILLIAM BAUSCH

Num. 11:25-29
James 5:1-6
Mark 9:38-43, 45,
47-48

"Whoever is not against us is for us."

Some friends who went deer hunting separated into pairs for the day. And that night one hunter returned alone, staggering under an eight-point buck. "Where's Harry?" asked another hunter. "Oh, he fainted a couple miles up on the trail, "Harry's partner answered. "And you left him lying there all alone and carried the deer back?" "A tough call," said the hunter, "but I figure no one's going to steal Harry."

And that story is cousin to the old exclamation, "If I've told you once, I've told you a million times not to exaggerate!"

It's what we call hyperbole, using extravagant language to get a point across. I introduce the story and mention the use of hyperbole because, as you heard in the gospel this morning, you were subjected to such outrageous, terrible sounding things as plucking out eyes and cutting off arms in order to get to Heaven. But we have to recognize that Jesus is using hyperbole here, severely exaggerated speech to make a point. Although it always makes me wonder about those who read this Bible literally. What do they do when they come to this passage? Obviously they make some adjustment. Because I haven't seen too many one-eyed or one-armed Fundamentalists around!

Anyway, the basic message beneath this hand-lopping and eye-plucking is radical decision. That's what the bottom line is. When Billy Graham's Crusade was travelling around the country he always gave his audience a final challenge: "Decide!" Cut away anything that prevents you from a radical decision for Jesus Christ! Decide for Christ!" That is pretty much this morning's Gospel message.

What are we to decide? To discover the answer we turn to a very famous picture that you've probably seen reproduced many times: the picture of Jesus standing outside a door overgrown with ivy. There's no knocker, no handle on the outside. The idea is that Jesus stands there and knocks but there's no way for him to enter unless someone on the other side of the door decides to open it and let him in. It's called "The Light of the World" and it's in St. Paul's Cathedral in London.

Those of you who have been to London know that St. Paul's has for a long time been situated in a very busy, commercialized area with heavy traffic. The result is that the picture got quite dirty. And so the Cathedral staff sent it to one of those places that restores art pieces. But when the restorers took the picture out of its frame to clean it, they saw something no one was intended to see. On the bottom, underneath the molding, the artist had written the words, "Forgive me, Lord Jesus, that I kept you waiting so long!"

The artist had known about Jesus and he had painted him on the other side of that door. He just regretted that he took so long to decide to answer and open up to him. Again, it's the same Gospel message: it's time for a radical decision. What decision? It's time to open the door to Jesus once and for all. And, like it or not, we must decide not just to open one door, but three: the door to the past, the door to the present and the door to the future.

First, to open the door the past is to face the reality that "what is done is done." That's it. What we did, you and I, the hurtful things, the heartbreaking things, the arrogant things, the unjust things—they're done and we can't undo them. The only way we can deal with past hurts and sins that haunt us is to open the door to Jesus. The name that tradition has for this opening is forgiveness.

There is a couple in one of Thomas Hardy's novels who has a daughter named Elizabeth and Elizabeth died. And they agreed, this couple, that if they ever had another child and if that child turned out to be a girl, they would name her Elizabeth. And so they did have another child and it turned out to be a little girl and they did name her Elizabeth. But it didn't help. They realized that they could have had fifty daughters and named each one of them Elizabeth and they would *still* miss Elizabeth. Some things in life you don't fix. You have to swallow that and accept it.

There are some things that you and I don't fix: a death, a divorce, a hurt, a stupidity, a betrayal, an infidelity. They're there. The only response to these is forgiveness. To decide to open the door to Jesus Christ-of-the-past is simply to go to Jesus and ask for forgiveness, and that's it. And you move in to the future. We cannot undo what's been done, regret it though we might. We can only submit it to the unconditional love of Jesus who can absorb all things.

Secondly, we must decide to open the door to the present and that means we ask ourselves, ""What's going on in my life right now? What has to be cut off? What has to be plucked out if I am to be whole? What has to be put in perspective?"

I remember years ago a missionary friend of mine telling me of his ordeal as a missionary in China. At that time he and a family—a mother, father, and two children—were under house arrest. They had been under house arrest living somewhat comfortably for years. Well, one day a soldier came in and said, "You can all return to America. But you may take only two hundred pounds with you, no more, no less.

Well, they had been there for years, as I said, Two hundred pounds! So they got the scales and the family arguments started with the husband, wife and the two children. "Must have this vase, must have this type-writer; it's almost brand new. Must have these books. Must have this, must have that." And so they weighed everything and took it off the scale. Weighed it and took it off, until, finally, right on the dot, they got two hundred pounds.

The soldier came the next day and asked, "Ready to go?" They said yes. He said, "Did you weigh everything?" They said yes. "Did you weigh the kids?" "No, we didn't." "Weigh the kids," he said. And in a moment, off went the typewriter, off went the books, off went the vase into the trash. The trash. The things that clutter our lives and separate us—into the trash. "Cut it off, pluck it out!" The time has come to decide to put things into perspec-tive. That's the moment you open the door of the present to Jesus.

Last week I met a woman up by the parish house and I was kidding with her. I said, "What are you doing up here?" She said, "I've come to see Sis-ter Pat for a massage." Sr. Pat Reynolds does healing and touch massage and teaches others how to do it. So, I kidded, "A massage, huh?" And suddenly she turned serious and said something that hit me in the gut. She said softly, "I live alone, and no one ever touches me."

And I thought about that. No one ever touches her. In effect she is paying someone to touch her, not with exploitation, not with violence, not with abuse, but with healing tenderness and affection. That must be a sore temptation for many people, since so many of us go off in different direc-tions and so many of us widen the gaps between us with accumulations, schedules, activities, and self-fulfilling careers. Some people who live in the same house are not very often touched. Sometimes they have to pay someone to touch them. And the Gospel comes back and shouts, "Cut it off! Pluck it out! If there are things between you and your loved ones that prevent you from touching as you should touch one another—make it your decision. Open the door to the present moment. "

The final door to open is the door to the future. This simply means to give yourself over to Christ. This is the Christ who said, "Come to me all of you who labor and are heavily burdened and I will refresh you." This is the Christ who said, "How often I would gather you as a mother hen gathers her chicks but you would not." This is the Jesus who says, "I am the Way and the Truth and the Life."

Decide. Decide what you have to cut off and pluck out to open these doors, these three doors. And the next time you hear this rather upsetting Gospel and remark to yourself, "My God, this sounds so gross and so awful!" just remember that this is Jesus's exaggerated way of saying, "Decide!" Decide what has to be chucked out of your lives in order to be free. Jesus stands at the door and knocks. With the artist we cry, "Forgive me, Lord Jesus, that I kept you waiting so long!"

So open the door of your past. There is forgiveness. Open the door to your present and take a look at all the unnecessary and divisive things you've got on the scale, and trash them. There is renewal. And open the door to the future. Hand over your life. There is promise. On the other side of all these doors stand the most unconditional Lover you'll ever meet.

"Behold," says that Lover, "I stand at the door and knock. Will you open up?"

This Gospel, in its own violent way, demands a decision.

Reprinted from More Telling Stories, Compelling Stories *by William J. Bausch,* ©1993. *Twenty-Third Publications. Used with permission. All rights reserved.*

GEN. 2:18-24
HEB. 2:9-11
MARK 10:2-16

"Therefore, he is not ashamed to call them brothers."

O*ne of my favorite books* in the Bible is the Letter to the Hebrews. It is written so beautifully, and it gives us theologians and preachers so much to fuel our imaginations.

Especially this morning. Did you notice it? We're told that there's good reason that "Jesus is not ashamed to call us his brothers and sisters." What a wonderful idea. What a beautiful truth: that God's becoming "one of us" is—far from something shameful—it is something God is actually proud of!

I have to ask myself, though: As proud as God is, *Is there anything that might make Jesus ashamed of calling us his brothers and sisters?*

Officially, no. God is never ashamed of being one of us. Our humanity is now, officially, and permanently, a part of God's identity. But I have to ask: *Do you think that there's anything that we do, or is there anything we fail to do, that makes Jesus just a "little less proud" of being our Brother?*

I'd like to suggest that there might be one thing: failing to forgive. Our failing to forgive might be the one thing that makes the Lord just a little ashamed of being our Brother.

Some years ago, we learned of a terrible tragedy in Pennsylvania. A man entered a schoolhouse and murdered the little Amish girls he found there.

I remember being *amazed* at the wide-eyed disbelief of some of our news-casters about that terrible tragedy. Everyone seemed literally amazed at how the Amish community was so forgiving of their daughters' murderer. They walked to the murderer's house—*on the very afternoon their daughters were killed*—and offered forgiveness to his wife and family. They even invited the murderer's wife to the funerals of their dead daughters.

Matt Lauer, on *The Today Show*, was completely flabbergasted: "I don't understand this," he said. "If someone had murdered my daughter, I know I couldn't forgive them."

Well, a rabbi had been invited to explain it—first, to Matt, and then to the television audience. The rabbi explained that the Amish people have a discipline, a daily practice, of forgiveness. They *practice* forgiveness every day of their lives. If you or I were, all of a sudden, dropped into this tragedy, without this life-long *practice* of forgiveness, we would probably find it next to impossible to do what the Amish do. But it's because they are in the *business* of forgiveness every day of their lives that, when this terrible tragedy struck their community, forgiveness came much more easily to them than it would come to us.

A famous man once said that every age has its 'ambassadors of cheap religion'—people who try to *explain* suffering by suggesting that God sends suffering to those who have sinned or displeased Him. This cheapens God, and cheapens religion by forcing those who are suffering to blame themselves for their predicament.

Well, religion *isn't* cheap. And neither is God. And, as we all know, forgiveness isn't cheap, either.

Forgiving a murderer is a lot harder than *blaming* him. Forgiving a murderer is a lot harder than blaming the *victims* or blaming their *parents*. But just because forgiveness is *hard*, doesn't mean that we shouldn't try it.

When the disciples asked Jesus to teach them how to pray, Jesus included asking God for forgiveness in the Our Father. And he also included forgiving one another in that same prayer.

When his disciples asked Jesus if forgiving someone seven times was enough, he told them, "No. It must be 70 *times* 7 times!"

And, perhaps, more importantly, is this: Jesus forgave *his murderers* on the Cross. Not because you have to be God to do such a thing—but because he was our Brother, and even as he hung dying, he was showing us how to be human.

Jesus is never ashamed of being our Brother. But I'm here to suggest that there's a way to make him proud.

The Amish, I think, often make Jesus proud of being one of us. We might not have noticed it, because it came dressed up in bonnets and aprons, and came riding down the street in a horse-drawn carriage. It all looked so quaint, so unreal. But it *was* real. It was *very* real.

How can *we* make Jesus proud of being our Brother? We Catholics can start *practicing* forgiveness—the way the Amish do.

We have to start the very hard discipline of *daily* forgiveness. Wives and husbands must start forgiving each other (and maybe many couples might avoid the problem Jesus speaks of in the Gospels). Parents and children must start forgiving one another. Brothers and sisters, neighbors and co-workers, and leaders of nations—we all have to start forgiving one another every day. We have to start doing it as a community. And, we can't do it as a community until we start doing it as individuals.

Let us pray, you and I, that he'll help us to start forgiving. Today. At this Mass. Now.

If we start practicing forgiveness, I'm sure the Lord Jesus will be very, very proud of being our Brother.

Wis. 7:7-11
Heb. 4:12-13
Mark 10:17-30

"Sell what you have, and give to the poor."

*T*his episode in the Gospels could go down as one of the great "unsolved mysteries" of the New Testament. We never hear what happened to the rich young man, never find out what he did, and never hear the rest of the story. We tend to assume that he was simply too attached to his belongings to give them up, and was never heard from again.

But I think that dismisses him too easily. If the Gospels teach us nothing else, it is this: an encounter with Christ changes people. The blind see, the paralyzed walk. It's entirely possible that this rich young man—in a sense, living with a different kind of blindness and paralysis—was also changed.

I think Mark leaves this story open-ended as a way of telling us that our lives, too, are open-ended. We have choices. What will we choose?

For the rich, Jesus said, the choice is especially hard.

But all things are possible with God. Consider, for example, the story of Brother Matthew Desme.

If you find yourself in southern California, you might drive about 20 miles south of Los Angeles, to St. Michael's Abbey, in Silverado, California. It is run by the Norbertine Order. There, you will find a number of young men in white robes doing the ordinary work that the Norbertines do. They get up at five every morning to pray. They chant the Mass. They dig trenches, mop, and mow lawns. They observe the "Great Silence" by not speaking for hours at a time. And at the end of each day, they retire to small rooms with a single bed, nightstand and sink. They own nothing.

One of these men is 26-year-old Brother Matthew—tall and slender, with close-cropped hair, and glasses. He's been a novice at the abbey for two years. He doesn't look any different from the other men in white robes, who walk the grounds and work the land. He's the sort of person you might not even notice. And that's the way he likes it.

He likes it because just a few years ago, everyone noticed him.

At that time,, he wasn't known as Brother Matthew.

He was known then as Grant Desme, and he was not a monk. In 2009, Grant Desme was one of the hottest rising stars in American baseball—a center-fielder playing for a farm team for the Oakland A's. During the minor league season in 2009, he hit 31 home runs. In November of 2009, he was voted the league's Most Valuable Player. When the opportunity came, he was drafted by the Oakland A's in the second round, and signed for a yearly salary of $430,000. He was looking toward a future which many young men dream about, one in which people would see him on cereal boxes and would line up to have him sign baseball bats and caps.

But just two months after signing that contract, Grant Desme announced that he was quitting. People were stunned. Since the age of four, all he'd ever wanted was to play baseball. But he realized that he wanted something else more.

He wanted to be a priest.

In the fall of 2010, he entered St. Michael's Abbey in Silverado. The man who seemed destined to be a household name *changed* his name. Or rather, he had his name changed for him.

He was given the name of Matthew. He asked his superior why. "He said it was because Matthew was a rich tax collector," Brother Matthew explained recently. "And I was a rich baseball player."

"I had everything I had ever wanted," he said. "But it wasn't enough."

One of his teammates put it this way: "His love for God took over his love for baseball."

People who know more about this than I do will tell you that what Grant Desme did is unheard of. Players with his kind of talent just don't do what he did. They just don't. It's unthinkable—or impossible.

But what did Jesus say in the Gospel?

"For human beings it is impossible, but not for God. All things are possible for God."

The blind see. The paralyzed walk. Grant Desme becomes Brother Matthew.

That's one reason I think the rich young man in the Gospel didn't do what you might expect. Maybe it didn't happen overnight. Maybe it took a lifetime. But I think he must have understood, as Grant Desme did, that he had all he wanted...but it wasn't enough. An encounter with Christ changes everything.

While the Gospel is about having, owning, and possessing—about the *things* that clutter up our lives and get in the way of our salvation—I think there is another message here, too.

Not all of us are burdened with wealth —and isn't that a burden we'd all like to have? —but there can be other things that get in the way of following Christ. Other things we possess. Maybe it's a fear of change, an inability to trust or to love. Maybe it's a stubborn attachment to a particular sin. Maybe it is something rooted in fear, or insecurity, or our own resistance to change.

How hard it is for us sometimes to give up those things, to let them go!

So often, the things we possess aren't *things* at all.

And often, we don't possess them rather, they possess us.

This Gospel asks us to let go of what we don't need, those "possessions" which keep us from following Christ completely.

Can we do it?

Will we do it?

Are we courageous enough to try?

Grant Desme did.

And today, as Brother Matthew, he will tell you: "All things are possible for God." Our restless hearts will find rest if we put our trust where it belongs—not in things, but in the *Creator* of all things.

This Gospel can serve as a timely reminder that faith is rooted not in what we see, or own, or have, but in something much deeper. It takes trust. It demands a kind of courage. The rich young man was asked to take a leap of faith. So was Grant Desme, and so are all of us.

But the rewards are incalculable. A life of faith, a life of surrender and sacrifice, can lead us to the place that all of us seek—the place that every baseball player knows is the ultimate goal.

It can truly bring us home.

Isa. 53:10-11
Heb. 4:14-16
Mark 10:35-45

"Can you drink of the cup that I drink?"

When I was a young man I went away to seminary in Cincinnati. I'd grown up in Kansas, and I felt that I was making a great sacrifice. They taught me history, literature, Greek, and Latin. Sadly, they didn't teach me any Spanish. I don't know why we were supposed to learn Greek and Latin. Who are we supposed to talk to? The next four years they taught me philosophy, which was good—it taught me how to think. For four more years they taught me theology.

During all of that time I was very well taken care of, and when I went home to Kansas I was the golden boy of all the family because I was going to be a priest. I was treated better than my brothers and sisters, I guess, and better than my cousins. "This is the one who's going to be the priest!" Nuns from Mexico did our laundry for us in the seminary. Then, later on, the Brothers did the laundry for those of us who were going to be priests. I was so well taken care of that I never had to worry about paying the bills for 13 years. I bet none of you ever had that luxury! That was seminary, a place to prepare us for ministry.

I'm very grateful for the many wonderful things this experience gave me. But I want you to compare this with the seminary that was just described in today's Gospel. It's a very different kind of training. In fact, I think you could conclude from this Gospel that you shouldn't even trust that anyone has anything to say—*unless* they have also drank from the same cup that Jesus drank from, and have been baptized with the same baptism which he was baptized. This is Jesus's only seminary requirement. It's not learning Greek and Latin. It's not having other people do your laundry for you. It's learning how to do something yourself, something that the ego doesn't want to do at all, which is to suffer.

You see, until you've been led to the edge of your own resources and learned what your real resource is, you really don't have anything to say about the Gospel. You don't. It's all just seminary textbooks, ideas and words. You think you believe them because you were taught them, but you really haven't lived them or risked anything for them. It's amazing how we can miss the point. Jesus is talking here about the ordinary vision of this school. He doesn't tell them, not that there's anything wrong with it, to go off and study philosophy and theology. He doesn't tell them to join some big institution, and then they'll have something important to say.

Jesus says, "You must drink of the cup that I will drink." In other words, you have to enter at least one situation in your life where you're not in control, you're not in charge, you're not right, you're not winning, you're not number one, or you're not the best, and see how you deal with that. If you can come through to the other side still happy, trustful, and loving, then you have something to say. Then you're ordained. That's the real ordination! And you know what? Some of you have the real ordination, and some of us standing up here have never been ordained in that sense.

In fact, we spent our whole life avoiding suffering—always looking good, always being on top, or always being number one. We go home and everybody bows and scrapes, "Yes, Father?." "What do you need, Father?," "How can I help you, Father?," "Aren't you wonderful, Father?" That's all I've heard my whole life. This is dangerous, brothers and sisters. It's dangerous for the ego because you start believing your own public relations program, and you start thinking that you really are wiser, better, smarter, and holier than everyone else.

The only requirement for having something to say about the Gospel is going through the mystery of death and suffering, and *then* coming out the other side better and more alive and more in love, and believe it or not, even happier and more free. Then, and only then, do you have anything to say. Otherwise, it's all just textbook knowledge. It's all just something you can learn in the university, but not anything that changes the heart. Yes, I'm picking on my own group—priests and clergy and ministers—but Jesus is primarily not about creating ministers or classes. He's about creating disciples.

There's only one class in the Church. We're all called to the same discipleship, and what I say about the priests and the ministers—now you know—applies also to you. You don't have anything to say. You don't have anything to talk about, until, once in your life, you've been led to the edge of your own resources, and learned how to rely upon the Source, God. Then you know, maybe for the first time, who you really are; it's not just you, but also the God who is in you, and with you, and for you, more than you are for yourself.

Once you actually experience the Gospel, you can freely do what Jesus says at the very end: "You don't come to be served, but to serve." You don't come wanting others to take care of you. Instead, you want to take care of others because of the way in which you have been so beautifully cared for.

JER. 31:7-9
HEB. 5:1-6
MARK 10:46-52

"Jesus, Son of David, have pity on me."

I am moved by the faith of Bartimaeus and his insistent cry for Jesus to have mercy on him. Here is a blind beggar sitting on the roadside; others are trying to quiet his pleas, those who think he is unsightly, too needy, or embarrassing.

I recognize this story as an external drama of the powers that be, trying to silence and make invisible those on the edges, those who sit on the roadsides of our awareness everywhere, those blind and begging for sustenance, who want to be seen and heard but whom are so quickly dismissed.

But I also recognize this concept as an internal drama, or a kind of archetypal image of our own inner multitude. This beggar is *me,* or at least the parts of my own inner world which cry out for healing, for attention, for presence and witness. The powers that try to silence this voice are those characters within, such as my inner judge or perfectionist, who have no room or tolerance for these ragged aspects of my inner life. These sharp critical voices don't want any expression of vulnerability or need.

So, Bartimaeus moves me with his refusal to be silenced, his rejection of the shouts of others who want to quiet him with their harshness, intolerance, and narrow vision of what is acceptable in this world.

I also find myself drawn to Jesus in this outer and inner drama, who is the voice of wisdom, and is symbolic of our own inner witness or highest self. He is the One within who is able to let all of the inner voices be present and have their say. He does not dismiss anyone as unworthy.

Jesus does not make assumptions about what the blind man needs or wants. He does not immediately move to heal his blindness, but instead, asks him "What do you want me to do for you?" He is asking him, *What is your deepest desire right now?* He yields to Bartimaeus's inner sovereignty, his ability to ask for what he needs, rather than anticipating what that might be. The blind man chooses sight, and Jesus's reply is, "Your faith has made you well." The power of healing was within him already, and was not reliant on external authority.

If Jesus is an image of our inner witness, or symbolic of our own True Self, then he is the one who empowers all the parts of us to ask for what we need, to not rely on victimization, nor to be silenced.

This Gospel story invites me to become more aware of my own inner multitude, to welcome the voices of need from the fringes of my being, and to not let the harshness of my inner critic silence this deep cry for healing. It is with this process that I make the long, slow journey toward wholeness.

In the Jeremiah text, the prophet proclaims that God is going to "gather them from the farthest parts of the Earth, among them the blind and the lame, those with child and those in labor, together; a great company, they shall return here." The blind and lame are included amongst those who are laboring and birthing. They again can represent the great multitude within us which have been fragmented and scattered, with the promise of return. The great gathering of this remnant will return to the archetypal Holy Land, the sacred center or point of inner convergence.

The passage from Hebrews offers a reminder that the high priest is called to deal gently with others, because he or she is mindful of their own personal limitations which bring compassion for others.

Christ did not glorify himself by becoming a priest, but was obedient to the appointment, a calling which is not a temporary vow, but one that endures forever. What if we are appointed by God for certain tasks because it is in our very nature to undertake them, woven into our creation? By claiming the work to which we are appointed, or called, we are not glorifying ourselves, but being obedient to our own enduring nature, and merely following the current to where it carries us.

What if all of our inner parts and selves were essential to living this call out in the world? What if extending generosity toward myself and others, toward the ragged and vulnerable parts of myself, as well as those faces I encounter in the world around me, call us to a great gathering, which is in turn a great inner and outer healing?

In the Christian monastic traditions, hospitality is about welcoming in the stranger as the face of Christ. It is in welcoming what is most tender and uncomfortable that we encounter the Divine presence.

Might this invitation to inner hospitality be a great portal to healing the world from within? In welcoming all of the voices inside of us, we bring more compassion and resources to the world around us. We remember our own vulnerability, and so deal with others with more tenderness and understanding. Those places of inner blindness offer us new revelation when listened to, rather than when they are rejected. They are essential to our own places of calling within the world.

These texts invite us to embrace our places of limitation, weakness, and vulnerability. What is the part of me or you right now on the edge of the road begging for sustenance, which has now claimed a voice for its own need, to demand it be paid attention to? What is it that you *most* deeply desire right now? What are the voices from the ragged edges of your inner being longing for? And how do they point the way ahead?

DEUT. 6:2-6
HEB. 7:23-28
MARK 12:28-34

"You are not far from the Kingdom of God."

I can't remember which teacher first taught me about the importance of showing my work. It was either Mrs. Whettle in 3rd grade, Mr. Reynolds in 4th grade, or Mrs Jackson in 5th grade. It was an early math class, I'm sure. Perhaps it was long division, word problems, or maybe beginning algebra. I can't remember when exactly it was that I learned the difficult lesson that you could have the right answer on the test, but if you didn't show your work then you would be marked off. You could say the right thing, but if you couldn't tell how you got there, you could still lose a few points. You may have the exact answer a bit wrong, but if you work the equations and follow the sequence, you can still gain quite a few points. You could figure it out all in your head, but if you didn't take the time to show your work so that others could see and understand and read your writing and follow your logic, then you would still be missing important lessons. At some point, showing your work became part of the exam.

In our Gospel lesson for the morning, Jesus is given an exam question from one of the Scribes. "Which Commandment is the first of all?" Jesus refuses to pick just one. "'Hear, O Israel: the Lord our God, the Lord is one; you shall love the Lord your God with all your heart, and with all your soul, and with all your mind, and with all your strength'. The second is this, 'You shall love your neighbor as yourself.' There is no other Commandment greater than these.'" It is a love of God, and a love of neighbor. It is devotion to God with every part of our being: heart, soul, mind, and strength. It is also devotion to our neighbors. This is the great commandment: love of God and love of the other. Or as Saint Augustine called it: the rule of love.

And it is best when you answer the question, to show your work. Jesus healing the sick. Feeding the hungry. Eating with sinners. Touching the outcast. Welcoming the children. Loving his enemies. Embracing the world with his outstretched arms there at the cross. Unconditional, self-emptying love. Willingly accepting the death that defines what it means to be human and not God. "Where you die, I will die" to use the expression from the Old Testament Book of Ruth. Or as recorded in the Gospel of John, "having loved his own who were in the world, he loved them until the end. Jesus answered, "the Lord our God, the Lord is one; you shall love the Lord your God with all your heart, and with all your soul, and with all your mind, and with all your strength. The second is this, You shall love your neighbor as yourself." And Matthew, Mark, Luke, and John, they record the homework. They show the work, which is Jesus's lesson on the rule of love.

The blessing and kindness of God are given a unique and glorious expression in the life and teaching of Jesus. Yes, in the Great Commandment and yes, in his life, death, and Resurrection. Yet, the very work of God, the Spirit of God, is given shape and form and substance in the rule of love in the here and now. This is through our life together, in our devotion to one another, and in our love for others. God's love made manifest here and now. Our love for God given hands and feet here and now. The blessing and kindness of God here and now.

Years ago in seminary, one of our classmates could go on for a long time telling the rest of us stories about the formalities of the family dinner table growing up. Everyone was dressed up for dinner, not just on Sundays. Proper manners were a must, as was proper posture. Mother would resort to a yardstick down the back of the shirt at the table to teach the children how to sit up appropriately. The conversation around the table was directed by their father, as if he happened to be conducting a concerto of some sort. He would lead with questions, sometimes about school, about the day, about the bible, about just about anything. At the meal, after the blessing, the only conversation came in response to a question.

There are many table rituals that people share at mealtime. Hopefully, most are less formal, not so oppressive, and contributing to more positive memories about family and relationships to be carried along the way. For some, it's a conversation about highs and lows of the day. Others start with the simple question "how was school today" and depending on the age and gender of your children, you might get a conversation going. All too many of us know and lament when the table opportunities overflow with the tensions that come with life together. Table rituals and table blessings are at the center of life and devotion and commitments one to another.

Like the family that sits long after the meal and shares memories through tears about the one whose chair is now empty. Or the grown-ups who happily give up on adult conversation at dinner for a season of life. Or the one who finds the courage to make the phone call to a friend or go to the dining room with others so as not to eat in silence. Or the folks who commit to having everyone at the table at least once a week or once a month.

Everyone can think of some table rules and practices that have little to do with a yardstick down the shirt but have everything to do with devotion, companionship, family ties, faith, and future. Here in the community of faith, when we come to this table, it is the rule of love that comes to the fore. God's love. The love of Jesus. And our love. "Hear, O Israel, the

Lord our God, the Lord is one; you shall love the Lord your God with all your heart, and with all your soul, and with all your mind, and with all your strength. The second is this: You shall love your neighbor as yourself." Here at this Table we enact, we embody the breadth of our love of God in a way that we can taste and see and smell and feel. Here we express our devotion and feast on grace. Knowing that it is only by such grace, and in the power of the Holy Spirit, that our lives will show our work. Show God's love. The very work of God given shape and form and substance in our life together. Our love for God given hands and feet here and now.

Most of us, I think, have been taught that the experience of Holy Communion is rather private. Indeed, it is the church's celebration but there is a spiritual privacy in all of the prayer and silence and formality that define this table. There is that sense that communion is about God and you. But like every other meal that we share, don't forget the conversation. This meal ought to take place surrounded by a web of conversation. Conversation about the rule of love and showing our work. The conversations, not just here in the liturgy, but the conversations in our life together. Discerning the rule of love and showing our work. It's what it means to be the church.

The rule of love and how we treat one another. At home, on the playground, at school, in the office, in our politics, in our sharing of resources with those we love and those no one loves. The rule of love. God's love made manifest here and now. At the border, in the neighborhood, on campus, with our enemies, around our tables, at this table, with children in worship, with those in the church who may disagree with us, when singing a hymn we don't like but someone else probably does. The rule of love. When crying out for peace and calling for an end to war, when speaking for those who have no voice, when welcoming all sinners and saints, when challenging the worlds priorities of wealth and success, when speaking out against acts of violence or racial hatred or state sponsored torture. If we don't talk about the rule of love here and showing our work here at the church, where else will you have the chance?

The blessing and kindness of God here and now!

Come to the Table and make sure you show your work.

1 KINGS 17:10-16	*"She contributed all she had,*
HEB. 9:24-28	
MARK 12:38-44	*her whole livelihood."*

This morning it is through the stories of the scribes, the widows and the two coins that we hear God's message of trust and letting go. So I am going to ask for your partial participation in this morning's homily! I would ask that you reach into your pockets and take out two coins and simply hold them in your hands; I will come back to them later.

Today's Gospel, broken into two sections, first introduces us to the scribes who are strutting around in their long robes, reciting their prayers, sitting in places of honor and taking financial advantage of widows. The scribes saw themselves as master teachers and future prophets; they were held in great esteem; and thus were not pleased that Jesus was cutting into their jealously guarded territory—seeing that Jesus had his own followers who were calling him rabbi and teacher. On top of all that, Jesus hung out with sinners, ate with the tax collectors, forgave sins, and seemed to do all this and more on the Sabbath Day, all while showing great flexibility with many of the Judaic laws. In short, not only was this radical Jesus cutting into the scribes means of revenue, but he was preaching against the current conventional wisdom by "rooting and anchoring" his followers in a new message. In today's passage, it is clear that the scribes were focused on themselves, their appearance, their money, and using a term from Luke's Gospel—their own 'mammon.' Their lives were focused on their own self-worth and desire for power, prestige and possessions.

In comparison, we have the figure of the widow who appears in the first reading, as well as in the Gospel. The Lectionary only gives you part of the widow's story, so in order to pull the full meaning from this reading taken from Kings, allow me to flesh out the whole story.

It begins with Elijah finding that King Ahab and his people are worshipping their own prosperity and wealth—their own 'mammon.' So Elijah prays to the one, true God to cease the rains in order that Ahab would learn that all we have comes from God, to whom we must place our trust. And so the rains cease, drought takes over the land—for three and half years. Eventually, even the stream that God gave Elijah to quench his daily thirst ran dry, so he brought Elijah to the city of Zarephath, where he meets a widow. Although she is running out of food and water, Elijah asks her to share her last meal with him, trusting that God will provide. So she feeds Elijah her last meal—she let's go of all that she has, so that God can give her even more! For the following year, Elijah, the widow and her son ate all which they required from a single jar of flour and a jug of oil. She was favored in her response to the prophet's need, and her ability to let go and trust in God.

In the second part of today's Gospel, we hear Mark's story of Jesus's last visit to the temple—a place now divided into courts of worthiness rather than a place centered on God. At this point the temple is the socioeconomic center of the city, accounting for 90% of its revenue. Thus, Jesus even calls the temple—the Treasury! It was designed to keep the rich in, and the poor and widows out. So we hear that Jesus and his disciples deliberately take a seat in full view of the collection box, and they watch as each person dropped in their donation. When the service ended, he pointed out the poor widow who put all that she had into the treasury—two coins, worth about a penny in today's currency. Just as the widow in the first reading, she placed her trust in God and let go of all that she had—allowing God to provide. It is in this emptying of all that she had, represented by the two coins, that Jesus praises her above the scribes who still held onto their own self-worth as being the most important.

So how do these readings speak to us today? At times, do we find it rather easy to get very comfortable with our surroundings…to be in control…to have things just the way we want them?

Society, fueled by a barrage of advertising and so called 'conventional wisdom,' reinforces the message each day for our need to have and want more; we feel that we need to have the latest gadget, the biggest car, the newest Blackberry, and of course, to have the finest clothes that we can strut around in so that everyone knows how well we are doing in life. Today's culture reminds us that we are measured by what we have, and that we always need more!

So what prevents us from giving our time and treasure to God's work? Could it be the fear of giving up control of our lives and letting God take over? It becomes very easy for us to spend our life building our personal kingdoms, holding onto our own 'mammon' and not letting go—and yet the message Jesus gives us today is that we must let go…we must empty ourselves of our desire for worldly goods. We must be completely free so that we can accept God's invitation to participate in something bigger than you and me! Spirituality is all about letting go; it's about letting go and placing our trust in God, and allowing God to work within us, and we in Him. We pray at each Mass for thy Kingdom to come…which requires, in turn, for each of us to let my personal kingdom to go.

So how do we begin this process of letting go? According to Biblical scholars, buried within today's Gospel is the key to God's answer to that question. We turn to the two coins in order to move away from the desire of holding onto the material world, to be able to let go of our wants and desires, and to cease focusing on conventional wisdom in the popular culture. It is the two coins that the widow holds which represent the two great Commandments that Jesus gives us in the passage from Mark, which appears just before this Gospel. "You must love the Lord your God with all your heart, soul, mind and strength...and Love your neighbor as yourself...there are no greater commandments." Our love needs to be focused on God and neighbor, not 'mammon.'

So this week, let us set aside a few minutes to reflect upon our own lives, our own direction, and our own journey. Do we find that there are times where we are holding onto our talents and treasures like the scribes? Do we find ourselves strutting around with all of our fine wear? Or are we more like the widows—sharing and letting go of what we have, placing our trust in God, and following the two greatest Commandments?

In closing, it is somewhat ironic that the widow gave all that she had—two coins worth about a penny, and placed her trust in God, while 2,000 years later we mint our pennies and all of our currency with the words, "In God We Trust." It does give one pause to think in whom and what do we place our trust?

Do you still have those coins in your hands? When the collection basket comes around after the Creed, I invite you to imitate the widow and toss in those two coins, along with your weekly offering. Let it be a symbol, a reminder of your commitment to let go, a reminder of the two great Commandments, a reminder of the widow's faith, and a reminder of being open to God's call to actively participate in a deeper, more meaningful spiritual journey with our Savior, Christ the Lord.

> *"But my words will never pass away."*

I am not a fan of apocalyptic literature. I appreciate it as a genre and have a little understanding of the elements of apocalyptic literature and how those elements work together to achieve a particular aim, which is usually to encourage those who are suffering to hang on in the midst of their dark hour. Just when things are getting to the point of being unbearable, God is going to jump in and turn things upside down (or, more to the point, right side up) again.

But I'm not a fan.

One of the reasons I'm not a fan is that once someone starts talking about "end times" and all that, the focus becomes narrowed intensely upon speculation about a future that we really cannot know about, often to the detriment of the present. It's all about what's going to happen at the end of the world, often accompanied by sometimes uncharitable hopes that people are going to get what they deserve, and the things that are going on now get lost.

In the case of this "little apocalypse" in Mark's Gospel, Jesus is trying to dissuade people from sitting around trying to interpret the signs in order to determine whether or not the end is near. Jesus asserts that we won't be able to miss it! We don't need to focus on nuances and tiny details to see if this could be the end. The end will be obvious. But in the meantime, no one knows when the end will be—not even Jesus himself, he asserts. So maybe we should just let that stuff go.

This all means that maybe we just ought to shift our focus from speculation about the times and scrutiny of the Heavens, and dwell on something more profitable. Maybe we ought to think about what we are doing here and now. Maybe we ought to think about what is going on in the world right now. Maybe we ought to think about the fact that God is giving us time to live out the Gospel instead of preparing for the destruction of the world.

In other words, repenting because the end is near is not an excuse to hunker down and wait for the blow. It's a mandate to go out now and feed the hungry, clothe the naked, visit the sick and imprisoned, now, while we can. Sitting around parsing this terrible thing or that terrible thing and wondering if they are subtle signs of the end of the world does nothing. Ministering to others in Jesus's name does everything.

Later in this Gospel, at the end of this discourse, Jesus reminds everyone that they must keep awake. No one knows when the time will come. But again, we are not to keep awake so we can see the destruction coming and correctly identify it as such. We are to keep awake to see signs of God's activity in the world and to go be part of that activity.

Lord knows in our world today we don't have any trouble keeping awake. There is an entire industry built around keeping us awake—coffee shops on every corner, soft drink machines everywhere, caffeinated confections offered and accepted as if they were nectar to the gods, not to mention all the cute coffee mugs and travel mugs or fancy coffee machines that we can even buy for our homes. We do what we can to keep awake.

But what Jesus wants for us is to be awake to God, to notice God, to notice the opportunities God is providing for us to minister to those around us. We are to keep awake to those opportunities so that we can seize them and can respond to them, because there are so many real people right now who need to feel God's healing touch, and for many of them, there isn't much time. Their lives are lessened, shortened and diminished by poverty, ill health, loneliness, mental illness, hunger, and incarceration.

When we are focused on interpreting signs or on speculation about who's going to finally get it in the end, then God's people go hungry and naked and live in isolation because we weren't able to see them while we were looking for something else.

So let us shift our gaze from the "end times" to our time, particularly to those in our time who are so hungry and thirsty for God's touch through our hands. The time is short for us to respond to the one standing right in front of us. Let us love as God loves now, today.

FEAST DAYS

DEUT. 4:32-34, 39-40
ROM. 8:14-17
MATT. 28:16-20

"And behold, I am with you always"

There was once an old Amish woman who went with her family to a mall for the very first time ever. The Amish family was mesmerized by the hundreds of stores, the lights, and the food court. And then, for the first time in her life, the old Amish woman saw an elevator. She watched as an elderly man approached the elevator doors and entered. The doors closed. A minute later, the doors opened and a handsome young man, who looked like George Clooney, exited the elevator. She saw another elderly man get on, and a minute later saw a man who looked just like Brad Pitt step out. A third elderly man went in, and out came a Ryan Gossling look-alike. Her daughter approached her and said, "Hey Mom, isn't this place great?" "Yes," said the old Amish woman. "Quick, go get your Father."

Our faith is all about transformation. We are transformed by the relationships in our lives. Our God is a relational God: Parent, child, and the love that exists between them. St. Augustine named them Lover, Beloved, and Love. The Trinity is the mystery which transforms us.

By any means, the Trinity is not an easy reality to comprehend. One of my old theology professors, Brian Daley, SJ, once told us, "The Incarnation is the reality of two-what's-in-one-who; the Trinity is the reality of three-who's-in-one-what." Jesus is both human and Divine. God is three persons in one God: Father, Son and Holy Spirit.

As young Jesuits, we had to undergo rigorous, comprehensive, oral examinations at the end of three years of philosophy, and again after three years of theology studies. My buddy, Dennis Ryan, was getting ready for the dreaded oral exams at the end of philosophy. We had to explain and defend dozens of philosophical theses covering topics like epistemology (the study of knowledge), metaphysics (the study of being or reality), and moral philosophy. We also had to select two readings from each of the areas of ancient, medieval, modern and contemporary philosophy.

Dennis put St. Augustine's *De Trinitate* (*On the Trinity*) down for one of his readings. I told him, "Dennis, that's crazy! No one understands that." Dennis said, "Yeah, I know. But they never ask any questions about it."

The exams were open. I was listening as Dennis got pushed around a little bit by the first of three examiners, who asked some tough and tricky questions. After that prof's twenty minutes, Roland Teske, a Jesuit from Marquette, took over the questioning. He showed mercy toward Dennis, and switched topics. "Dennis," he began, "I see you chose Augustine's *De Trinitate* as one of your readings. I just wrote an article on it."

"Oh, Oh," I thought. "This could be bad."

Teske continued, "Dennis, Augustine re-read his *De Trinitate* thirty years after he wrote it, and even he said he couldn't understand it."

Dennis, without missing a beat, replied, "Well, I can see why."

The teaching of our faith that God is Triune, Three in One, is the way we make sense of human existence. The doctrine of the Trinity explains how God's loving us is revealed in Jesus, and continues through the actions of the Holy Spirit poured out into our hearts (Rom 5:5).

Catherine LaCugna, the brilliant theologian who died much too young, put it succinctly in her book on the Trinity, *God For Us*. So does Notre Dame theologian Richard McBrien in his magisterial tome *Catholicism*, where he writes:

> *"What the mystery of the doctrine of the Trinity means, when all is said and done, is that the God who created us, who sustains us, who will judge us, and who will give us eternal life is not a God infinitely removed from us. On the contrary, our God is a God of absolute proximity, a God who is communicated truly in the flesh, in history, within our human family, and a God who is present in the spiritual depths of our existence as well as in the core of our unfolding human history, as the source of enlightenment and community (1981, p 361).*

The doctrine of the Trinity is not easy to understand, but it is possible to experience. The reality of our relational God is experienced in the relationships of our lives, especially the relationship between parent and child.

The older I get, the more in awe I am of parents. The love and largesse which parents lavish on their sons and daughters amazes me. Having lived in the First Year Dorms for more than a decade, every year I witness the amazing reality of "Move In" day. Moms anxiously hovering; Dads fixing chairs and tightening already tight bolts on the bed; the son or daughter desperately wanting them to leave, while also just as desperately desiring that they can all just go back home. These loving parents have loved this child into adulthood, and now need to let the child go. The love between the child and parents is palpable in the air, even as all involved tend to shy away from naming and claiming how emotionally charged the whole day actually is.

God loves us the way parents love children, the way the Father loves Jesus. The love of Jesus for God, for Mary and Joseph, for his family and friends, for all of us, is the Holy Spirit. The Holy Spirit is the transformative, Divine power remaking all and saving us from all disaster, destruction and death.

This love of parent for child is exquisitely expressed in this moving essay by Bruce Lawrie, who writes of his relationship with his severely disabled little boy, Matty:

> "My six-year-old son and I share a nightly ritual, just the two of us alone in the fading light of his bedroom. Matty, who is severely mentally retarded, loves routine because life comes at him as if blasted from a water cannon, the millions of sights and sounds we all unconsciously assimilate every second of every day an undecipherable roar. Even more than most children, Matthew craves the safety that comes from learning the rhythms of his life, thrives on repetition. And of all his daily routines, winding down to bedtime might be the best. For a few minutes every night, I can turn down the white noise for him, and help him ease into the peaceful joy of drifting off to sleep. We start out sitting on the floor with his favorite board book about monkeys drumming on drums, dumditty, dumditty, dum, dum, dum...The book is worn with love, all four corners gnawed off—Matthew chews up books the way other kids do grilled-cheese sandwiches, starting at the corners and working his way to the center. As we reach the last dumditty on the last page, he lets out a sigh that tells me everything's right in his world and he's looking forward to climbing into bed."

Bruce sings to Matty, as his little boy drifts off to sleep, and movingly muses on what life must be like for his beloved son.

> "I finish the song and stand up and wonder what Heaven will be for my son. Maybe it'll be a place a lot like here, a place where his own son will run from him across a wide open field of green, every nerve-end in his little body singing, where afterwards, Matty and I can tip back a beer together at a pub. Where he has a healthy body and a lovely wife, and our family can linger long over pasta and home-

made bread and salad and red wine. Where his son, my grandson, will fall asleep in my lap, a sweaty load of spent boy pinning me to my chair on the deck, the night sounds stirring around us, the stars rioting in the dark sky."

"I look down on Matty's peaceful sleeping face. So often peace has eluded him: the operations, the I.V.s, the straps tying his hands to the hospital bed rails so he wouldn't pull the needles out, the countless blood draws when they couldn't find the vein, all the insults descending out of the blue onto my little boy who couldn't understand why the people around him had suddenly begun torturing him. But he is at peace right now. And a time is coming when he will have peace, and have it to the full. And all the other things he's been robbed of. Meeting a girl. Playing catch with his father and his son. Making love. Calling his mother's name aloud. Talking with his twin sister. Eating a pizza. Drinking a beer. Running. And I'll get to be there with him. God will carve out a little slice of eternity for us, our own private do-over where the breeze carries the smell of fresh-cut grass, where the sky is bluer than you ever thought it could be, where the air feels newborn. Soon, Matty. Soon."

Like all good parents, Bruce Lawrie wants the best for his son, Matty. So, too, does our loving, Triune God, desire the best for us. God is love, and that love exists primordially and powerfully in the relations of the Trinity. Love will transform us all. Let us pray.

EXO. 24:3-8
HEB. 9:11-15
MARK 14:12-16, 22-26

"Take it; this is my body."

It may interest you to know that today's liturgical feast of the Body and Blood of Jesus Christ is a late one. It was established in the 13th century. Question: why, after 1100 years, did the Church feel it necessary to do this? A parable will explain why.

Once upon a time there was a very gracious and very wealthy man who always threw a dinner party once a month for his close friends. These were times of wonderful food and vintage wine, a time of joy, great intimacy and sharing. Well, it so happened that on one occasion a few of his closest friends got sick at the same time and were unable to attend.

The man felt bad but nevertheless he wanted them to have a memento of the celebration they missed so he took a bottle of his best wine from the table and put it in a special ornate box and set it on the sideboard where it could be seen. He knew his friends would see it, open the box, and enjoy the wine knowing that they had not been forgotten. So he went to his servant and told him, "Pierre, be careful of that box and make sure that you treat it with respect because what's in there will gladden the hearts of my friends and they will always think of me."

The servant wasn't quite sure what the master meant, but, being of rigid mind, he took his words too literally so that every time he passed the box, he bowed to it. Eventually the bowing became a habit. Well, it so happened that that very week the master suddenly died, but he had often expressed his wish that his friends would continue those monthly meals in his memory, and so they did. When they arrived in good spirits at the next gathering the servant pointed out to the jovial friends the special box. They were intrigued, but they couldn't help but notice how the servant bowed each time he passed it. Unsure why he was doing this, it wasn't long before they too began to bow to the box before they sat down to dinner. For some reason—perhaps a sense of awe—none of them ever asked what was in the beautiful box.

As time went on, that box, sitting there silently on the sideboard for all to see, had a depressing effect. The meals began to grow less and less joyous and more and more quiet, more solemn, to the point where, finally, instead of celebrating being together as friends, they began to eat in silence and to gaze with respect at the box never, ever knowing that a bottle of the best wine, meant to be happily shared among them in the wealthy man's name, was inside unopened and unused.

End of parable. That's what happened to the Eucharist. In earlier times people had a very close and intimate relationship with this sacrament. It was, after all, a shared meal reflective of the intimate Last Supper. They would even take home some fragments for consumption by the family during the week. Some, even children, would bring the sacred Bread hidden on their persons to Christians in jail. But by the thirteenth century, all that history had been forgotten. By that time, the Eucharist, in its ornate tabernacle box, still sitting there, had become an awesome and remote mystery, something to be bowed to and approached with fear and trembling and then only very rarely and by very specially chosen people. The people felt they were not worthy.

So the Eucharist became something hidden inside the box or to be looked at with bowed heads from afar—such as when the priest elevated the host in Mass—and that was all. All this, of course, was a far cry from the generous and intimate fellowship meals Jesus shared with the poor and the unworthy—so much so that the Pharisees complained that he ate with publicans and sinners. It was a far cry from the Last Supper, where there were only rough fishermen present when Jesus broke bread and shared wine. The bar for approaching Jesus was obviously set pretty low. So, centuries later, why were people staying away?

The Church slowly began to realize this sad state of affairs and finally had to legislate that people receive the Eucharist at least once a year and to establish feasts like this one we're celebrating today—the Body and Blood of Christ—in the hopes that the people would remember its meaning and Jesus' desire to be near us and, so to speak, unlock the box.

So we are here today to remember. There are lots of things we could remember about the Eucharist, but let us focus on two key words: unity and mission.

Unity. In this regard, I call your attention to something quite unnoticed but profound that happens at Mass. Before he holds up the host and the chalice and says "Behold the Lamb of God," the priest breaks off a small piece of the host and drops it into the chalice. Why does he do that? He does it because it's a custom that goes back to the old papal Masses when a piece of host from the previous papal Mass was placed in the chalice to signify continuity with the Mass that went before. Even more, on Sundays and feast days the pope would send a small piece of the host he had to the other churches in Rome.

It was a gesture that signified unity: all ate the same Eucharistic Bread. All were bound by a common faith. All were united in one Church. So if you happen to notice my dropping a piece of the large host into the chalice—and I'll be deliberate about it today—think what you are meant to think when you see it: we are connected with all those throughout the world who this day are celebrating the Eucharist whether openly in cathedrals or secretly, at the peril of their lives, in internment camps or private homes—and this is happening more and more today as Christians are daily being severely persecuted in many lands. We are connected to one another through this Mass. Yes, here all are united in one global faith, one Lord. We belong to something larger than ourselves. We are brothers and sisters to all those who this day break bread in the name of the Lord. It's a powerful thought.

Mission. "Do this in memory of me" are words always said aloud at every Mass. Question: what should we do in Jesus' memory? Meet in assembly and celebrate this ancient ritual of course, but it goes deeper than that, much deeper.

Remember that before the words "Do this in memory of me" are these words: "This is my body given for you…my blood shed for you." That's what we should do in Jesus' memory: As he has given his body and blood for us, so we should give our body and blood for others—in his memory. That is to say, justice, mercy, and sacrifice should characterize those who have received these gifts from Christ himself. That's our mission: to be sent out from here bearing the gifts of faith, hope, and love.

The Eucharist is unity and mission. Unity says we are connected to those Christians in China, Yemen, Iraq, and Africa who today celebrate Mass in secret and in terror. Mission says we are sent, sent to share what we have celebrated. The parting words say it all: "The Mass is ended, go in peace." That word, "Mass" is the Latin word for "mission." Therefore, when we leave here, in a very real sense our Mass just begins.

FEAST OF THE ASSUMPTION

FR. JAMES J. GREENFIELD, OSFS

REV. 11:19; 12:1-6, 10
1 COR. 15:20-27
LUKE 1:39-56

"Blessed are you among women, and blessed is the child you will bear!"

*I**t's challenging to understand the** physics of the Feast of the Assumption, but it's comforting to hear the singing of the Magnificat by the
one whose feast day we celebrate today. Before touching on Luke's mas-
terful Gospel for today, my all-time favorite explanation of the Assumption
comes from a typical teacher-student exchange. The teacher asks, "Who
can tell me what the Feast of the Assumption is all about?" A little boy
offers this response, "It means that Mary was so holy that we just assume
she went to Heaven."

That little boy's thinking about Mary being so holy is deeply resonant with
the Scriptures we hear proclaimed for this feast. Her holiness is steeped
in the fact that, as a first-century Galilean woman, she simply recognizes
that God is doing great things in her and through her—isn't this what all
disciples are called toward? So, to be *who* we are, and to be *that* well is
the stuff of personal holiness, even sanctity! Accepting the implications
of achieving holiness in the here and now, present-tense moments of
our lives simply by living each day well in the zip code where we live is
liberating.

Mary certainly stands with anyone—past, present, or future—who recognizes and honors that God *does* work wonders in and through individuals

who allow their own ordinariness to be the stuff of radical holiness. Dietrich Bonhoeffer, commenting on the Gospel for today, said that Mary's song "has none of the sweet, nostalgic, or even playful tones of some of our Christmas carols. It is instead a hard, strong, inexorable song about collapsing thrones and humbled lords of this world, about the power of God and the powerlessness of humankind."

I was so touched by a man who spoke on the news after a terrible hurricane, standing amidst all the rubble of what was once his home, alongside his wife. He said very simply that the hurricane had not taken what is most important—and then he turned and embraced his wife. In that news snippet we learned that richness is not counted by what you have, but it is counted by whom you have standing by your side. Mary's Magnificat is sung to address this very experience that when one stands with God, who is the author of life and love, then no matter how lowly the world may make one feel, no matter how devastating the circumstances of one's life, we are rich in the eyes of God. Theologian Elizabeth Johnson rightly suggests that even though Mary is socially insignificant in the eyes of the world, she is still highly favored by God. Mary also mirrors our final destiny in Christ, to be raised up in the Communion of all the Saints, with Christ who reigns.

On this Feast it seems that we are also given a glimpse of Heaven. In the Book of Revelation, there is a woman described as being clothed with the sun, and with the moon under her feet. What I especially love is the next image of the red dragon ready to devour the child. It reminds me of the wonderful children's book by Maurice Sendak, *Where the Wild Things Are*. In this book, a little boy named Max sets out on an amazing adventure wrestling with the "wild things" of his imagination only to discover that by doing so he actually finds out the true meaning of home. Aren't the "wild things" what the dragon symbolizes for all of us? We are all encouraged to ride that dragon, to wrestle with the wild things, trusting our destiny, like Mary's, is that God has good things in store for us! American author and journalist, Margaret Mitchell, suggesting there are two handles to every problem, says that "you can grab it by the handle of fear or the handle of hope."

This Feast day encourages us to literally grab the problems we face each day, and to wrestle with the wild things of our imaginings by the handle of hope. There have been many studies conducted on the effects of fear and anxiety on the baby in its mother's womb. Just imagine some of the worries that Mary had to face for herself—and even the concerns she had for her elder cousin who was pregnant! Yet, even after her arduous trek to visit Elizabeth, Mary and her cousin realized that their pre-natal babies were leaping for joy in their wombs! We see the full blossoming of hope announced by Elizabeth as she delighted in the fact that Mary was blessed because she believed that the promises of the Lord would be fulfilled.

Mary's willingness to believe that the promises of the Lord would be fulfilled is a posture that she assumes for the rest of her life, and it is one that we also need to take on as we reflect on our own particular situation and vocation in life. Writing about Mary in his book *Jesus: A Pilgrimage*, James Martin reminds the reader that "Mary was told that her son would be the Son of God, not that he would be tortured, put to death on a cross, and then rise from the dead. Mary says yes to a future that she does not know. She is an example of letting God do God's work, without trying to figure it out." Sometimes I wonder whether we spend too much time trying to figure life out instead of trusting that God will work it out.

The scene of these two women embracing, while the children in their wombs are leaping for joy, serves as prelude to the beautiful canticle which Mary was about to sing. As Martin Luther observed, "she sang it not for herself alone, but for all of us to sing it after her." Thus, discovering, as did Mary, that God is as real as the problems we face each day, we come to know and love God whose "mercy is from age to age" and has "lifted up the lowly."

Mary says it so well: "The Almighty has done great things for me, and holy is God's name." As that little boy said so unassumingly, this Feast is all about assuming Mary went to Heaven because she was so holy. We, too, know that in sharing in the holiness of God, we ultimately come to know ourselves as we truly are and then strive to be that well.

SOLEMNITY OF ALL SAINTS

FRAN ROSSI SZPYLCZYN

REV. 7:2-4, 9-14

1 JOHN 3:1-3

MATT. 5:1-12

"Blessed are the poor in spirit."

*T*he names and ethnicities are varied, as are the dates of birth and death. The list is long—365 names, one for each day. Some names are familiar, while others are not—in fact, some have no proper name, and many do not bear the "official" title of canonized Saint. *Père Vincent Lebbe, Rahab, St. Benedict,* and *The Syrophoenician Woman.* After each name, a designation: *Apostle to the Chinese, Faithful Prostitute, Monk, Faithful Witness.* Thus reads the canon of saints—those formally canonized, and those otherwise. All are to be remembered here on this day when we celebrate the Solemnity of All Saints.

These names come from the table of contents from Robert Ellsberg's book: *All Saints: Daily Reflections on Saints, Prophets, and Witnesses for Our Time.* I love this book because it is a reminder that those we often think of as "the saintly other," even if it is in the best way, are not as "other" as we might think. Many of us think of the saints as "other," don't we? It is a classic 'us and them' scenario, but instead of 'us versus them' going against one another, in this case we long to be more like them. Many of us do not believe that such a thing is possible. We pray with the psalmist, *"Lord, this is the people who longs to see your face."* We know that all things are possible with God, and so maybe we are all saints?

Did you hear the words in the first reading, from the Book of Revelation? *"I had a vision of a great multitude, which no one could count…"* Immediately we are invited by God to imagine that the multitudinous list of names in Ellsberg's book, which contains many names, might possibly include our own.

Another hint comes along in the form of *"salvation comes from our God,"* which is something all saints and holy people know well! It is God who does all the heavy lifting; all saints—including us—are simply responding to what God initiates. When I was a little kid, I thought that to be a saint meant to *make yourself perfect*. As adults, we know that we can do all that we want, but it is only God who brings forth perfection. The challenge comes because our cooperation is necessary. God's promise is that this will happen frequently, and with mercy through Christ. All who are saints recognize that surrender and cooperation with God are essential elements of holiness.

So how do we respond to this call to sainthood? We are invited to worship God and to live with joy, full of expectation and hope. These things are easier said than done, and no one knows that better than our saint friends. Their struggles and challenges were as real as our own. So how did they do it? And how do we follow?

The key to this might be found in today's Gospel, which may be the most antithetical passage to our way of life today. Listen to the words, "blessed are the poor in spirit…" or "blessed are those who mourn." What about "blessed are the meek?" Or "blessed are the peacemakers?" Poor in spirit, or otherwise? Mourning? Meek? Peace-making?

Some of these things are viewed with suspicion in our culture, if not outright contempt. With the ideal that we should get more, do more, be more, have more, things such as mourning, poverty and meekness are out of place. Even the best of us may see poverty as something calling for a charitable response, but we typically eschew being poor. Can we acknowledge our own poverty of spirit?

If we cannot enter into our poverty, our meekness, our mourning and more, then we cannot enter into God's deepest presence very easily. God is patiently poised to bring us closer, leading us to our inheritance, our sainthood. Yet our response may often be to act like a willful toddler, who does not want to cooperate.

I think about the names in the book: *Père Vincent Lebbe, Rahab, St. Benedict*, and *The Syrophoenician Woman*. Somehow each of these people, on whose shoulders we all stand, came face to face with vulnerabilities, fears, control issues and more, and somehow they turned it all over to God.

Pere Vincent, for example, inspired the ire of his fellow missionaries when he tried to carry his own bag when he arrived in China. He realized that most of his compatriots felt superior to their flock, never learning the language or culture. Rahab, a prostitute, went against the king and helped the Israelites, who were technically her enemies. This "marginalized outsider" had faith in a God in which she had only heard about. The list goes on and on, and we find example after example of the saints who may end up reminding us of ourselves.

Instead of spending time thinking about how unworthy we are to claim the title of saint, can we reorient ourselves to travel in a new way? That is what Jesus asks of us—to be saints by following him. His way means a complete turnaround, to change our route, alter our path, change our direction. If this becomes our focus, our own sainthood progresses, free from angst or false piety, and full of the Spirit!

With Jesus at our side as friend and brother, we have a hand to grasp as we enter into the places that we typically avoid. Yes, I am weak; yes, I am arrogant; yes, I am prejudiced; and yes, I am afraid. Yes, I am selfish; yes, I am needy; yes, I am broken and yes, I am dishonest. With each admission of what blocks us, we allow God to dismantle the boundary that stands between us and our sainthood.

Today when you leave, I urge you to go look at a book of saint names, or find something online—you can even look at your church calendar. Read the names aloud, learn some of their stories, and let the details of their lives sink in. When you do so, imagine yourself there as part of the great multitude, bigger than can be imagined, known as the children and friends of God. Imagine yourself there because that is where God longs for you to be. As you let God work in you, that is where your saintliness will be found.

FEAST OF ALL SOULS

JAN RICHARDSON

WIS. 3:1-9

ROM. 5:5-11

JOHN 6:37-40

"The faithful will abide with him in love."

For many years I have had a fascination with the trinity of days in which we now find ourselves: Halloween, the Feast of All Saints, and the Feast of All Souls. These days have become for me what Celtic folk have long called a *thin place*; a space where the veil between worlds becomes permeable, and Heaven and Earth meet. I have learned that it pays to be attentive as these three days unfold; each year, something occurs that offers insight into what my life has been, and a glimpse of what it may yet hold.

It was during this thin place that, thirteen years ago, I began dating the man who would become my husband. A remarkable singer, songwriter, and storyteller who toured nationally, Gary became my partner in ministry, our lives and vocations intertwining in wondrous ways that would forever change us.

Last year, the Feast of All Souls found Gary and me preparing to go to the hospital. Several months earlier, we had discovered that Gary had a brain aneurysm. He had experienced no symptoms of the aneurysm; it was spotted in the process of checking out something else that proved not to be a problem. *How fortunate*, we thought. *How providential*. The aneurysm had been found; it could be treated; life could return to normal, all the more graced for knowing what a potential disaster we had dodged.

During an eleven-hour surgery, Gary suffered a massive stroke and was placed in an induced coma. The following days would bring further complications, two more surgeries, and the most painful vigil of my life. I learned again, this time with a vengeance, how strangely time moves in hospitals. It both expands and compresses, stretching out even as it speeds past, offering thin places where love and grace move in the midst of agony and fear.

But for all its turnings and openings, time finally ran out. Gary never regained consciousness. Eighteen days after the initial surgery, he died, encompassed by our family and by the God who had entrusted him to us.

After Gary died, I stayed in the room as his nurse removed everything that had helped to keep him alive during the awful and beautiful vigil that we had kept with him. I watched as she put away the ventilator tube that had kept him breathing, watched as she took out the seemingly innumerable lines that had delivered medications. Finally Gary was shed of everything that had kept him living, everything that had tethered him until it became clear that nothing would return him to us. I placed my hand against his chest and commented to the nurse that it felt so strange to feel a heartbeat and know that it was only my own pulse.

His heart beats in you now, she said to me.

The path I am traveling in the wake of Gary's death is akin to the vigil I kept with him before it, in that it is both terrible and beautiful. As I make my way—slowly, slowly—through the labyrinth of grief, trying to absorb the unfathomable loss and to keep breathing through it, I am mindful of the grace that makes itself known in the midst of the anguish, and the love that stubbornly persists in finding me. Again and again, the nurse's words return to me, bearing their remarkable grace and wisdom anew:

His heart beats in you now.

The Feast of All Souls invites us to remember our beloved ones whose hearts beat in us. This day asks us to pay attention to their pulse that abides within our own pulse, to listen for how they linger with us and continue to bless us, even when their physical absence bewilders us and breaks our hearts still.

This day reminds us that as we reckon with the loss of those we love, gifts come to us through the thin places. These gifts are unbound by time and have small regard for chronology. Instead, these gifts spiral around to us and move through time in ways that we cannot contrive or foresee, asking us to remember just how fragile the veil is. Here's a story about such a gift.

I have a blog called *The Painted Prayerbook*, where I offer art, reflections, and blessings that accompany the lectionary readings. The Sunday before Gary went into the hospital, the Gospel was Luke 20:27-38. In this passage, religious leaders come to Jesus with a question about what would happen in Heaven to a woman who, in the custom of levirate marriage, had been wedded to a succession of brothers. Jesus knows the question the leaders have posed to him is a political one, wrapped in theological trappings. As ever, he responds to what lies beneath the trappings.

Jesus tells his questioners that, in the eyes of God, there is no question of the dead versus the living, "for to [God]," Jesus says, "all of them are alive."

As I wrote my reflection for that Sunday, I thought about how, on this side of the veil, we feel the distinction between the living and the dead so keenly, and Jesus does not dismiss or disparage this. Bent as he is on breaking down the walls of division, however, he cannot resist pressing against this one, the wall we perceive between the living and the dead. Nearing his own death and Resurrection, Jesus pushes against that wall, shows it for what it is, challenges us to enter anew into our living and into our world that is so much larger, so much more mysterious than we dreamed.

This is the blessing I wrote as part of that reflection. I had no thought of how much I would need it for myself, and how soon. This is the last blessing that Gary saw. Its words continue to spiral back around to me, inviting me to listen for the heartbeat of the beloved who continues to bless me. On this Feast of All Souls, I offer this blessing as a gift to you. In the thin place of this day, may you remember with gladness those who bless you and breathe with you still, their heart beating in you.

God of the Living
A Blessing

When the wall
between the worlds
is too firm,
too close.

When it seems
all solidity
and sharp edges.

When every morning
you wake as if
flattened against it,
its forbidding presence
fairly pressing the breath
from you
all over again.

Then may you be given
a glimpse
of how weak the wall

and how strong what stirs
on the other side,

breathing with you
and blessing you
still

forever bound to you
but freeing you
into this living,
into this world
so much wider
than you ever knew.

FEAST OF THE IMMACULATE CONCEPTION

SR. SIMONE CAMPBELL

GEN. 3:9-15, 20
EPH. 1:3-6, 11-12
LUKE 1:26-38

"Where are you?"

*G*od called out in the Garden of Eden looking for Adam and Eve, "Where are you?"

What a great image: God looking for us! But this wasn't just an event in Biblical mythical times, it continues to this day.

In our very rich nation, I often sense that God is calling to us and asking, "Where are you?" Today, God is looking for us. The Holy One asks us, "Where are you when we have hungry people? Where are you when an economy is favoring the few at the expense of the many? Where are you when violence in our cities is tearing us apart? Where are you when people are denied healthcare because of the political preference of a few politicians? Where are you?"

And like Adam and Eve, I am inclined at times to make excuses. But at the root of all my excuses seems to be Adam's response: "I was afraid, so I hid." I imagine that you, too, have had that experience.

Overwhelmed at the clear view of injustice, my fears get the better of me. It is fear that actually drives me from any sense of the Garden, because fear cripples me and separates me from others. Fear takes root when I think that I am in control and in charge. And because I can't measure up to the task, I have a tendency to blame others for my incapacity to face the anguish around me. I sometimes become "sick with fear" and look for a snake to blame. However, blaming snakes does nothing to alleviate fear.

In today's Gospel, Mary shows us a different way forward. When the angel Gabriel goes looking for Mary his opening line is, "Do not be afraid!" Mary demonstrates an alternative response. In the face of mystery she is curious, not closed. In the face of mystery she asks, "How can this be?" It is because she is willing to turn and face this puzzlement that our God has taken root in her. God grows within her because she is willing to be open to something new. She is the model of the antidote to fear and hiding, but she did not do it alone. She went immediately to her cousin, Elizabeth. Mary's way is to connect with others and respond to their needs. This "other-centeredness" is at the heart of wholeness.

In Detroit recently, I met a modern-day Mary. Her name is Kristina. She has struggled with dyslexia and other learning disabilities all of her life. But rather than closing in on herself, she has stayed curious and engaged. At a literacy center, sponsored by the Adrian Dominican Sisters, she has overcome her learning challenges and reaches out to engage others. Rather than keeping her head down and hiding her struggle, she looked me in the eye and with an electric smile, she volunteered that only together with her colleagues at the center could she have ever made the academic progress that she has achieved. I marveled at her clarity and willingness to share her struggle.

But, then I heard more. Adult student after student lauded Kristina as being the reason that they, too, have made progress. Kristina's warmth and "other-centered" curiosity got her engaged with her peers. When engaged, they all achieved something more than any one of them could do alone. They have realized their dreams of reading and being contributing members of our society.

My sense is that Kristina is unknowingly birthing God in this literacy center. She is creating community, sharing her struggle, and making something new. She is not focused on herself; rather she focuses on including others and creating opportunity. She sees around her Marcella, Elizabeth, Ms. Perry, Brandon, Antonio and so many more. And in their turn, her colleagues reach out to add more people into the community of nourished individuals.

For me, the mystery of Mary's willingness to live an "other-centered" life is a direct parallel to the story of Kristina. By being curious beyond her limitations, Kristina helps to create community in the face of struggle. At the heart of it, Kristina is living the truth that when we share our limitations we create community. She responds vibrantly to those around her, releasing hope and healing into our world. This was an incarnational moment in Detroit which I delighted in experiencing.

It made me wonder, though, what is my response, what is our response, when God comes looking for us and calling out, "Where are you?"

Do I dive into personal guilt and try to hide? Or do I, or we, engage in community, sharing our gifts, vulnerabilities and curiosity, and merely call out, "Over here!"

It is an "over here" response that we desperately need in our nation. An "over here" response means that rather than focusing on our individual selves or our judgments and limitations, we are engaged with those around us. An "over here" response means that we visit the sick and in the process are healed ourselves. Calling out "Over here!" means that we are in the midst of fellow humans struggling to create something new. We do not have time to be fearful and hide.

This new moment of engagement becomes, as Paul says to the Ephesians, "Thus God chose us in Christ...to be adopted children." "Such is the richness of the grace which God has showered on us in all wisdom and insight." Wisdom and insight come in community when we open up to the needs of others, and let go of our fear and desire for control. This is the incarnational mystery and promise that God lives among us and within us.

Immersed in the reality of living the Gospel in our world, we leave behind fear and hiding. We are prepared when we hear God call. When we hear, "Where are you?", we need only call out from the midst of caring, "Over here!"

CHRIST THE KING

FR. RICHARD ROHR, OFM

DAN. 7:13-14
REV. 1:5-8
JOHN 18:33-37

"I am the Alpha and the Omega."

L et me give you a little of the history of this Feast which might give you an unexpected perspective. In the 1920's the Franciscans, my own Order, urged Rome to mark this as a feast day. However, the Feast of Christ the King of the Universe was not universalized until the 1960's by the Vatican Council. After the First World War, when the kings of Europe had been destroying one another—all in the name of Christianity, it seems—the Franciscans realized that we needed a bigger pattern. We needed something that would hold Christian civilization together.

They recognized that most Christian understanding was based on what I'm going to call *Plan B. Plan B* is what most of us implicitly or explicitly grew up with—the notion that everything started with a big mistake, which is a terrible way to start history. Adam and Eve ate the apple, dang it! So God had to send his son into the world to redeem the whole thing and turn it around. In effect, according to the *Plan B* perspective, Jesus was the mop-up exercise to correct Adam and Eve's terrible fault.

Scripture shows a much broader view, though for some reason it has mostly gone unnoticed. In the Second Reading we are told that this Christ is the Alpha and the Omega—Alpha being the first letter of the Greek alphabet, and Omega being the last.

There has to be a correspondence between how the universe began and where it's going. There has to be a trajectory created, a meaningful direction, and an end goal made clear. *Plan A* says the direction and the meaning were set from the very beginning. The story of creation didn't start with a problem; it started with God's clear blueprint, which was called the Logos, "the first idea in the mind of God", as it were. I don't know if God has ideas, but that's how Scripture writers seemed to see it (See Colossians 1:15-20, Ephesians 1:3-14). Christ was *Plan A* and God's incarnation did not depend on a mistake, but was pure revelatory gift from the very start.

Did you notice that the official name of the feast is "Christ the King of the Universe?" The feast points to a universal understanding of what's going on. What does this thing called history mean? Where does it come from and where is it going?

Here is what the Franciscans proposed. They said that the first idea, the Alpha of history, is that God wanted to materialize. God—who is Spirit, shapeless, and formless—wanted to take form. That's *Plan A*, that this material universe reveals the invisible God. That's what it means for Christ to be the King of the Universe. Christ is the first revelation of what's going on, the pattern of how things work, or the inner DNA of everything.

Because we were preoccupied with kings in most of history, we used the word "King." But as we see in the Gospel, Jesus in effect rejects this title. He says as it were, "That's not what I'm about. I just came to reveal the big truth, not to be a king in your worldly sense."

The Christ is not the same as Jesus. Now don't be shocked, don't be scandalized, don't think I've lost faith. Jesus has existed only for 2,000 years. The Christ, the King of the Universe, the pattern of all things, has existed, according to our present understanding of the universe, for 14.6 billion years.

From the best we know through science, the Big Bang is when God first decided to show God's self. That's the original Incarnation, or the Alpha point. We're the first people who ever had a name and approximate date for it. Now our telescopes reveal that this universe is still expanding. After 14.6 billion years it's still moving outward from the first explosion. The Christ is still unfolding, just as Paul said in Romans (8:18-23). Perhaps the Second Coming of Christ is when, as scientists predict will happen, the whole thing stops expanding and in a quick moment everything will implode and return to the Source. Science is saying a lot these days that sounds an awful lot like good theology.

I don't know if this is how it will happen. We don't need to know. Last week's Gospel said this very thing. We don't need to worry about it. It's not our problem. But what we do know is that the Alpha and the Omega are the same thing. What God revealed as *Plan A*—the Christ, to reveal who God is in the universe, in creation, in every creature, in everything that exists on this planet and all planets right now—is a revelation of the mystery of God from beginning to end.

I hope you recognize what this means. It means that you are inside something very sacred, very beautiful, and inherently holy. We ourselves don't make it holy because it already is. You are the in-between of the Alpha and the Omega, you are the becoming-in-time of the eternal Christ. In other words, Christ is indeed the pattern of the universe. Life has meaning and direction and purpose! This is what our postmodern world no longer enjoys.

So Jesus doesn't come to proclaim any kind of domination or warrior status or control of history. He simply says, "I am naming the deepest meaning of history and the deepest meaning of humanity." That's why, in a moment of time, this eternal Christ mystery came as a person that you and I call Jesus. Creation itself is the timeless Incarnation which we call

Christ, and Jesus is the personal Incarnation born in a moment of time when we could begin to understand and love a person. Christianity is the religion which dares to believe this. Do you realize what a daring belief system we have?! Can you really believe that one ordinary looking man, born in a little dusty town in Palestine, is the eternal blueprint of what God has been doing since the beginning of time "in Christ"? That is what we believe when we say we believe in both "Jesus" and "Christ".

That's a big act of faith. And maybe that's why Jesus asked Pilot, "Do you believe this of yourself, or have others told you of this?" Maybe we have to ask ourselves the same question. *Are you just here because others have told you that you should be Catholic or Christian, or do you really believe that the Christ reveals what is happening all the time and everywhere? Or that this is happening even in you, and even now?* This, I believe, is the deepest, biggest, and vast meaning of the Feast of Christ the King of the Universe.

THEMATIC CROSS REFERENCE

Adversity: 131

Authority: 187, 267

Baptism: 263, 53

Beatitudes: 301

Community: 209, 239, 309

Compassion: 131

Conversion: 153, 131, 249

Courage: 259

Creation: 53, 313

Death: 85, 263

Discernment: 63, 147, 205, 227, 259, 309

Discipleship: 147, 159, 219, 231, 239, 93

Eucharist: 293, 211

Faith: 167, 191, 195, 201, 223, 53, 43

Family: 39

Fear: 191, 309

Forgiveness: 111, 147, 249, 255

Freedom: 191

Glory: 131

Grace: 89

Gratitude: 17

Grief: 305, 97

Healing: 163, 179, 183, 235

Holy Spirit: 141, 287

Hope: 7, 11, 69, 81, 103

Hospitality: 127, 267

Humility: 119, 93, 43

Incarnation: 115, 175, 293, 313, 29, 35, 39

Journey: 277

Joy: 7, 11, 17, 107, 115, 135, 39, 35

Judgment: 171

Justice: 163, 271, 277, 281, 47

Kingship: 313

Lament: 59

Life: 215, 223

Light: 39

Listening: 63, 147, 243

Loss: 305

Love: 81, 119, 127, 227

Mercy: 75, 111, 281, 29

Ministry: 195, 205, 281

Mystery: 85, 183, 263, 43, 287

Obedience: 153

Peace: 29

Poverty: 215, 267, 301, 47

Power: 159, 201, 227

Prayer: 17, 179, 209

Preparedness: 7

Reconciliation: 127, 171

Redemption: 75, 211, 271, 135

Relationship: 123, 147, 163, 239, 249

Renewal: 107

Repent: 59

Resurrection: 103, 107

Revelation: 271

Saints: 301, 297

Salvation: 175, 195, 301, 29, 107, 103

Service: 85, 215, 93

Silence: 179

Sin: 171

Stewardship: 277

Suffering: 97

Surrender: 69, 23

Temptation: 219

Threshold: 305

Transformation: 119, 123, 163, 175, 187, 243, 287

Trinity: 287

Trust: 69, 159, 167

Truth: 23, 123

Unity: 183, 211, 293

Virgin Mary: 23, 297, 43, 309

Vocation: 205, 211, 259

Wilderness: 59, 219

Witness: 115, 235, 135, 97

Wisdom: 75, 235

THE CONTRIBUTORS

FR. WILLIAM J. BAUSCH is a parish priest of the diocese of Trenton, New Jersey. He is the award-winning author of numerous books on parish ministry, the sacraments, Church history, storytelling, and homiletics. His book, *Traditions, Tensions, Transitions in Ministry* received an honorable mention in 1983 from the Catholic Press Association; *Storytelling: Faith and Imagination* was awarded second place in 1985 for best pastoral work; *The Total Parish Manual* won first place in 1995; *Brave New Church* first place in 2002; and *Once Upon a Gospel* won third place in 2009.

He was awarded the President's Award in 1996 from the National Federation of Priests' Councils for Parish Leadership, the Catholic Library Association's Aggiornamento Award for Notable Contribution to Parish Life in 2004 and the Walter J. Burghardt, S. J. Preaching award in 2008 for his contribution to Catholic preaching. He has lectured and given workshops at such colleges and universities as Notre Dame; Sacred Heart in Fairfield, Connecticut; Boston College; Charles Carroll in Cleveland; and in most U.S. dioceses as well as abroad. His latest book is *The Story Revealed*, a book of homilies.

First and foremost, however, though retired from the pastorate, he remains happily engaged in his first love: being a parish priest active in assisting at three parishes, writing, and giving lectures and retreats.

ROB BELL was named one of *Time* Magazine's 100 Most Influential People in the World in 2011. Rob Bell is the author of a number of books, including *Velvet Elvis, Drops Like Stars*, and the *New York Times* Bestsellers *Love Wins* and *What We Talk About When We Talk About God*. The founding pastor of Mars Hill, an innovative church in Grand Rapids, Michigan, his Nooma short film series has been viewed by over thirty million people around the world. His sold-out speaking tours of clubs and theaters have repeatedly taken him around the English-speaking world and in 2013 he launched CraftLab, a leadership event designed to help executives, writers, artists, and activists develop and create compelling new content. He and his wife Kristen live with their three children in Southern California. For more information on Rob go to: *www.robbell.com*.

MARGARET (MAGS) BLACKIE, PHD is a spiritual director, a scientist and an educator. She is the author of *Rooted in Love: Integrating Ignatian Spirituality into Daily Life*. She worked for four years as a spiritual director in the UK before returning to South Africa.

She holds an academic position at Stellenbosch University near Cape Town. Currently her challenge is to hold together medicinal chemistry, science education and Ignatian spirituality, and allowing cross-pollination between these rather disparate fields! She recharges by walking in the mountains of the beautiful Western Cape.

REV. JOEL BLUNK is Associate Pastor at the State College Presbyterian Church in Pennsylvania, where he led the Fellowship in Senior High (FISH) youth group from 1994 to 2012. Beginning in 2012, Joel launched a new outreach ministry known as the *WheelHouse* (www.scpresby.org/), which seeks to help people find that place where their "deep gladness and the world's deep hunger meet." Professionally, Joel has enjoyed being an athlete, coach, singer/songwriter, pastor, and spiritual director. His focus is now devoted to men's groups, rite of passage experiences for youth and young adults, helping older adults embrace the second half of life, and tending to the sacred threads that weave one's soul. He enjoys basketball, playing guitar, hiking with his wife Kristen, and playing disc golf with his three sons. He is a graduate of Duke University and Vanderbilt Divinity School. His music is available on iTunes.

FR. GREGORY BOYLE, SJ was born in Los Angeles and is one of eight children. He entered the Society of Jesus (Jesuits) in 1972 and was ordained a priest in 1984. He received his BA in English from Gonzaga University, an MA in English from Loyola Marymount University, and advanced theology degrees from the Weston School of Theology and the Jesuit School of Theology at Berkeley.

He has taught at Loyola High School in Los Angeles, was chaplain in the Islas Marias Penal Colony in Mexico and at Folsom Prison, and worked with Christian Base Communities in Cochabamba, Bolivia. He was appointed pastor of Dolores Mission Church in the Boyle Heights neighborhood of East Los Angeles in 1986, where he served through 1992. Homeboy Industries was born in 1988 and is now the largest gang intervention, rehabilitation, and re-entry program in the United States. (www.homeboyindustries.org)

Fr. Boyle is the author of the *New York Times* Bestselling book *Tattoos on the Heart: The Power of Boundless Compassion*. His debut book has been honored by SCIBA (Southern California Indie Booksellers Association), Pen USA, *Publishers Weekly*, and Goodreads Choice Awards.

Fr. Boyle has received numerous honorary degrees, awards, and recognitions, including the Civic Medal of Honor, the California Peace Prize, Humanitarian of the Year from *Bon Appetit* magazine, and in 2011 was inducted into the California Hall of Fame.

the Sellinger School of Business and Management, Loyola College in Maryland to serve as interim president of Loyola University New Orleans in academic year 2003-04. From August, 2000 until June, 2003, he was pastor of Holy Trinity Catholic Church in Washington, DC. From 1982-1992, he was president of The Catholic University of America.

He holds a doctorate in economics from the University of Maryland, two theology degrees from Woodstock College, a bachelor's in philosophy and master's in economics from Saint Louis University, and a certificate in educational management from Harvard. He was the 1999 recipient of the Association of Catholic Colleges and Universities' Theodore M. Hesburgh Award for his contributions over the years to the advancement of Catholic higher education. In that same year he received the Council of Independent Colleges' Academic Leadership Award. He holds 30 honorary degrees.

Father Byron writes a syndicated bi-weekly column ("Looking Around") for Catholic News Service Syndicate. He is the author of numerous books including: *Faith-Based Reflections on American Life* (Paulist 2010); *One Faith, Many Faithful: Short Takes on Contemporary Catholic Concerns* (Paulist 2012), and *The Word Received* (2012) and *The Word Proclaimed* (2013) homilies for Sundays in Years C and A (Paulist Press).

SR. SIMONE CAMPBELL, SSS, has served as Executive Director of NETWORK, A National Catholic Social Justice Lobby, since 2004. She is a religious leader, attorney and poet with extensive experience in public policy and advocacy for systemic change. In Washington, she lobbies on issues of peace-building, immigration reform, healthcare, and economic justice. Around the country, she is a noted speaker and educator on these and other public policy issues.

During the 2010 congressional debate about healthcare reform, she wrote the famous "nuns' letter" supporting the reform bill and got 59 leaders of Catholic Sisters, including LCWR, to sign on. This action was cited by many as critically important in passing the Affordable Care Act. She was thanked by President Obama and invited to the ceremony celebrating its being signed into law.

In 2012, she was also instrumental in organizing the first "Nuns on the Bus" tour of nine states to oppose the "Ryan Budget" approved by the House of Representatives. This budget would decimate programs meant to help people in need. NETWORK's "Nuns on the Bus" received an avalanche of attention across the nation from religious communities, elected officials and the media. Last year, she led a new cross-country Nuns on the Bus trip (May 28 through June 18, 2013) focused on comprehensive immigration reform. More "Nuns on the Bus" journeys are planned.

In 2012, she was also instrumental in organizing the first "Nuns on the Bus" tour of nine states to oppose the "Ryan Budget" approved by the House of Representatives. This budget would decimate programs meant to help people in need. NETWORK's "Nuns on the Bus" received an avalanche of attention across the nation from religious communities, elected officials and the media. Last year, she led a new cross-country Nuns on the Bus trip (May 28 through June 18, 2013) focused on comprehensive immigration reform. More "Nuns on the Bus" journeys are planned.

Sister Campbell has often been featured in the national and international media, including recent appearances on *60 Minutes*, *The Colbert Report*, and *The Daily Show with Jon Stewart*. She has received numerous awards, including the "Defender of Democracy Award" from the international Parliamentarians for Global Action and "Health Care Heroes Award" from Families USA. In addition, she has been the keynote or featured speaker at numerous large gatherings, including the 2012 Democratic National Convention.

Prior to coming to NETWORK, she served as the Executive Director of JERICHO, the California interfaith public policy organization that works, like NETWORK, to protect the interests of people living in poverty. She also participated in a delegation of religious leaders to Iraq in December 2002, just prior to the war, and was later (while at NETWORK) part of a Catholic Relief Services delegation to Lebanon and Syria to study the Iraqi refugee situation there.

SR. JOAN CHITTISTER, OSB is one of the most articulate social analysts and influential religious leader of our times. For 40 years she has put her energy into advocating for the critical questions impacting the global community. Courageous, passionate and charged with energy, she is a much sought after speaker, counselor and clear voice across all religions. A best-selling author of more than 50 books, columnist and noted international lecturer, she has received numerous honors for her work on behalf of peace, human rights, women's issues and church renewal including Notre Dame University's, Dr. Thomas A Dooley Award. She currently serves as co-chair of the Global Peace Initiative of Women, a partner organization of the UN, facilitating a worldwide network of women peace builders and was an advisor for the groundbreaking report, "A Woman's Nation," led by Maria Shriver.

Her doctorate is from Penn State University in Speech Communication Theory and she was an elected-fellow of St. Edmund's College, Cambridge University.

Sister Joan is a member of the Benedictine Sisters of Erie, PA, and the animating force behind MonasteriesoftheHeart.org, a web-based movement sharing Benedictine spirituality with contemporary seekers, and the executive director of Benetvision, a resource and research center for contemporary spirituality located in Erie. She served as prioress of the Benedictine Sisters of Erie for 12 years.

REV. DR. DAVID A. DAVIS is currently the senior pastor of the Nassau Presbyterian Church in Princeton, New Jersey. He has served that congregation since 2000. David earned his Ph.D. in Homiletics from Princeton Theological Seminary. He is currently the Chairperson of the Board of Trustees for the Presbyterian Foundation. His academic work has focused on preaching as a corporate act and the active role of the listener in the preaching event. Before arriving in Princeton, he served for fourteen years as the pastor of the First Presbyterian Church, Blackwood, NJ. David is married to Cathy Cook, a Presbyterian Minister who is Associate Dean of Student Life at Princeton Seminary. They have two children, Hannah and Ben.

David is an adjunct faculty member in preaching at Princeton Theological Seminary and a contributor to various journals in the discipline of preaching and has had published of a collection of his sermons. The book is titled *A Kingdom You Can Taste: Sermons for the Church Year.*

You can follow David's weekly homilies at: *www.nassauchurch.org/worship/sermons.php*

DEACON BILL DITEWIG, PHD, is a deacon of the Archdiocese of Washington, DC, but currently is Executive Professor of Theology at Santa Clara University and serves as Director of Faith Formation, Diaconate, and Pastoral Planning for the Diocese of Monterey. A retired Navy Commander, Bill also served as Executive Director of the Secretariat for the Diaconate at the United States Conference of Catholics Bishops. He is the deacon of St. Joseph Parish, Spreckels, California. Bill and his wife Diann have four children and fourteen grandchildren.

MSGR. MICHAEL DOYLE was born on a farm in Rossduff, County Longford, Ireland. Ordained a Catholic priest in Wexford, Ireland, he came to the Diocese of Camden in 1959, where he taught high school and assisted in various parishes. In 1974, Msgr. Doyle was appointed pastor of Sacred Heart Parish, where he continues to serve.

Fr. Doyle earned a Master's Degree in Education from Villanova University in 1962 and received an honorary Doctorate in Humanities from Villanova in May 2007. He has a lifelong commitment to peace and justice. In 1971, he participated in the "Camden 28" peace action against the Vietnam War at the Federal Building in Camden and was arrested. He was acquitted two years later in a trail where he acted as his own defense. Anthony Giacchino directed and produced a documentary about the "Camden 28" in 2007.

He has been the subject of television programs such as *60 Minutes'* "Michael Doyle's Camden" in 1983 and *CBS Sunday Morning*, December 1995, and of newspaper articles such as *The Philadelphia Inquirer's* series on inspiring preachers, 1996.

During his tenure at Sacred Heart, he has established a free medical clinic serving those without medical benefits; founded the Heart of Camden Housing, which renovates abandoned houses and assists low-income families to become homeowners, and helped to establish Camden Churches Organized for People, CCOP, a church-based community organizing effort. He has written numerous magazine and newspaper articles and pens a monthly "letter" that is mailed to thousands on his mailing list. A collection of his letters was published in March 2003 in a book called *It's a Terrible Day, Thanks Be to God*.

MICHELLE FRANCL-DONNAY is a professor of chemistry and a writer. Her reflections on the joys and struggles of attempting to live a contemplative life in the midst of the everyday chaos that being a wife, mother, and teacher brings appear regularly at the Philadelphia Archdiocese's *CatholicPhilly.com*. She is an occasional contributor to *Give Us This Day* and a regular columnist for the science journal *Nature Chemistry*. Her essays have appeared in several print collections, including *Professing and Parenting* and *The Open Laboratory* 2009, and online at *dotMagis* (www.ignatianspirituality.com/author/francl-donnay/) and *This Ignatian Life* (ignatianlife.org/author/mfranci/). Michelle gives the occasional retreat and blogs about prayer, God, and laundry at *Quantum Theology* (quantumtheology.blogspot.com).

FR. JAMES J. GREENFIELD, OSFS, is an Oblate of St. Francis de Sales and has worked in a variety of educational roles at the university level, and also as director of a number of Salesian programs for his community prior to his present ministry as its provincial superior of the Wilmington-Philadelphia Province, a position he has served since January 2008. He is also the president of the Congregation of Major Superiors of Men and enjoys working with fellow religious in the United States. He now lives with his local Oblate community in Wilmington, DE. Fr. Greenfield followed his undergraduate degree in politics from DeSales University with master's degrees in divinity and counseling from DeSales School of Theology and George Washington University, respectively. He later returned to GW to earn his doctorate in human development.

Working many years in Washington, D.C., Fr. Greenfield has served in a number of parishes for weekend ministry, where he greatly enjoys preaching and celebrating Mass. He has traveled throughout the various regions of his province leading parish missions, retreats, and days of recollection. He is a certified pastoral counselor and author of a number of articles on religious life, seminary formation and the intersection of spirituality and human development.

FR. PAUL A. HOLMES, STD, was ordained a priest for the Archdiocese of Newark in 1981and is now Distinguished University Professor of Servant Leadership at Seton Hall University. In 1992, Father Holmes helped inaugurate Clergy Consultation and Treatment Service, an interdisciplinary outpatient treatment program for priests at St. Vincent's Hospital in Harrison, New York, and has recently returned to serve once again as the program's Spiritual Director.

Father Holmes was invited to be the first occupant of the Carl J. Peter Chair of Preaching at the North American College in Rome. He has published articles in numerous journals and was invited to create *This Sunday's Scripture*, the first homily service of Twenty-Third Publications. He has also offered a number of "Authentic Preaching" practicums to deacons and priests from around the English-speaking world. In collaboration with the National Leadership Roundtable on Church Management, he has developed the Toolbox for Pastoral Management, offered twice a year, teaching new pastors the administrative skills needed to lead a vibrant Catholic parish in the 21st century.

FR. DANIEL P. HORAN, OFM, is a Franciscan Friar of Holy Name Province, a columnist at *America* magazine, and the author of several books, including *The Last Words of Jesus: A Meditation on Love and Suffering* (2013), *Francis of Assisi and the Future of Faith: Exploring Franciscan Spirituality and Theology in the Modern World* (2012), and *Dating God: Live and Love in the Way of St. Francis* (2012). In addition to his award-winning popular writing, Fr. Dan has published dozens of articles in scholarly journals including *Theological Studies, New Blackfriars, Worship, Cistercian Studies Quarterly*, and *The Merton Annual*, among others. He has previously taught in the Department of Religious Studies at Siena College and the Department of Theology at St. Bonaventure University. A frequently sought-after speaker, Fr. Dan has lectured, directed retreats, and led workshops around the United States and in Europe. He is currently completing a Ph.D. in Systematic Theology at Boston College. Additionally, Fr. Dan is currently a member of the Board of Directors of the International Thomas Merton Society. His blog is *www.DatingGod.org*, and you can follow him on: Facebook *www.facebook.com/DanHoranOFM* and Twitter @ DanHoranOFM. For more information, visit *www.DanHoran.com*.

DEACON GREG KANDRA is the Multimedia Editor of Catholic Near East Welfare Association (CNEWA), a pontifical society founded by Pope Pius XI in 1926. He oversees all online content for the agency and edits its award-winning quarterly magazine, *ONE*. Deacon Greg is also the author of the popular blog "The Deacon's Bench," carried on the spiritual website *Patheos*.

Before joining CNEWA, Deacon Greg spent nearly three decades in broadcast journalism, most of that time at CBS News, where he was a writer and producer for a variety of programs, including *48 Hours, 60 Minutes II, Sunday Morning* and *The CBS Evening News with Katie Couric*. He was also the founding editor of "Couric & Co.," Katie Couric's blog at *CBSNews.com*. In addition to his work with CBS News, from 2000 to 2004 he also served as a writer and producer on the live finales of the hit reality series *Survivor*.

In 2002, he co-wrote the acclaimed CBS documentary "9/11," hosted by Robert DeNiro, which told the story of firefighters on September 11, 2001. The film showed the only footage shot inside the World Trade Center that day, and featured the last images of Fr. Mychal Judge, moments before he became the first official fatality of the attacks.

In print, Deacon Greg's radio essays were featured in Dan Rather's best-selling book *Deadlines and Datelines*. His spiritual writing has been published in *America, U.S. Catholic, Catholic Digest, Reality* and *The Brooklyn Tablet*. He contributes homiletic reflections to *Connect!*, the award-winning parish resource published by Liturgical Publications, and writes spiritual reflections for the monthly prayer guide *Give Us This Day*.

Deacon Greg has received every major award in broadcasting, including two Emmys, two Peabody Awards and four awards from the Writer's Guild of America. He has been honored three times by the Catholic Press Association.

A Maryland native, Deacon Greg graduated from the University of Maryland with a B.A. in English. He was ordained a deacon for the Diocese of Brooklyn in 2007. He and his wife live in Forest Hills, New York, where he serves at Our Lady Queen of Martyrs parish.

You can follow Deacon Greg on his blog at *www.patheos.com/blogs/deaconsbench/*

DEACON JIM KNIPPER is a Roman Catholic deacon serving the Diocese of Trenton, N.J. When not serving his faith community at St. Paul's in Princeton, he is CEO of J. Knipper and Company, Inc., and a principal of Clear Faith Publishing LLC and editor/contributor of this book.

In 1981, Jim graduated from the University of Scranton with a degree in Chemistry, and in 1984 he received a Master's in Business in the Pharmaceutical Industry from Fairleigh Dickinson University. He will earn his Masters in Theology from Georgian Court University in May 2015.

He is a member of the Board of Trustees for Georgian Court University, the only Catholic University in the Trenton Diocese, and a former member of the Board of Trustees for the University of Scranton, one of the 28 Jesuit colleges and universities in the United States.

Deacon Jim lives with his wife, Teresa, in Princeton and Cape May, NJ, and is father of four sons.

You can follow him and his homilies on his blog site: *teachbelief.blogspot.com*, Facebook page: *www.facebook.com/teachbelief*, Twitter @jjknipper

MICHAEL LEACH is publisher emeritus and editor-at-large of Orbis Books. A leader in Catholic publishing for more than 30 years, he has edited and published more than two thousand books. His authors include Nobel Prize winners, National Book Award winners, and hundreds of Catholic Book Award winners. He has served as president of the Catholic Book Publishers Association and the ecumenical Religion Publishers Group. Before joining Orbis as director and publisher in 1997, Michael was president of the Crossroad/Continuum Publishing Group in New York City. In 2007, the Catholic Book Publishers Association honored him with a Lifetime Achievement Award. Dubbed "the dean of Catholic book publishing" by *U.S. Catholic* magazine, he has also authored or edited several books of his own, including the bestsellers *Why Stay Catholic?*, *A Maryknoll Book of Prayer*, *The People's Catechism*, and *I Like Being Married*. He is a columnist for the *National Catholic Reporter* (*ncronline.org/authors/michael-leach*). A popular speaker at Catholic conferences nationwide, Mike lives in Connecticut with his wife of forty-five years, Vickie.

FR. RICHARD G. MALLOY, SJ, aka "Mugs," was born at Temple University Hospital in Philadelphia, and earned a doctorate at in Cultural Anthropology from Temple (He didn't go very far in life!) His dissertation was an ethnographic study of Puerto Rican leaders in Camden, NJ.

After being educated by the Sisters of Mercy in grade school, he went on to the Jesuit high school in Philadelphia, St. Joseph's Prep. He attended Lafayette College in Easton, PA, and then entered the Jesuit Novitiate in Wernersville, PA. While in Jesuit formation, he spent two years teaching high school in Osorno, Chile, and one year in pastoral work in Santiago.

For 15 years (1988-2003), Fr. Malloy lived and worked at Holy Name Church in Camden, NJ, as a member of the Jesuit Urban Service Team (JUST). From 1994 to 2008, he also taught at St. Joseph's University in Philadelphia.

In September 2010, he was sent to the University of Scranton, where he serves as the Vice President for University Mission and Ministry, working with campus ministry, community outreach, service learning, and international service trips. He teaches cultural anthropology, lives in a freshman dorm (anthropological fieldwork!), and plays his guitar to awaken students who fall asleep in class or during his homilies.

Fishing is his passion in life, and he prays for the day when he will catch a 10 lb. trout or a 47 inch Muskie. He is convinced that such a catch, the Eagles winning the Super Bowl, or the Phillies beating the Yankees in the World Series would all be sure signs that the second coming of Jesus is at hand.

You can follow Fr. Malloy on his blog: *jesuitjottings.blogspot.com* and Twitter @FrMalloy.

FR. JAMES MARTIN, SJ, is a Jesuit priest, author, and editor-at-large of *America*, the national Catholic magazine. Father Martin is the author of several books, including *The Jesuit Guide to (Almost) Everything*, which was a *New York Times* bestseller and won a Christopher Award in 2010. His memoir *My Life with the Saints*, which also received a Christopher Award, and his book *Between Heaven and Mirth: Why Joy, Humor and Laughter are at the Heart of the Spiritual Life*, were both named among "Best Books of the Year" by *Publishers Weekly*. His newest book is *Jesus: A Pilgrimage*. His books have been translated into Spanish, German, Chinese, Portuguese, Korean, Polish, Lithuanian, and Slovenian.

Father Martin entered the Jesuits in 1988, after graduating from the Wharton School of Business and working at General Electric for six years. During his Jesuit training, he worked in a homeless shelter and with the seriously ill in Boston; at a hospice run by the Missionaries of Charity in Kingston, Jamaica; with street-gang members and with the unemployed in Chicago; as a prison chaplain in Boston; and, for two years, in Nairobi, Kenya, with the Jesuit Refugee Service, where he helped East African refugees start small businesses. He received his Master's Degree in Divinity (M.Div.) and in Theology (Th.M.) from the Weston Jesuit School of Theology in Cambridge, Mass. and was ordained a priest in 1999. Since his ordination he has received honorary degrees from several colleges and universities.

Father Martin has written for a variety of publications, both religious and secular, including *The New York Times*, *The Wall Street Journal*, *The Boston Globe*, *Slate*, and *The Huffington Post*, and has appeared on all the major networks, including venues as diverse as CNN, BBC, the History Channel, and Vatican Radio. He has also been featured on such programs as NPR's *Fresh Air with Terry Gross*, PBS's *NewsHour*, Fox TV's *The O'Reilly Factor*, and Comedy Central's *The Colbert Report*. Father Martin blogs regularly for *America* magazine's "In All Things," posts to a public Facebook page (FrJamesMartin) and tweets under @JamesMartinSJ.

BROTHER MICKEY O'NEILL MCGRATH, OSFS, an Oblate of St. Francis de Sales, is an award-winning artist, author, and storyteller. He is a popular presenter and frequent keynote speaker at conferences, parishes, and retreat centers throughout the United States and Canada. Using his own paintings and the stories which inspired them, Bro. Mickey makes deep and often humorous connections between art, social justice, and religious faith around a wide variety of themes and subjects.

Bro. Mickey also paints on commission for parishes and schools, and his most recent commissions can be viewed on his website. He has created illustrations and/or written articles for many of today's leading Catholic publishers, including *America Magazine*, *Commonweal*, and *St. Anthony Messenger*. In 2010, his painting "Christ the Teacher" was presented to Pope Benedict XVI. God only knows where it is now.

Mickey's first and foremost love, however, is books, in all aspects: illustrating, writing, publishing, and promoting. In 2014, his book, *Go To Joseph* (WLP) was honored with four awards from the Catholic Press Association and Association of Catholic Publishers. He was also honored beyond measure to have launched his first publication with Clear Faith Publishing, *Good Pope John XXIII*, a copy of which was presented to Pope Francis soon after its launch. Bro. Mickey sees his work as being at the service of Catholic social teaching. To that end, he has created posters for the United States Conference of Catholic Bishops to promote immigration reform and home missions and has licensed his work to Catholic textbook publishers. He is a recipient of the Thea Bowman Black Catholic Education Award in recognition of his work on Sr. Thea Bowman, his great spiritual mentor and inspiration.

Mickey also offers workshops on the creation of mandalas and other forms of artistic meditation. Since 1987 he has been a summer faculty member at the Grunewald Guild in Leavenworth, Washington, an interfaith art guild where he is officially designated a "Guild Master."

Bro. Mickey currently lives and works in Camden, NJ. You can visit his website at *www.bromickeymcgrath.com.*

REV. CAROL HOWARD MERRITT is the award-winning author of *Tribal Church: Ministering to the Missing Generation* (Alban) and *Reframing Hope: Vital Ministry in a New Generation* (Alban) and a frequent contributor to books, websites, magazines, and journals. She is a regular columnist at the *Christian Century* where her blog, "Tribal Church," is hosted. She's a Presbyterian (USA) minister whose dynamic writing, speaking, and teaching is anchored in theological and sociological insight. Twitter: @CarolHoward Visit: *http://www.carolhowardmerritt.org/*

REV. PENNY A. NASH serves as Associate Rector at St. Stephen's Episcopal Church in Richmond, Virginia, where she is primarily responsible for pastoral care and small groups ministry and serves as pastor to the evening community (Celtic Evensong and Eucharist, community supper, and sung Compline). After completing her priestly formation and M.Div. (with a Certificate in Anglican Studies) from the Candler School of Theology at Emory University, she was ordained in 2008 in the Episcopal Diocese of Atlanta. Penny writes for various Forward Movement publications, contributed to a collection of essays called *Letters to Me: Conversations with a Younger Self*, and was one of the original Celebrity Bloggers in the annual Lent Madness online devotional (*www.lentmadness.org*). An amateur photographer, she posts daily prayers, reflections and visual meditations at "One Cannot Have Too Large a Party" (*www.penelopepiscopal.blogspot.com*) and is an avid user of social media to build community and spread the Gospel. Follow her on Twitter @penelopepiscopal, Facebook *www.facebook.com/penny.nash.733*, and Instagram @penelopepiscopal.

MSGR. WALTER E. NOLAN is a retired Catholic priest within the Diocese of Trenton, N.J. He received a BS degree in Pharmacy from Fordham University, a Masters Degree in Divinity from Pope John University in Massachusetts, and a Masters Degree in Pastoral Counseling from Iona College. He served as Associate Pastor of St. Gregory's, Chaplain and Athletic Moderator of Notre Dame High School, Chaplain at Rider University, Director of Priest's Personnel for the Diocese, and served the Catholic community of Princeton as pastor of St. Paul Church for fourteen years before retirement. He continues to host the *Trenton Diocese Catholic Corner* radio and TV show.

CHRISTINE VALTERS PAINTNER, PhD is the online Abbess at *www.AbbeyoftheArts.com*, a global monastery without walls and an online gathering place for the Holy Disorder of Dancing Monks. She is the author of seven books on contemplation and creativity, including *The Artist's Rule: Nurturing Your Creative Soul with Monastic Wisdom* and *Eyes of the Heart: Photography as a Christian Contemplative Practice*. Christine is a teacher, pilgrimage guide, spiritual director, and Benedictine oblate, and she lives out her commitment as a monk in the world with her husband John in Galway, Ireland.

JAN RICHARDSON is an artist, writer, and ordained minister in the United Methodist Church. She serves as director of The Wellspring Studio, LLC, and travels widely as a retreat leader and conference speaker. Known for her distinctive intertwining of word and image, Jan's work has attracted an international audience drawn to the welcoming and imaginative spaces that she creates in her books (including *Night Visions* and *In the Sanctuary of Women*), blogs, and public events.

Jan serves as the Visiting Artist at First United Methodist Church of Winter Park, Florida, is on the faculty of the Grünewald Guild in Washington State, and belongs to Saint Brigid of Kildare Monastery, a community that draws from Methodist and Benedictine traditions. She makes her home in Florida. Visit her primary website at *janrichardson.com.*

FR. RICHARD ROHR, OFM is a globally recognized ecumenical teacher bearing witness to the universal awakening within Christian mysticism and the Perennial Tradition. He is a Franciscan priest of the New Mexico Province and founder of the Center for Action and Contemplation (CAC) in Albuquerque, New Mexico. Fr. Richard's teaching is grounded in the Franciscan alternative orthodoxy—practices of contemplation and lived kenosis (self-emptying), expressing itself in radical compassion, particularly for the socially marginalized.

Fr. Richard is author of numerous books, including *Everything Belongs, Adam's Return, The Naked Now, Breathing Under Water, Falling Upward, Immortal Diamond,* and *Eager to Love: The Alternative Way of Francis of Assisi.*

Fr. Richard is Academic Dean of the Living School for Action and Contemplation. Drawing upon Christianity's place within the Perennial Tradition, the mission of the Living School is to produce compassionate and powerfully learned individuals who will work for positive change in the world based on awareness of our common union with God and all beings. Learn more about Fr. Richard and CAC at *cac.org.*

MARY ELIZABETH SPERRY holds a Master's Degree in Liturgical Studies from the Catholic University of America and a master's degree in political science from the University of California, Los Angeles. She has worked for the United States Conference of Catholic Bishops since 1994. She is the author of *Bible Top Tens* (Our Sunday Visitor), *Ten: How the Commandments Can Change Your Life* (Franciscan Media), and *Scripture in the Parish: A Guide for Minister*s (Liturgical Press), and *Real Life Faith* (Liguori Publications). Her articles have appeared in on the *America* magazine website and in the *Liguorian Magazine, Emmanuel, Today's Parish* and other publications. She has spoken in the Dioceses and Archdioceses of Baltimore, Los Angeles, Dallas, Harrisburg, Greensburg and Orange and has given talks and retreats in numerous parishes. She has been interviewed about the Bible on National Public Radio, CBS Radio, *Catholic Community of Faith, The Drew Mariani Show,* and *Seize the Day.*

REV. MARTHA STERNE has been a parish priest for over 25 years including serving for a decade in midtown Atlanta, where her ministry bridged the worlds of the church and the poor and marginalized of the city. She is a celebrated preacher and has written two books, *Alive and Loose in the Ordinary* and *Earthly Good.* She and her husband divide their time between Atlanta and a family farm outside of Natchez, Mississippi.

FRAN ROSSI SZPYLCZYN is a writer, retreat leader, and public speaker with a focus on how spirituality intersects with daily life. By day she is the Pastoral Associate for Administration at the Church of the Immaculate Conception in Glenville, NY. Fran worships at St. Edward the Confessor in Clifton Park, NY, where she is involved in liturgical ministry and catechesis. In May of 2013, she received her MA in Pastoral Studies from St. Bernard's School of Theology. Her work has been published in *The Evangelist* (*www.evangelist.org*), the newspaper of the Roman Catholic Diocese of Albany (*www.rcda.org*), in the *Albany Times Union* (*www.timesunion.com*) and in the *National Catholic Reporter* (*www.ncronline.org*). She is also an on-going contributor to the *Give Us This Day*. She lives in Clifton Park, NY with her husband, Mark, and step-daughter, Erica. You can explore her work at her personal blog, *There Will Be Bread* (*breadhere.wordpress.com*). Follow Fran on: Twitter @FranSzpylczyn and Facebook: *www.facebook.com/fran.szpylczyn*.

PATRICK J. WENRICK graduated with an M.Div. in Mission Specialization from Catholic Theological Union in 1982 and was ordained a priest in October of the same year. Since that time he has been in various ministries within the Church, including being a Vocation Director and Assistant Pastor of two churches in NJ, as well as an Assistant Rector of a religious community. In 1997 he graduated from LaSalle University with a Master's Degree in Pastoral Counseling and went to work first as a therapist and later as Program Director for a drug and alcohol outpatient facility in Bucks County, Pennsylvania. While Program Director he also taught World Religions as an adjunct faculty member at Bucks County Community College. In 1998 he also established his own clinical practice in New Jersey and was licensed in the state as a professional counselor.

In July 2003, Rev. Wenrick married his lovely wife Susan in Princeton, NJ, and together they moved to the Tampa area with their daughter, Allyson. He continues to witness marriages, perform baptisms, and to be available for visiting the sick and dying in hospitals and nursing homes. A gifted preacher, Rev. Wenrick and his wife also continue to tend to the poor and needy of the community through donations of food and clothing, and by assisting with other needs. He has been a member of CITI Ministries and the International Council of Community Churches since 2004.

While in Tampa he has served as Director of an Allied Health Career School, and a tutorial program for licensed practical nurses who wish to become registered nurses. He also has served as a chaplain with a hospice in Lakeland, FL. He has given numerous workshops and talks on life-span development, spirituality, and bereavement issues. He has weaved a healthy spiritual-psychological approach to the issues that confront contemporary society.

THE CHARITIES

CITIZENS ACTING TOGETHER CAN HELP

CATCH has been a cornerstone and anchor in the South Philadelphia community since 1979. As a well-established and credentialed provider of Community Behavioral Health and Developmental Disability Services, CATCH has an ongoing responsibility to serve and to enhance the community at large.

With its mission to provide continuous care on the ladder of independence for individuals with disabilities, CATCH wrestles with the dichotomy of evermore finite and diminishing resources and the community's real and expanding needs for its unique human services.

Newly designed programs continue to strengthen CATCH's base of offerings. There are increased efforts toward the employment of the developmentally disabled; long-term, interventional, emergency, and geriatric resident programs continue throughout the City; ongoing outreach in consultation to brother and sister agencies; and the expanded transportation department specializing in the delivery of residents to medical health care providers are just a few accomplishments of which we are especially cognizant and proud.

www.catchinc.com

HOPEWORKS 'N CAMDEN

Working in one of America's poorest and most violent cities, Hopeworks 'N Camden is a nonprofit that has been working for over 15 years with Camden youth. Utilizing an advanced training curriculum in website design/development, GIS and Salesforce, Hopeworks works with youth ages 14-23 to get back in school (the estimated high school dropout rate in Camden is close to 70%).

At Hopeworks, justice is connected to brain health. We understand that toxic stress directly impacts the brain health of our youth and our community. Endemic poverty, violence, abuse and neglect lead to toxic situations that directly impact the Camden community, the organizations that work here and all who live here. Hopeworks believes that without addressing the traumatic issues in a youth's life especially as they manifest in habitual patterns of protection i.e. disengagement, disconnected emotional state, anger, emotional eruptions, etc. youth will not be able to take full advantage of opportunities in their lives. Fundamentally, we can either work on creating new opportunities and "hope that there are youth who can succeed in them" or we can work on helping youth heal who will then be able to take advantage of new opportunities. We are choosing the latter!

As part of our program, Hopeworks runs three businesses, offering a complete array of web site design, development, maintenance and hosting services, along with online mapping products, and a complete set of salesforce administration offerings. These businesses have helped to generate over 450 youth jobs!

http://www.hopeworks.org/

RELIGIOUS MINISTRIES PHCS

A partner of Princeton HealthCare System, Religious Ministries PHCS is a community-based non-profit serving the spiritual and emotional needs of the wider Princeton-Plainsboro community through the Medical Center, Princeton House, and Hospice. Working with a multi-faith board of local clergy and community members, the chaplains comfort those who grieve, tend to the souls of those making end-of-life decisions, help patients with cancer find meaning amidst their illness, help those with mental illness find coping skills with their spirituality, and celebrate the gifts of life that are present even in a place of suffering. In addition to providing care to the patients, chaplains also provide support to families and staff, who walk alongside the patients.

http://www.princetonhcs.org/phcs-home/who-we-serve/patients/pastoral-carereligious-ministries-.aspx

SAINT CAMILLUS CENTER

The Mission of Saint Camillus Center for Spiritual Care is to accompany people in the midst of suffering with holistic healing and hope. As chaplains we support, affirm, and challenge each other in a spirit of collaboration. We commit ourselves to be Church in its preferential option for the poor in the L.A. County/USC Medical Center.

St Camillus has provided full time and professional interfaith bilingual chaplains to the Medical Center since 1955 and we provide 24/7 emergency care to a number of cancer centers in the area. We helped establish the Interfaith Communities United for Justice and we provide support to the East Lake Juvenile Hall near to us.

We provide an accredited interfaith urban clinical pastoral education training program. We make connections between our patients who come as immigrants, uninsured or underinsured patients along victims of burns, abuse and lack of prenatal or early childhood preventive care.

We appreciate all forms of partnership that empower persons and groups and we practice this in the context of daily interfaith reflection and shared lunch to provide a community of reflection and integration. We value nonviolence in word and action at bedside and in the global struggles. Spirit is respected in various formulations but puts us all into the larger history, picture and world view.

www.stcamilluscenter.org